The HISTORY TEACHER 2.0

Awakening Our Innate Lovability, Worthiness, Adequacy and Empowerment

FRED PHILLIPS

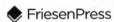 FriesenPress

Suite 300 - 990 Fort St
Victoria, BC, V8V 3K2
Canada

www.friesenpress.com

Copyright © 2016 by Fred Phillips
First Edition — 2016

All rights reserved.

No part of this publication may be reproduced in any form, or by any means, electronic or mechanical, including photocopying, recording, or any information browsing, storage, or retrieval system, without permission in writing from FriesenPress.

ISBN
978-1-4602-9548-9 (Hardcover)
978-1-4602-9549-6 (Paperback)
978-1-4602-9550-2 (eBook)

1. YOUNG ADULT FICTION, SOCIAL THEMES

Distributed to the trade by The Ingram Book Company

CHAPTER 1:
YOU SAID WHAT?

And it's one, two, three
What are we fightin' for
Don't ask me I don't give a damn

— Country Joe McDonald, *Feel Like I'm Fixin' to Die Rag*

The imaginative teacher sat alone in the faculty lounge patiently waiting for the bell to ring. At the precise moment when he reckoned all of the students would be in the classroom, he made his move.

He had been preparing for this day for weeks. He felt confident, like a matador about to enter the ring to face the raging bull. He had read the reports and he understood that he was going to have his hands full with this group of students, particularly Matt, a seventeen-year-old thug with a police record who had been bounced from several schools.

Yes, there would be many challenges and he needed to be at the top of his game. There was the girl with ADHD, the boy with Asperger's Syndrome... a condition he was still trying to wrap his head around... and several others who exhibited signs of oppositional defiance and other behavioural issues.

Although it appeared daunting, the exuberant teacher was brimming with enthusiasm as he rose confidently from his chair, strode down the hallway, opened the door to his classroom, and like the poised matador, bravely marched in. "*Good morning,* everyone!" he said.

It took a few seconds for the students to take notice, clustered as they were in several small groups, talking amongst each other. "Holy fuck!" he heard one of them exclaim in a whisper. "Who the fuck is this?" another one muttered.

The object of their shocked curiosity stood before them, fully decked out in a black tuxedo, riding chaps and top hat. His knee-high boots had been shined to a sparkling finish. He looked as if he was heading to the royal ball rather than a classroom full of misfits deemed too incorrigible to teach.

"I'm John Stevens, your new teacher. You may call me Mr. Stevens, or you may call me John, or you may call me sir, or you may address me in whatever manner you deem appropriate."

"Is it okay if I call you weirdo?" one of the students asked.

"Do you feel that addressing me in such a manner is appropriate?"

"Well, you look like a weirdo."

"What's your name?"

"Scott," replied the rebellious looking kid, eyeing the man at the front of the room.

"Thank you for your honesty, Scott."

"How about Teach?" asked a short, brown haired kid sitting behind Scott.

"That seems appropriate," John replied. "What's your name?"

"Josh."

"Yes, Teach would be fine, Josh. Now, before I ask the rest of you to introduce yourselves I would like to show you three videos." John had arranged to have a flat-screen TV and computer brought to the room earlier that morning.

First, he showed them a video of Country Joe McDonald performing *Feel Like I'm Fixin' to Die Rag* at the 1969 Woodstock music festival. The video started with Country Joe's famous fish cheer… 'gimme an f.' Several of the students echoed the f, and they did the same when he followed up by directing the audience to 'gimme a *u*, gimme a *c*, gimme a *k*,' although, when Country Joe asked, 'what's that spell?,' the students were wise enough not to repeat the entire *f* word!

Next up was a video of comedian Robin Williams explaining how the Scots invented golf. Several of the students were familiar with the routine and laughed heartily throughout the piece.

Finally, he showed them a clip from Eddie Murphy's nineteen-eighties standup comedy performance, *Raw*. None, of the class had seen Eddie's act and most of them laughed hysterically.

At the conclusion of the last video, Teach turned off the computer and pushed the TV stand into the front corner of the room. "What did you think of those performances?" he asked, turning and addressing the class.

"They were pretty funny," one of the students replied.

"What's your name?"

"Eric," answered the tall, scraggly blond-haired teen sitting near the back of the room.

"Thank you, Eric. I'm glad you enjoyed them. And what did they all have in common?"

"There was a lot of swearing, yep" said another student, appearing quite agitated.

"What's your name?"

The young fellow looked away without answering, but judging by his appearance and his reluctance to speak, John assumed it was Adam Dinnage. Adam was heavy set and wearing an oversized sports jersey and baggy blue jeans. He was the boy with Asperger's.

"He don't like to talk to strangers, do you garbage?" taunted a student sitting nearby.

Adam immediately covered his ears, buried his face in his lap and started rocking back and forth.

"You are such a bastard, Stuart," snarled one of the girls. "You know he hates that word!"

"Shut up, stupid!"

"Hold on," the teacher interjected as all eyes turned to the front. "We're not going resolve anything yelling at each other." Aware of the potential volatility of the situation and not wanting to lose the group or the point he was about to make, John decided it would be best to let this go for now. He would get to the principles of kindness and feeling good about yourself later when he felt they were ready to listen.

"Let's move on shall we? Stuart would you please refrain from speaking unkindly to your classmates."

The smirking teen turned his head and looked out the window.

"Any swear word in particular that stood out?" the teacher continued, noticing that Adam had stopped rocking.

"The *f* bomb," said one of the boys sitting at the back.

"You can say it," the teacher encouraged.

"I can?" replied the boy, looking somewhat shocked.

"Certainly, it's just a word! Three consonants and a vowel. What's your name?"

"Tom." Tom Powell had several visible tattoos, which provided a sharp contrast to his Buddy Holly style glasses.

"Thank you, Tom. The word in question is very effective," Teach continued, as the students looked at him warily, clearly surprised with his enthusiasm for this taboo word. "It's the most versatile word in the English language. It can be used as a noun, a verb, an adjective, an adverb, or just about any other way you want to use it."

"It's an awesome word," agreed a baby-faced teen with a bit of a smirk. He was sitting at the front of the class.

"Shut up, dickhead," snapped the boy beside him.

"We all have a right to express our opinion," countered John, diplomatically.

"Ya, tell that to my dad," the boy snarled, looking away.

"What's your name?" Teach asked the second boy.

"Blair."

"And yours," he asked, looking at the other chap.

"Mike."

Blair Anderson had 'CHALLENGE' written all over him, just as his assessment had concluded. In the last few years, no teacher had been able to connect with him and he had performed miserably. He seemed to have a penchant for making life difficult for himself and everybody around him.

Mike Green on the other hand had the appearance of a good kid with good intentions, but just couldn't get it together at school. The report in his file concluded that he was a little slow, eager to please and had difficulty thinking for himself.

"Do you two have an issue with each other?"

"No," replied Blair. "I'm just messin' with him."

John nodded his head, not fully convinced he was being truthful.

"In addition to being versatile, no word conveys how you truly feel like the *f* word. If you say to someone, 'that was a great movie,' they've got a pretty good idea of how you felt about it. But if you say, 'that movie was f'n great,' they know exactly how you feel. The inclusion of the *f* word pretty much removes any doubt about the meaning of what you are trying to convey."

"So why does everyone get so uptight and angry when we say, fuck?" asked a tough looking, sandy-brown haired girl sitting three seats back to the teacher's right. "People don't care when we say, friggin'."

"I guess, at some point in time, our society decided that it was an inappropriate word to use, particularly in public."

The girl continued to look at him. "Caitlyn," she said, stone-faced.

"Pardon?" John replied.

"Caitlyn. My name is Caitlyn. I thought I'd save you the bother of asking."

"Yes! Caitlyn Jones!" he acknowledged, quite aware of her fiery demeanour.

"It was probably my parents who decided it was inappropriate."

"I think it was decided long before your parents appeared on the planet."

She stared expressionless at him for a few seconds, then curled her lip and huffed, before dropping her eyes to look at her desk."

"So why are you wearing the tux?" Scott inquired.

"What did you think when you first saw me?"

"I thought, 'for shits sake, what's this idiot up to.'"

"I thought, 'here we go again, another teacher trying to show us who's boss,'" added Terry. Terry Williams was tall, with an athletic build and short, curly black hair. He had a mischievous smile and an easygoing manner.

"I thought, 'loser,' cause you look kinda silly," said Jessica, a thin, talkative girl with an ever-present smile. She was not so kindly described as ADHD on steroids and Red Bull. She had a big heart, but had great difficulty containing herself. She talked constantly and was very impulsive.

John Stevens patiently acknowledged each of their responses with a smile and a nod. "Well, to answer your question, I wanted to show you that things aren't always as they appear to be. I'm guessing that you wouldn't have expected a teacher in a tuxedo to come in here and start talking about the *f* word."

"I wouldn't have expected that from any teacher," agreed Jordan. Jordan Thomas was tall and lean with short-cropped black hair. His inclusion in the class was quite odd. Although he struggled with reading and writing, he was intelligent and quite perceptive. John's immediate assessment was that he seemed personable. He was puzzled that the bright young man didn't perform better in school.

"Well, life is kind of like that. Sometimes things aren't as they appear to be and you've got to look past the illusion to see the truth. Life is about contrasts and quite often we need to experience the opposite of what we want in order to understand and appreciate what it is we truly desire."

"What do you mean by that?" Terry inquired, looking doubtful.

"Many people grow up in circumstances and environments that are less than ideal. Our challenge is to step outside of our suffering to see the gift in the experience."

"That sounds like bullshit," countered Stuart. "What gift is there when your dad yells at you every day?"

Stuart Carter, a thin, sandy brown haired kid, was Blair Anderson's sidekick. He was a follower and as much as the school wanted to separate the pair, they felt that he could benefit from this program, so they took a risk and included him in the group.

Just then the bell rang, signaling the end of class.

"One more thing," John added, before the students could get out of their seats, "the *f* word has another benefit."

"Oh ya, what's that?" Mike asked.

"Swearing helps relieve stress."

"Hey, I saw something about that on TV a while ago!" Scott said.

"Studies have actually demonstrated it."

"Awesome!" remarked Blair. "I'll be swearing all the time."

"We'll have to continue this discussion tomorrow. In the meantime, swear discretely and have a great day," the jubilant matador shouted, hoping everyone would hear him above the loud chatter that had erupted.

Nobody acknowledged him, so he simply nodded his head as they filed out of the room.

After all the other students had left, Matt walked up to the teacher's desk and stood menacingly before him. At six foot six and sporting multiple tattoos and a shaved head, he was an imposing figure, especially when he was standing inches away. "You might just be an okay guy," he said, taking John Stevens by surprise.

"Thank you, Matt!"

"I hope you're not bullshitting us." Not waiting for a response, he turned and walked out of the room.

I guess I might have a chance after all, Teach thought, grinning to himself.

As Blair and Stuart walked up the hallway towards the cafeteria many students stepped aside not wanting to get in their way and risk being humiliated or roughed up. "Hey watch this," Blair said as he walked over and punched a chubby, red-haired kid in the arm. "You're a dickhead, Trevor," he mocked, as the other boy grimaced in pain.

Trevor was too terrified to say anything, particularly when the two troublemakers were together. The pair harassed a lot of kids at the school. Not getting the response they were hoping for, Blair gave the terrified teen a shove, taunting him with "wimp," before continuing on.

"He might be okay," Stuart said, continuing their conversation.

"He's a fuckin' teacher. They're all idiots."

"Well, he seems different."

"He's different all right. That stupid-ass cape. What a jerk!"

"You can't blame him for trying, man."

"Ya, right. Let's see what he's like tomorrow."

"I bet he's for real."

"Don't start goin' soft on me, man."

"I'm not going soft. I just think he's okay."

"Have you ever liked any teacher?"

"No."

"Well, this one's not gonna be any different."
"Ya, I guess."

"What happened to your big plan, gentlemen?" asked Tom, joining the group that had congregated outside the gym.

"Teach got us!" replied Josh.

"He certainly did," agreed Tom with a chuckle.

"I didn't see that coming," remarked Eric.

"That was very clever," observed Ryan. "What could you say, man?"

"He came in with both barrels blazing," said Tom. "The outfit and the videos."

"Ya, man. I mean, how could we give him a hard time after that?" asked Scott.

"I don't think you're gonna get to this guy like most teachers," said Ryan.

"He's knows his stuff," added Josh.

"This is going to be an interesting year," said Tom with an approving smile.

"You got that right," agreed Eric.

Before leaving the school, John Stevens paid a visit to Principal Clark's office. He was still getting adjusted to the new Principal, although, he instinctively liked him. John had a good relationship with Neil Glover, the former Principal, but Clark was far more progressive and seemed more spiritual in nature. He felt confident they would work well together.

"How did it go today?" the Principal inquired in a very business-like manner.

"Awesome, Ken! I connected with the students as well as I could have hoped."

"They're a tough group. Perhaps the most challenging class of students I've ever seen. I understand your costume took them by surprise."

"Yes! I would say it shocked them a bit."

"Given the importance of this initiative, that might be a good thing."

John recalled the end of the previous school year when he had been summoned to Neil Glover's office. Glover informed him that he was moving on to another school and that John had been selected to teach a special class. The school board was impressed with the results he had achieved, particularly in winning over the students and inspiring them to get more out of their education. By challenging the status quo and standing up to the resistance they faced, he and the students, had in essence created a new, more interesting curriculum that was more relevant and applicable to the students. By doing so, they had won over the school board and parents alike. So the Board decided to put this success to the test to see if he could salvage these students.

The innovative Stevens saw an opportunity to create a new program for classroom instruction, so he was quick to accept. He long held the opinion that the existing educational model was built on a premise of conformity, control and economic gain, which was no longer relevant. It did not serve our evolving society, one that was awakening in consciousness and developing a growing interest in spirituality, wisdom and truth. He felt that we needed an education system that focused on enlightenment and bringing awareness to the true purpose of our existence. One that dedicated itself to nurturing the innate creativity within each of us, while honouring the unique individuality of each soul within our overall oneness. John felt in his heart that before this could begin, people needed to feel good about themselves. This was critical if change was to be accomplished. "Yes, it certainly is," he agreed. "But we've still got a long road ahead of us."

"One other thing," Clark said. "We've got a new Director of Education at the school board. His name is Jonathan Fox and that's all I know about him right now."

"That's a little unusual isn't it?" remarked a very surprised Stevens, "replacing the Director on the first day of school."

"Highly unusual," agreed his new boss, looking a little distressed.

John was feeling quite puzzled as he left the school. His sixth sense was telling him something wasn't quite right.

An important element of John Stevens' transformation from an angry, disillusioned victim to a spiritually conscious man who experienced more inner peace and joy, involved letting go of the emotional pain that he had been holding on to since his childhood, particularly the rage, hatred and shame he was feeling towards himself for growing up feeling inferior and cowardly. He had to acknowledge that anger was a big part of his life and he had to release the emotional energy that lay underneath the anger that was getting him into so much trouble and causing him so much unhappiness. He also had to acknowledge that this was a process that could last a lifetime.

John could see that the same approach was critical with the new group of students he had been assigned to teach. Each one of them was seething with anger and in many cases, it was clearly boiling over. In their minds, they had been victimized their entire lives and they still felt like victims. Being in this class reinforced their feelings of victimhood. It made them feel marginalized and unwanted; feelings they had been experiencing since childhood. It made them feel like outcasts.

Aware that he was sitting on a powder keg, he needed to use a delicate touch in order to guide these kids to their own inner peace and joy. He needed to help them understand that in order for each of us to heal any unpleasant condition or life situation, we must understand and heal the fear, faulty beliefs and emotional pain that are at the root of the condition. He was facing a huge challenge with this fragile group.

John was feeling very cheerful as he pulled into Sandra's driveway. He had enjoyed an awesome day and life in general had been amazing for some time now. He had settled quite comfortably into this town and he was pleased with his initial interaction with the new class. Most of all, he was really enjoying his relationship with Sandra Connors. They had been dating for over a year and he was very much in love. Life couldn't have been better. He hopped easily out of the truck and almost sprinted up the walk to her front door. Opening it, she looked as beautiful as ever. He stepped into the front entranceway and gave her a long embrace. As he held her closely she felt somewhat tentative. She didn't hug him in the usual manner.

"Are you okay?" he asked, as he released her and stepped back.

"Of course, I'm fine," she replied, with a forced smile.

Her response was less than convincing, but he thought better than to press her at the moment. He removed his shoes and followed as she turned and made her way into a spacious, well-appointed kitchen.

She began telling him about her day, but she talked nervously and she spoke with her back to him.

"Something is going on and you need to tell me what it is?" he insisted.

She hesitated for a moment. "Yes, there is something going on," she admitted, looking away.

John Stevens felt his heart jump up into his throat. He had no idea what was coming, but he sensed it was not good news. A flood of thoughts came crashing into his mind. He didn't know if his girlfriend was sick or if she wanted to end the relationship or what it was, so he stood quietly waiting for her to speak.

"It's been my lifelong dream to teach art at the university level," she began, now trying to look bravely into his eyes.

"Yes," he acknowledged hesitantly.

"But I thought that I was never going to realize this dream. A few years ago I applied to several colleges, but had no luck. Then I landed the position at PLJ High and I've been quite happy teaching here, especially since you arrived at the school."

In that moment, he realized what was coming and he immediately felt a pang of anxiety. His throat constricted and his hands began to tremble. It had been a long time since he had felt this way and he was overwhelmed by it. He took a deep breath and tried to centre himself, but it seemed that the anxiety was out of control. It was overpowering him, so he allowed himself to feel it, as unbearable as it was.

"This morning I received a call from one of the country's most prestigious art schools, offering me my dream job, teaching contemporary art."

"That's wonderful," he said, trying to seem happy and sincere.

"I couldn't believe it. I had given up hope that it was ever going to happen and I stopped thinking about it after I met you. I haven't been able to focus or think clearly all day."

He walked over and wrapped his arms around her. His emotions were mixed and his mind was racing. He knew that this was an incredible opportunity, but the thought of her moving away was more than he could imagine. "How did this come up?" he enquired, clearly puzzled, "And how did they know where to contact you?"

"Someone I worked with years ago is now the arts director at the school and he called me," she explained, looking away.

"Oh," he replied, quite surprised that she had never mentioned this before.

"Yes, I haven't seen him for five years, but we've stayed in touch."

A wave of jealousy hit him like a prizefighter and he suddenly released her and stepped back. "You've stayed in touch?"

"Yes, on *Facebook*."

"Of course," he acknowledged, trying not to sound mistrusting.

"We taught at the same school for several years and we both had dreams of teaching at an art college."

This was the first time he had heard of this person and Sandra seemed to be talking evasively. He wondered if she had been romantically involved with him. He also wondered if this guy was still interested in her. Perhaps that was why he offered her the job. He needed to know from where she was coming. He couldn't tell if her feelings were mutual, if she was truly considering the job because of him or simply because it had been her dream. He was feeling very confused and distressed, but he didn't want to show it. He waited for her to continue.

"I'm sorry to throw this at you right now, but I don't know what to do."

"Then don't do anything," he suggested. "At least not right now. Not until you've had a chance to consider everything."

"I need to make a decision by Friday and as much as I enjoy teaching at PLJ, this would be an easy decision if you weren't in my life."

John was taken aback by the urgency of the situation. "Why so soon?"

"They need to fill the position immediately."

"What happened to whoever was in the job?"

"Apparently, she left suddenly."

He thought it quite a coincidence that this was happening on the first day of school ... the same day the Director of Education had been replaced.

"This is so difficult. I'm a mess."

He took her in his arms again and held her closely. He was torn, wanting to feel happy for someone for whom he cared so intensely, but also feeling very betrayed. He did not want to lose her.

"What should I do?'

"I don't know… I don't know," he replied looking desperately upward.

The rest of the evening was a blur. Driving home, John remembered very little of the conversation, other than that Sandra was seriously considering the offer. The fact that she was, left him feeling quite let down… and angry… but he wasn't sure who or what he was more angry at… Sandra Connors or life.

It seemed like this was constantly happening to him. Every time things were going well, he got kicked in the teeth. He remembered how he was feeling when he arrived at her place earlier that evening. He had been riding a wave of confidence and joy… as joyful and confident as he had ever felt in his life. And now this. "Damn it!" he screamed, pounding the steering wheel. "Why are you always doing this to me? Why are you always creating so much heartache?"

And then it suddenly struck him. Heartache! Heartache… the emotional pain that seemed to constantly haunt him. It was at the core of these experiences. Heartache was why he was never able to experience sustained joy. It was why he was continually being betrayed by life.

But he was not the powerless victim here, reminding himself of the five essentials and the fact that we're always being tested. Rather, he was now the conscious architect of his experiences. He, and he alone, was creating them through his beliefs and only he could create change. He was in charge of his life. He was responsible for his beliefs. He just needed to stay in the moment and try to understand what was at the root of it.

In that moment, he felt empowered by this epiphany and the anger subsided.

CHAPTER 2:
TAKING CHARGE

And to my mind
Everything's stinking
Stinking without you

— The Cranberries, *Miss You When You're Gone*

As John walked into the classroom, he had very mixed emotions. He was still feeling upbeat about his initial interaction with the students on day one. He felt certain that he had connected with them and he was looking forward to the day's discussion. He was particularly encouraged by Matt's comment at the end of the class.

But he was also still reeling from Sandra's admission that she was considering a teaching position at another school. Despite the epiphany he experienced on the drive home, he still felt confused and angry with her. He would have to muster up a tremendous amount of focus and courage in order to teach effectively today.

"Where's your tux?" inquired Scott, snapping the beleaguered teacher back to reality.

"Back at the rental shop," he replied.

"I thought it suited you. You should have worn it!" said Caitlyn.

"I'll give your suggestion due consideration, Caitlyn," Teach smiled, trying to be cheerful and non-confrontational with his response. He sensed that she had a great deal of anger boiling just below the surface and he knew instinctively that connecting with her would require a delicate touch.

She eyed him for a moment, before turning her attention to her cell phone. She appeared to be looking at a text message. He noticed that a couple of other students were in the midst of texting. "Okay everyone, would you kindly finish up with your text messages and turn off your phones so we can begin class."

Josh and Stuart turned off their phones and placed them in their pockets while Caitlyn continued texting.

"Caitlyn, would you put your cell phone away, please."

Again she ignored him.

"Caitlyn!" he said.

"This is important, man!" she snapped.

Feeling that she was testing him, he walked over to her desk and held out his hand, "Would you give me your cell phone please."

"No way."

"This is not something for which you have a choice."

"I'm not giving you my phone," she repeated, jumping out of her seat and backing away a few paces.

"You can't take her phone," said Blair.

"Ya, man! No way," agreed Stuart as the rest of the class joined in the protest, hollering and banging their desks.

John realized immediately that he had stepped into a hornet's nest. Caitlyn was openly challenging his authority with the support of her classmates. All the time and effort he had put into connecting with these kids could be undone right at this moment if he didn't take appropriate action. "Come with me, everyone!" he commanded walking out the door.

"Alright!" he heard one of the boys shout, as the students followed him down the hallway. "We're goin' on a field trip."

Several of the boys were pushing and jostling each other and the entire group was talking loudly and behaving inappropriately. That is, until they rounded the corner heading towards the main office. All of a sudden, things got very quiet.

Teach opened the door and without breaking stride, walked right into Principal Clark's office. He winked at the Principal who sat quietly letting the teacher take the lead.

Josh, who was leading the group, stopped in the doorway, not sure if he should enter.

"Come in," John directed.

They crowded hesitantly into the office, not uttering a word.

Teach waited patiently until they were all inside before speaking. "Your behaviour was entirely inappropriate! When you are ready to conduct yourselves in a proper manner, you are welcome to come back to the classroom." Then without saying another word, he left.

As he made his way down the hallway, he could only imagine what was going through the students' minds. Their Principal was a former college wrestler and football player. While he was very personable, he was nobody to mess with.

Moments after arriving back at his desk, the first of the students, Matt and Tracy, walked through the door.

They were followed in short order by Josh, Ryan, Tom and the rest of the class. Caitlyn was the last one to return.

After they were all seated, John walked over to her. "May I have your cell phone please?"

"No," she said defiantly.

"Caitlyn, you have a choice. You can hand me your phone or you can go back to the office."

She looked at him for a moment, then took her phone out of her pocket.

"I'll give it back to you at the end of the class," he promised, holding out his hand.

"Fine," she huffed, handing it to him.

"Thank you."

The rebellious young woman turned her head and looked out the window.

At that moment, John realized that he had focused so much of his attention and preparation on connecting with these kids that he had forgotten something very important. In his zest to show them that he understood their problems, he had neglected to establish who was in charge of the classroom. He hadn't communicated the boundaries for acceptable behaviour, which was particularly important for this group and he needed to do it right now. Caitlyn and some of the other students had issues with authority and needed fair and clearly established boundaries in order for the class to function effectively.

"Given what just took place, this would be an appropriate time for me to tell you what my expectations are for your involvement in this class."

"Great," scowled Terry, "another control freak tellin' us how it's gonna be."

"This isn't about control, this is about what I need from you in order to be able to teach this class effectively."

"So what do you want us to do?" asked Scott, "Sit here quietly like good little boys and girls?"

Scott Pearson was quite small for his age, but he had a constant smile and was rarely serious about anything. Unfortunately, his cavalier attitude was constantly getting him into trouble. His previous teachers wanted him to be more serious.

"Not quite. Actually, it's very straightforward. What I need from each of you is two things. First, I would ask you to participate. The more you get involved, the more you will get out of everything we do. It's just that simple. Second, I need you to be as attentive as you can be. Again, the more attentive you are, the more you will get out of this class.

"Those are the two things I need you to do. What I encourage you to do, is your best. If you do your best, generally speaking, everything will work out just fine," he stated with conviction, noticing that Caitlyn appeared to be listening to the conversation, although not looking directly at him.

"If you do your reading assignments and your homework, complete your projects and prepare for your tests, you will be successful and I have no doubt that you will move to the next level. If you choose not to do the work, you will have to deal with the consequences. I am not here to babysit you. You, and only you, are responsible for your results."

"Is that it?" asked Tom.

"Not quite. There are two things I will not allow you to do in this classroom. I will not allow you disrupt the class and I will not allow you to bother another student. If you do either one of these things, I will simply ask you to go sit in the main office until you are ready to participate appropriately."

"So you're gonna punish us," observed Tracy.

Tracy Morrow was another student with which John had difficulty understanding her inclusion in the class. Dark haired and slightly heavy set, although, attractive, her report indicated that she was bright, conscientious and personable. But she was also rebellious and challenged authority, not always in a constructive way. She seemed to have trouble fitting in to mainstream. "You won't be punished. Nor will you get a detention or lose your privileges. You will simply be asked to sit in the office until you are ready to participate. When you have decided that you are ready to take part you will be welcome to return to class."

"What if I don't want to come back to class?" asked Blair.

"Then you can remain in the office. Again, you are responsible for your work. Whatever you miss during class, you will be responsible for catching up on. But I can assure you, the more you participate and the more time you spend in this class, the more you will get out of it and the less you will have to do in the evening."

John Stevens stood silently waiting for an objection. "Does this sound fair?"

Several of the students nodded their heads. There were no objections.

"What about respect?" asked Tom. "Don't you want us to respect one another?"

"Respect for others starts with respect for yourself. If you don't respect yourself… if you don't feel good about yourself… you can't possibly respect others. But I can't force you to respect others just like I can't force you to feel good about yourself."

"Do you mean we have to have high self-esteem?" asked Eric.

"Yes, that's another word for it."

"I don't understand what that means… to feel good about yourself," said Jessica. "Does that mean you're supposed to feel happy?"

"Feeling happy actually comes from feeling good about yourself. Feeling good about yourself means that you feel lovable… that you believe you are capable of being loved. It means that you feel worthy… that you are deserving of everything life has to offer. It also means that you feel adequate... that you feel good enough to do anything you want to do. And lastly, it means that you feel empowered. It means that you feel like you are in charge of your life. I believe that nothing is more important on a day to day basis for our health and happiness than how you feel about yourself. If you don't feel good about yourself, nothing else matters."

"How do you know when you don't feel good about yourself?" inquired Mike.

"There are many ways to tell. The most obvious is by how you treat yourself and others and by how you let others treat you. If you mistreat people, if you mistreat yourself, or if you let others mistreat you, it's hard to imagine that you're doing it because you feel good about yourself."

"When you mistreat someone else you actually feel worse about yourself, don't you?" asked Tracy.

"I don't!" Blair said snidely.

"That's quite true," replied Teach ignoring the comment for the moment. "For most people, mistreating someone else just adds more shame and guilt to how they already feel. You can also tell how you feel about yourself by the type of relationship you're in and by the job you work at."

"You mean if you're in a lousy relationship or if you work at a job that sucks it's because you don't feel good about yourself?" asked Terry.

"Yes! It can reflect a lack of self-love and self-worth."

"I guess that makes sense," agreed Ryan.

Ryan Carr was another student whose report indicated extremely high intelligence with an inability to fit into mainstream. John was pleased that his first contribution to the discussion was a positive one. In the previous year, he had been kicked out of the classroom on many occasions, mostly for being critical of his teacher, and by the end of the term, was being home-schooled.

"How else can you tell that you don't feel good about yourself?" asked Josh.

"If you complain a lot. If you have a bad attitude. If you compare yourself to others. If you don't act with integrity. And to bring this conversation full circle, your behaviour also reflects how you feel about yourself."

"What do you mean by that?" asked Josh.

"People act out and behave inappropriately because of low self esteem. They misbehave, they drink and put harmful things into their body. They become workaholics, even when they don't like their job."

"Acting like a jerk just gets you in trouble," observed Scott. "I kind of know that from personal experience."

"Yes, that's true. So why would someone act out if it's just going to hurt them?"

"My dad said I misbehaved because I was a little shit who wanted attention," answered Eric.

"Your dad sounds like a real nice guy," scorned Blair.

"He's not so bad sometimes."

"My uncle drinks cause he's trying to avoid what's bothering him," added Mike. "At least that's what my old man said."

"We do these things unconsciously, without really understanding our behaviour. A rational mind wouldn't do something that brings harm to him or herself, but our minds aren't necessarily rational. We behave this way when we grow up feeling unloved, unwanted, unaccepted and unappreciated, mostly as a result of a dysfunctional or non-existent relationship with one or both of our parents. When we grow up feeling this way, quite often we believe we must be bad. If our parents don't love us, don't want us, don't accept us and don't appreciate us, there must be something wrong with us. And this leads to self-hatred."

"I don't get that," said Eric. "Just because we don't love ourselves, doesn't mean we hate ourselves, does it?"

"In all things, there are polarities… opposites. If we don't love ourselves because our parents didn't teach us how to, and if we believe we are bad because our parents told us we were, on a certain level, we must hate ourselves. If we didn't have self-loathing, we wouldn't do self-destructive things that get us into trouble."

"Um, that's pretty messed up," Josh piped up. Although Josh was quick-witted, he sometimes had difficulty following instructions and articulating what was in his mind. He also had a habit of using humour inappropriately, although at the moment, he was playing it straight.

"It certainly is. If we only realized that that there's nothing wrong with us, that it's actually our parents who have the issues."

"That sounds like crap," snorted Blair. "Why do your parents want to mess you up? Why would they have you if they didn't want you?"

"A lot of kids are mistakes," observed Jessica. "My friend Joanna is a mistake. She told me so."

Jessica's admission brought a few snickers from the class.

"We're talking about two different things, although they're related. Yes, it's true that children frequently arrive in the world unplanned. They may be born to adults who are unwed, married couples who are not quite ready to begin a family, teenagers who are dating and people who have one night stands without using protection. But whether children are planned or not, quite often their parents are unable to connect with them, love them and want them due to their own emotional woundings. Many parents had dysfunctional relationships with their parents that left them incapable of having healthy relationships with their children. Or it may be that some parents were forced to get married because of a pregnancy and they hold resentment towards that child."

"There are a variety of factors involved, but the net result is that we've created a society that collectively doesn't feel good about itself."

"So that's why my old man yells at me," observed Stuart. "He doesn't feel good about himself. All of a sudden I don't feel so bad."

"Nor should you," agreed Tom.

John was pleased that Stuart had figured out the answer to his question on his own.

"Man," observed Mike, "we started off arguing about cell phones and ended up talking about our messed up society. How did that happen?"

"That's how things seem to work, Mike. When you look at our individual behaviours and when you examine the root cause of these behaviours, you start to understand why there is so much suffering going on in the world."

"Is this what we're supposed to get out of this class?" asked Tom.

"That's certainly part of it. There are many things I'm hoping you will learn and one of the things I would really love, is for you to have fun because that is what life is really all about… having fun."

"You're kidding, right?" asked Caitlyn.

Teach was surprised but pleased that she had finally joined the conversation. "Yes, I know, school is not exactly fun for most kids, but we can make the most of it. We can make it an enjoyable experience. It's totally up to us."

"If you can figure out how to make school fun, you'll be a fucking hero," said Matt.

At that moment, the bell rang. "Perhaps tomorrow we can figure out how we're going to make this school year fun."

"By closing down this rat hole," scoffed Caitlyn, as her teacher returned her phone.

"I don't think that option is available to us." She ignored John's comment and headed out of the classroom.

Caitlyn stood quietly in the smoking area at the side of the school ignoring the conversations around her. She saw her friend approaching from across the parking lot. Jessie Hall was her only real friend. They had known each other since Grade 4 when Jessie's family moved to town. Her parents split up two years ago and since then she had spent all of her free time with Caitlyn. Despite some of the difficulties the spritely girl had experienced she remained upbeat, at least in public, and she was actually quite optimistic about life. It made the pair a bit of an odd match.

"How was your class with Mr. Stevens?" Jessie asked.

"I hate him and I hate his class," replied Caitlyn.

"Why, what happened?"

"He's a dickhead. He tried to take my cell phone away from me."

"Why did he do that?"

"I was texting."

"Well, you're not allowed to text in class, girl."

"Fuckin' school rules. They were created by conformist control freaks who want us all to be sheep. I hate them."

"Ya, I know. Sometimes they suck."

"All the time they suck. They just keep people down."

"Give it time, girl. I hear Stevens is different. He's not like the rest."

"They're all the same. They're all part of the system."

"I don't know. you should give it time. What have you got next?"
"Math. What about you?"
"Drama class."
Caitlyn finished her cigarette and tossed the butt on the ground. "I gotta go."

At the end of the day, John Stevens paid a visit to Principal Clark's office to thank him for his support. The student's were unaware that the two had prearranged John's impromptu trip to the Principal's office in order to establish who was in charge and what the protocol was for their inclusion in his class. Their plan had the desired effect! They discussed the incident at length and agreed that it was a powerful way to deal with such situations.

They also discussed Adam. John was uncertain as to how to connect with him. Clark assured the concerned teacher that it would take time and that the unique teen would get involved when he was ready.

Later, he stopped by Sandra's classroom, only to discover that she wasn't there. She had called in sick. He called both her home and cell phones and got no reply from either. It wasn't like her and he was at a loss. When she also failed to respond to his text messages, he felt his anxiety level rise. He missed her desperately. He wanted to talk to her. This whole situation was very unsettling. Teach spent a fitful evening at home. He tried to reach her again by phone and text message without luck.

He considered driving over to her house to make sure she was okay, but thought better of it. He assumed that if she wasn't answering his calls, she must be doing it intentionally. By the time he went to bed that night, he was a mess and he had a restless sleep.

CHAPTER 3:
LET'S HAVE SOME FUN

Always in a hurry, I never stop to worry
Don't see the time flashin' by
Honey, got no money
I'm all sixes and sevens and nines

— The Rolling Stones, *Tumbling Dice*

John's mind was running at a million miles an hour as he walked into the school. He was certain that Sandra was planning to accept this prestigious job she had been offered. He felt unglued, almost out of his body. He couldn't understand why this was happening, particularly at this point in time when everything had been going so well. It seemed that all he had learned on his spiritual journey was temporarily lost, replaced by intense anxiety and foreboding. To get through the day he needed to be very diligent about staying present.

As the frazzled teacher rounded the corner heading towards his classroom, he suddenly heard a blood curdling scream. Thinking one of the students had been seriously injured, he bolted up the hallway and was nearly run over by Adam who came charging out the door screaming at the top of his lungs.

John quickly wheeled and chased the hysterical teen down the corridor, right into the boy's washroom. By the time he got inside, Adam was on his knees in the corner, clutching his head, sobbing uncontrollably.

Teach knelt down beside him. "What happened, Adam?" he asked calmly.

"They put garbage on my desk!" he howled.

"Who did?"

"The boys."

"Which boys?"

"I don't know!"

John thought quickly. "The garbage isn't here now, Adam."

"What?"

"The garbage isn't here. It can't hurt you."

The sobbing boy let go of his head, opened his eyes and looked at his teacher. "Is it still on my desk?"

"I don't know," John replied, wanting to be honest. "Let me go find out. While I'm checking, where would you like to wait?"

"Here!"

"Alright. But if anything happens, you go to the office and I will come and get you there. Is that okay?"

"Yes."

When he walked into the classroom, many of the students were milling about, but they quickly returned to their seats, prepared for the repercussions. "What happened here?" he asked.

Silence.

"Would anybody care to explain the garbage on Adam's desk?"

"We were just having a little fun, Teach," admitted Josh.

"Shut up, man," whispered Blair.

"Do you have anything you would like to add, Blair?"

The troublesome teen hung his head, refusing to respond.

"Thank you for your honesty, Josh, but clearly you can see that this wasn't fun for Adam."

"We didn't know he would freak out so badly," said Scott.

"Man, that was weird," added Eric.

"Do you understand Asperger's Syndrome?" John asked.

"No," Eric replied.

"Then we need to learn about it." John Stevens understood why the students had pulled this gag. They lacked self love. In his experience, people who feel good about themselves don't mistreat others, for any reason. This incident also reaffirmed the whole purpose of this class and the need to teach these kids to feel lovable. "And we also need to understand kindness and why people act unkind."

Teach asked for volunteers to clean up Adam's desk, after which, he retrieved him from the washroom. Several students offered apologies, which brought a smile to his face and seemed to break some of the tension in the room.

After things settled down, John proceeded with the talk he had planned. "When we ended our last discussion, I said that my first wish was for you to have fun this year. A couple of you expressed some doubt about the likelihood of this. But you know what, I believe it's possible to have fun in school. In fact, I believe anything is possible."

"I guess that would make you an optimist!" Travis observed.

Travis Morrison was an only child who grew up without his father. He was likeable, but had severe anger issues according to the report in his file. "And a believer," the teacher added.

"But not much of a realist," said Caitlyn.

John looked at her and mustered a faint smile, feeling the irony of what he was trying to accomplish with these students given his situation with Sandra. "If you observe young children, you see that they are constantly learning and much of what they learn is done on their own, particularly with preschoolers. One of the challenges with the education system is that it creates a very structured learning environment ... a sort of rigid, one dimensional learning environment because everyone is forced to learn the same way, about much the same things, whether it interests them or not.

"The dilemma is that we don't all learn the same way or at the same speed and our interests are quite different. Some people are auditory learners, some are visual learners and some are cognitive learners. Some students like math, others like history, while others might be interested in computers."

"Some of us don't want to be in school, period!" blurted Blair.

"That's very true, but can we come back to that later, Blair? It's an important point to address."

" Sure," he replied, pleasantly surprised by his teacher's response.

"Our minds don't all work the same. Some people are more creative in their thinking, others are good problem solvers, some comprehend really well, while others excel in their ability to memorize."

"Some people have photographic memories," remarked Josh. "Click, boom, bam. Locked in forever like an elephant."

"That is quite true. We all have these abilities. We just have them to varying degrees. What is more, in many courses students aren't really learning. Rather, they are memorizing, and quite frankly, it seems that a lot of what students are forced to memorize, is a bunch of meaningless facts about things that kids have no interest in, nor will they ever use when they finish school.

"That's not to say that memorization isn't important. It is. The ability to memorize saves us time. For example, if you know that ten plus ten equals twenty, you don't have to write it down on a piece of paper or pull out a calculator to figure out the solution."

"Or count your fingers and toes," joked Mike, bringing a few snickers from his classmates.

Throughout his oration, John noticed that the students were glancing at each other with puzzled expressions, perhaps wondering where he was going with this discussion or perhaps thinking he was a bit bonkers.

"Why is it that pre-schoolers enjoy learning?"

"Cause nobody's telling them to," replied Tracy.

"That's true. Quite often, when we're forced to do something, we resist it."

"And a lot of stuff, they need to learn," said Scott, "like tying their shoes."

"Yes, much of what children learn is useful… even necessary."

"And a lot of what they learn is fun, like throwing a ball," added Tom.

"That is an extremely important factor. Much of what children learn is more like play and it's something that interests them."

"When was the last time anybody got to play at school?" asked Ryan. "Everybody takes school so freakin' seriously. None of the teachers I've had know how to have fun."

"How would you like it if school was more like play? If you could learn what you want at your own pace and have fun doing it. What if you could learn about things that really interest you… things that are meaningful?"

"There's nothing at school I want to learn," noted Adam, surprising his teacher with his unexpected contribution. "Yep, school is stupid."

"Nothing, Adam?"

"Well, I like music."

"Do you take music class?"

"No."

"Why not?"

"They want me to play the trumpet."

"What instrument would you like to play?"

"Basically, guitar."

"And if you could play the guitar, would you?"

"Yep."

"Music class is full of losers!" Blair said.

"Perhaps Bono and a few others might take issue with that statement," Tom retorted.

Blair eyed Tom with contempt, then turned and looked out the window.

"Janis Joplin was actually considered a bit of a loser when she was in school," offered Tracy.

"She's one of the best singers ever," agreed Jessica. "I love her. She's awesome man!"

"There's far more to it than just being good at something," John interjected before Jessica could go off on a run. "Have you ever considered that through the guitar, you can learn a little about history, geography, science, physics and mathematics?"

"Ya, I guess," replied Adam, after pausing a few seconds to think about it.

"If you really have a passion for the guitar, there is plenty to learn. You could spend twenty years playing the guitar and still not know everything there is to know… different musical styles… rock, hip hop, metal, jazz… different playing styles… strumming, picking, open chords, bar chords and power chords. You could literally spend your lifetime, playing the guitar and still not know everything."

"That's true," agreed Mike. "My brother told me about how Keith Richards of the Rolling Stones learned about open G tuning and used it to create the unique Rolling Stones sound, especially on songs like Honky Tonk Woman, Brown Sugar and Tumbling Dice."

"What's open G tuning?" asked Adam.

"It's a cool way of tuning the strings of the guitar so that you can play a G chord without having to fret the strings. You just strum the strings open."

"That is cool, yep!"

"What's even cooler," Mike continued, "is that Richards learned about open G tuning after the Stones became famous and he modified it by removing the top E string."

"You mean he plays a five string guitar?"

"Yep. On some songs. Very cool, eh?"

"That's for sure. Where did he learn about open G tuning?"

Teach was more amazed by the moment with Adam's participation in the discussion. Fascinating what could happen when you sparked someone's interest.

"He first heard about it from Don Everly of the Everly Brothers, but Ry Cooder actually showed him how to do it."

"Are you serious?" asked Stuart. "Their music was so cheesy. I can't believe Keith Richards actually learned something from the Everly Brothers."

"Richards actually thought Don Everly was a really good rhythm guitarist... one of the best."

"Cool!"

"It just goes to show you that you can learn from anybody," John added.

"Who is Ry Cooder?" asked Jessica. "I've never heard of him. But he's got a cool name!"

"He's an American guitarist," replied Mike. "Plays blues, country, folk. A lot of different stuff. He's been around since the sixties."

"So what's your point?" asked Matt, directing his question at Teach.

"My point is that if we're interested in something, we'll learn about it, especially if we're allowed to learn at our own pace, without pressure. And we won't just memorize a bunch of facts, we'll actually learn it. We'll understand it. We'll be able to talk about it without having to refer to a book or a fact sheet. And what's even more important is that we'll have fun doing it. We'll actually enjoy it."

"Are you saying that we can learn anything we want?" asked Terry. "Cause man, that sounds too good to be true."

"As long as it doesn't involve breaking the law, the answer is yes. But you will be responsible for deciding what you want to learn, how you're going to learn it and demonstrating what you've learned. I'll be here to guide you and assist you along the way. If there is something you want to learn that I don't have the expertise to help you with, I'll direct you to someone who does. This is an innovative project that the school board is undertaking to create a more relevant curriculum for all students."

"That's how my brother described Keith Richards," noted Mike. "Innovative!"

"Doing something or learning something you like is fun in itself. Being innovative with it takes it to an entirely different level of enjoyment."

"But why us?" asked Tom.

"Each of you is in this classroom as a part of this initiative because the education system, I believe, has not served you."

"You got that right," said Scott.

"It has not motivated you to learn. Nor has it supported when you needed it. It has not recognized the challenges you face both inside and outside the classroom."

"I don't get it," said Josh. "How is this gonna work? What if we all want to learn something different?"

"That's kind of what we're here to figure out. As I said, this is an innovative initiative."

"So you have no idea what you're doing!" remarked Caitlyn.

"I have some ideas on how things can work and we're going to test these ideas."

She eyed John suspiciously, but didn't respond. "The purpose of elementary and secondary school the way they are currently structured, is two-fold: to educate you about specific 'core' subjects, such as mathematics and history, and to prepare you for post-secondary school life, whether that is to continue your education or enter the workforce. The purpose of the education system, as a whole, is to educate people so they can make more money for themselves, the companies they work for and the governments that supposedly serve us."

"So it's all about money," observed Ryan.

"It certainly seems that way. What the education system doesn't do very well, is understand and develop your unique special talents. It doesn't really try to understand what interests you. It doesn't teach you about kindness, compassion, acceptance, forgiveness, our innate sensitivity or any other basic human attribute that is so important to creating a loving society; one that strives to protect each other and this planet we live on.

"Nor, quite frankly, does it do anything to help you feel good about yourself, and as I said yesterday, this is the most important thing for each of us. It doesn't teach you what this means, why we don't feel good about ourselves, how we can recognize when we don't or what we can do to change how we feel."

"Schools don't care about what's going on in our lives either," remarked Tracy. "I know kids that are terrified to come to school because they're being bullied."

"And a lot of kids are going through really hard times at home and don't want to be at school," added Josh. "I mean, how important is school when your parents are splitting up cause your dad has a new girlfriend and he's moving to another town?"

Teach was pleasantly surprised at how seriously Josh was taking this discussion, given his history of turning everything into a joke, quite often, at inappropriate times.

"Society is changing, man," said Mike, "but schools aren't."

"Ya," said Eric. "Look at all these kids with autism and Asperger's and ADHD. My parents said they didn't have any of this when they were kids. Now the schools are full of them."

"I have ADHD," said Jessica. "I drive my parents crazy cause I talk all the time and I can't sit still."

Jessica's admission of what was quite obvious to everyone brought a few snickers from the class.

"Aw, shut up you guys," she grumbled.

"You're the one that needs to shut up," retorted Blair.

"Speaking of compassion!" said Caitlyn, staring at him.

"What? She talks all the time."

"At least she doesn't hurt people," said Tracy.

Her comment seemed to sting the boy, because he hung his head without responding.

"Well, now that we've gotten that out of the way," John interrupted.

"Some people say that there are more kids with autism because docs are doing a better job of diagnosing the condition," said Travis.

"If that were true then where are all the adults with autism?" asked Ryan.

"Good point."

"As you can see from this exchange, just talking about the education system brings up a lot of emotion and contentious issues."

"It's true that kids hate school," said Tom. "But nobody seems to be concerned about us. Our parents just want us to get good marks. They could care less if school is meaningful and they don't seem to care how we feel about it. They just go along with the system without questioning it."

"It's the same with teachers," added Jordan. "They just go with the flow, maybe because they're afraid of losing their jobs."

"I agree with Tom and Jordan," said Ryan, suddenly taking an interest in the conversation. "There are some fundamental flaws with the system. I've hated school and teachers all my life."

"Why is that, Ryan?"

"How about because my Grade 1 teacher used to beat the shit out of us and nobody did anything about it!"

John was not startled by Ryan's admission. There are too many bully teachers in schools and given that they are unionized they're quite often hard to identify and weed out.

"Why didn't you say something?" asked Jordan.

"Are you kidding? We were all terrified of her. And besides, if I told my parents that I got in trouble at school, I'd probably get it even worse."

"That sucks," sympathized Josh.

"Bully teachers are a big problem in schools," observed Tom.

"Yes, they're one of the things that needs to change," agreed John. "They're another symptom of a society that doesn't feel good about itself. And Tom and Jordan are both right. Everybody is focused on marks and grade point average, forsaking all else."

"If kids felt good about themselves, as you suggested," remarked Ryan, "wouldn't marks improve by extension?"

"I'm sure they would."

The jubilant teacher couldn't quite believe what he was witnessing. The students were participating in the discussion and behaving in a way that he thought might never be possible, given what he had read in their files. And it seemed the only thing he did was to initiate a relevant conversation.

"I don't believe anyone has the courage to step up and say, 'Hey, the education system isn't working,'" remarked Tom.

"Perhaps we can change that. It seems that we have chosen a good group of students for this project. You have expressed some very strong feelings about this issue."

"What do you plan to do about it?" inquired Matt.

"Let me explain. This initiative will have three elements. First, as we've been discussing, each of you will be able choose something that you would like to learn about, be it related to arts, music, sports, computers, business, nature or whatever. You will not be limited to the school's current curriculum. You will be responsible for selecting your topic or area of study and for determining your objective. I will help you with both of these."

"That's good, cause I'm gonna need some help figuring this out!" said Jessica.

"We'll help you," Tracy offered.

"Thanks, Tracy. I need lots of help." Jessica was smiling from ear to ear at her classmate's kind gesture.

"Second, we will also focus on self-image, or as I talked about earlier, the importance of feeling good about yourself. We will delve deeply into what this means, how you can tell when you don't and what you can do to ensure that you do."

"I've never heard anyone talk about that kind of thing before," admitted Jordan.

"Quite frankly, it's the most important thing there is to talk about. If we don't feel good about ourselves, how important is anything else?"

"What's the third thing?" asked Travis.

"Third, we will learn about compassion, acceptance and other important attributes. We'll learn from the perspective of how it applies to each of us, as well as how it applies to all of humanity."

"What about the rest of our classes?" inquired Ryan.

"You still require a certain number of credits in order to graduate. This is just one credit, so you will have to take other courses from the standard curriculum."

"That sucks," complained Blair.

"Hey, it's better than nothing," countered Stuart.

"I'd rather not be here at all."

"Then it will be a pleasure to have you serve me when I pull in for gas ten years from now," Tom kidded.

"I'd rather pump gas than be in school."

"You might say that now, but I don't think you would after twenty years of it, buddy" countered Stuart.

"I only care about right now man."

"Maybe that will change," remarked Jordan.

"I doubt it."

At that moment, the bell rang signaling the end of class. "We'll have to continue this discussion tomorrow," Teach said, as the students filed out the door. "Have an awesome day!"

Their teacher's cheerful comment prompted several of the students to nod their head. Even Caitlyn appeared to give him an approving glance.

"What do you make of what Mr. Stevens talked about?" Mike asked Tom, standing outside the school.

"Let's just say, it sounds interesting," Tom replied.

"You don't trust him?"

"I don't trust anything schools do. They continually make promises, but nothing ever changes."

"Ya, you're right. They're like the freakin' government."

"Besides, he didn't seem to have his heart in it. He wasn't exactly very convincing."

"Ya, it seemed like he wasn't totally there. So what do we do?"

"Nothing right now. Let's just see what happens."

"Do you really think anything will happen?"
"You heard the man, anything is possible!"
"I guess."

As John Stevens walked out of the classroom at the end of the day, he was feeling some uncertainty about the attitude of the class. He felt that he had begun developing a connection with them and even though he was encouraged by their participation, he sensed that there was still some reluctance, particularly with Blair and Caitlyn. Doubt about the sincerity of the school system or John's sincerity perhaps or his ability to make this happen. Maybe they were sensing his anxiety. He felt that he had done his best to hide the angst he was feeling about Sandra, but it was very difficult and he sensed this group was very intuitive. He was also concerned that the anger and resentment that characterized much of their lives could undermine things. He also knew that whatever path they chose would be the right one for them. Yet, he couldn't help but want to give them some guidance that would enable them to trust him.

As he rounded the corner and headed down the main hallway towards the front door, he ran into Matt who was just coming out of the change room.

"Still at school?" the cheerful teacher asked.

"Ya, man. I was doing some weightlifting."

The burly student had his hands full with books and binders, including a folder that was balancing precariously on top of the pile.

"Would you like a little help carrying some of this stuff? I could carry the binders and that folder."

"No thanks. The folder has my… um… poems in it," he said hesitantly.

"You write poems?"

"Ya. Sort of."

"Would you mind if I have a look at a couple of them?"

Matt paused for a moment. "Ya, I guess that would okay."

John took the folder off the binders, pulled out a poem and began reading it. "This is quite good," he said. Then he pulled another one out and read it. "Your work is extraordinary. How long have you been writing poetry?"

"Since I was eleven. Actually, I wrote one on the weekend and I think it is meaningful. Would you mind looking at it?" he asked, pulling a piece of paper out of one of the binders.

"I would love to." He took the poem and began reading. After he was finished, he stood silently. It touched him deeply and for several moments he was unable to speak.

The towering teen stood quietly awaiting his assessment. "I call it, *the wisdom of the night sky*."

"Wow! This poem is incredible!"

"Thank you."

"It is very significant and I would love to share it with the class. Would you be okay with that?"

"Um… I guess that would be okay," he said, stuffing the poem into his folder.

"Great."

"I'm sorry, but I've got to go or I'm gonna be late for work."

"No worries. See you in the morning."

Teach watched as the budding poet hustled out the front door and headed towards the street. He wondered what the other students are going to think when they find out who he really is. They're in for quite a surprise. Then he had another thought, *Man, I love my guides!*

Before leaving the parking lot, John sent another text to Sandra. He simply said, *I hope you are doing well. I love you!* About a half an hour after he had arrived home, he finally received a reply. *I'm sorry that I haven't been in touch. I hope you can understand. I need to be alone in order to make this decision. Will call you.*

He felt both relief and anger. He was thankful to know that she was okay, but angry that she had shut him out. He was shocked that she was capable of this behaviour. He didn't see it coming.

He waited by the phone all evening, but her call never came. He was devastated and took it very personally. He felt like he was on a rollercoaster ride of emotion… very gratified with his experience with the students, yet deeply upset with his girlfriend and himself for forgetting his spiritual teachings. It was well after midnight when sleep finally came and he was deep in anguish.

CHAPTER 4: HEALING THE HEART

Well, I think you're smart
You sweet thing
Tell me your sign
I'm dying here

— The Flys, *Got You Where I Want You*

John Stevens became aware of a familiar presence in the room. He felt peaceful and calm knowing intuitively there was nothing here to fear. And then she came into view. It was the beautiful angel who had visited him many times before, bringing him comfort and understanding around troubling issues. She was smiling at him. And then she spoke.

"I am present with you today, with great gratitude for the opportunity to offer a new opening… a new door opening… in your experience of healing the heart. This entire process upon which you are about to embark is of the heart… around the heart… engaging the heart. This is where I ask you to draw your attention. This is, in a sense, all you need to know. This is the future of your power and the present focus of your healing. Your heart has been crying out for this and now the time is here.

"We misunderstand the nature of our hearts. We think of them as physical organs that are custodians of life and death, a pump, like a mechanical object, and yet, deeper within the body lies the source of life ... the seat of the soul. The heart holds the soul, embraces it, and speaks for it upon its journey."

John was again in awe of this wondrous celestial being. He felt beautifully tranquil and safe in her presence. As he bathed in her warmth, the angel continued.

"You have come in this life to achieve mastery and nothing less. Hence, the intensity of the drive you experience on a daily basis. This mastery, this urgency, to achieve it, is both your great gift and your wound, awaiting awareness. For the journey, of course, is towards the recognition of the mastery that already lies within you but, is presently in denial. It is this denial to which we wish to speak today.

"If you take a creature of great power, a horse for example, and you harness this animal, you keep it under bridle, halter, rein and saddle. These are instruments of control, intended not to support the power of the being itself, but only to make use of it, to address the needs of others… those who would take its power for their own. This is a familiar sensation for you. You have been this animal and you have worn these constraints. You know how it feels to have a bit in your mouth… to have a saddle tied around your girth. You know what it feels like to have a whip cracked over your head and to have your neck turned from side to side by the pulls of a rider who thinks you are nothing more than a vehicle for his own desires.

"You have in this life, an opportunity to be a great leader, and yet, there is a very important and large step that awaits you before you can undertake this task, for your leadership is to stem from the awareness and the openness of the heart. At this time, your perceptions and your awareness and your energies are focused elsewhere. They are focused within the mind and the body. The heart is distinct from both these places, and yet, it encompasses all. The body is simply form... it is a means of expression... it is beautiful... it is a profound gift. But the body does not tell us who we are. It is to be honoured and respected, but it is only form.

"The mind is our servant. Yes, there is tremendous power here, and humankind is on the verge of discovering this, and yet so often in this attempt to understand the use and the purpose of the mind, we cannot see beyond our own blindness... we cannot see beyond the limitations and the fears that are so deeply embedded that they are not yet conscious... they are not yet visible to the awakening soul. And so, we assume that the mind must come first, that it is the mind that will lead us to the heart, when in fact, it is always the other way around... hence, the importance of understanding the true nature of the heart."

The words which the angel was speaking were having a profound affect on John. He could feel his heart pounding as if the emotional pain contained within was about to explode from his body in a triumphant flight to freedom. He might have thought he was having a heart attack, so incredibly intense as the pain, and yet he trusted that he was well, so the angel continued.

"The purpose and the essence of our experience is of the heart, because it is always the heart that brings light into all aspects of our being.

"When imbalance is present, it may be experienced in so many ways. This is the primary reason for the levels of what you might term dysfunction on the planet today. There are so many beings opening themselves toward wholeness, simultaneously on the planet at one time… so many souls reaching together to create a united flame. And we do this through great acts of courage, including those which may be defined in various cultures as hindrances, disabilities, limitations, illnesses, fears and challenges. All of these are simply aspects of growth and they rise on the planet now because our Mother and our Father desire it to be so."

He wondered if the acts of courage of which the angel spoke are all the brave souls who are coming to the planet experiencing autism, Asperger's, ADHD and other conditions, in order to help guide humanity to the next stage of our evolution. Where we begin to live in awareness of who we really are and why we're really here on the planet, and where we live in peace, love and joy… where we live with compassion and acceptance.

"And so, if you consider yourself only a part of this great wave you can in all honesty give thanks and offer gratitude for your new understanding of the role you have chosen to play. There is great beauty in the opportunity for healing that you have waited so long to enact. But it is new, and it will take time, understanding and the deepest surrender.

"If we return to the horse, how can this horse ever be its totality and its magnificent power if he is so constrained? The nature of the horse is not as servant to man. This is the conjoining of the wound of the horse and the wound of the man and this is where love has been found and where awakening begins. There has been so much pain in this union… far more pain for the horse than for the man. We humans have not yet had the readiness or the awareness to recognize the immensity of the pain that we have given to other species. We think of them as our tools and our assistants. And so, they are… their sacrifices are beyond words. And in this case, our horse has given himself to our rider. But he does not entirely give himself willingly, as this is part of the dance. He is present and he fights.

He expresses and he is controlled. He is the mirror of the rider and the counterpoint of the rider, and he has a greater power than the rider will ever know.

"And so, we ask you to take your focus away from the rider you have been and enter the being of the animal itself. Your task is to unburden yourself of every strap and binding that has held you… not just in this life, but in many lifetimes. It is to return to your natural organic power… that which you know very well, but you have yet to name and to see and touch. The horse is your teacher. He is the part of you that is already free and it is this knowing to which you are about to return."

It seemed to John that the angel was asking him to step out of the ego-based human mind where he was spending too much of his time fretting about the past, worrying about the future, worrying about his finances, mired in too many negative thought patterns, and instead focus on the heart by living in the present moment, because this focus would lead him to healing the wounds in his heart, where he could live joyfully and in peace.

"We know that in your heart, your greatest desire is to assist the children with whom you interact. You see them, and you know them, because they are you. They are not just you in that you are someone who understands youth and you are patient and kind. They are you because energetically there is a powerful connection. You have been these children and they will be you. They come to you because they are coming home. You call them to you because you know this too. Understand that the greatest gift you can give to any one of them is your own self-awareness.

"Resist the need to understand more… the need to document, define and research. This is, in fact, the principle area of your form that requires rest and nourishment in order to make way for something much more powerful. A healed heart will facilitate so much of your overall healing. Sit in silence… and stop. You have no idea how much power you will find in this experience of stopping… allowing. The mind is a tool of the heart, and that tool will be ready when the heart is ready to pick it up again.

"All ailments originate in the heart. Scientists will tell us about injury, trauma, deficiency, abuse and a long list of physical factors and experiences. But each of these begins with a hunger in the heart that attracts these experiences, this chemistry and this imbalance. Let us begin at the source and let us understand what the heart is here to heal, and that is fear … fear that affects us on so many levels. In a way, it is as simple as that.

"Your journey at this moment is to become the originator of how you experience, through awareness. And awareness does not live in the mind, it lives in the heart. Begin by taking time each day to live in the present moment. Your mind will judge this and tell you that this is not possible because it is so used to the mind chatter. All that is asked of you is to love whatever experience you have. Simply observe … and smile.

"This will feel very foreign to you and that too, is fine. You are so beautiful and yet you do not realize that it is because of your heart that your beauty is visible to all. You need do nothing else, but allow your heart to speak and you will reach anyone and everyone with your desire to heal."

John felt that the angel was directing him to focus his attention on himself. To heal his own *heart* woundings, first, so that he would be better able to help others. His priority was healing and releasing the anger that had been so detrimentally present his life. Only then would he clear the way within himself to assisting others with their healing.

The angel concluded by saying, "Your heart asks at this time, for rest, conversation, exploration and a blind trust. You are surrounded by guides who will facilitate this with you at all times."

And then she was gone.

As he thought about the angel's message, he had a sudden epiphany. He realized that when we are holding on to deeply embedded emotional pain in our hearts from experiences of profound wounding, quite often it is those closest to us, and in particular, the *love of our life* who *co-creates* an experience with us that brings our awareness to this wounding. If he blamed Sandra, he would place himself in victimhood and would miss the opportunity to heal, just as the archer who momentarily takes his eye off the target unleashes his arrow wide of the mark. As difficult as this was going to be, he had to take ownership of this experience. He had to stop being angry with her, accept the experience and thus, initiate the healing of his heart.

Unresolved emotional pain was at the root of his heartache and it was shaping the destructive attitude that was presently working against him. He recalled the story of Victor Frankl, the WWII concentration camp survivor, who stayed alive because he was able to find meaning in the experience. He remembered Frankl's famous quote, *We don't always get to choose our experiences, but we do get to choose our attitude towards that experience.*

One of the key factors in shaping our outlook he reckoned is our self-image. If we feel good about ourselves, we will naturally have a positive demeanour… it's pretty hard to have a negative attitude when you are in a state of self love… and this seemed like a pretty good place to start with himself and the students.

As painful as it was, he knew in his heart that Sandra was bringing him a gift and he needed to allow this situation to unfold as it was meant to. Whether she stays or leaves is almost irrelevant, he reckoned. This was about his journey and the need to heal his heartache. He needed to trust that he would be okay.

The early morning meeting on the top floor of the Board of Education involved only two men.

"He must not succeed," implored the visitor ... the middleman.

"I understand," acknowledged the host.

"Are you aware of what is at stake here?"

"I am."

"Some very powerful people in important places have directed me to communicate this to you."

The host nodded his head.

"The status quo must be maintained and you were appointed to this position to ensure that it does."

"I will do whatever is necessary."

"We are in the process of addressing any, shall I say, potential obstacles."

The host nodded again.

"Good. Then we have an understanding."

"We do."

"I will let them know."

The two men stood and shook hands, before the visitor quickly departed.

CHAPTER 5:
SELF-IMAGE

*Like a fool
I fell in love with you
Turned my whole world upside down*

— Derek & the Dominoes, *Layla*

John stood quietly before the class, waiting for everyone to take their seats. Despite his outward calm, he felt very excited. Today's topic of discussion was very close to his heart. It had become his raison d'etre.

He was also feeling a touch of anxiety because the students' acceptance of the concept he introduced a few days earlier was critical to everything that followed. If they rejected his ideas, he could be in for a long uphill struggle with them.

"A couple of days ago," he began, "I suggested that the most important thing for our health and happiness is how we feel about ourselves ... that is, our sense of self-image ... and that we feel lovable, worthy, good enough and empowered. Today, I would like to expand on this notion."

"You know what I think?" interrupted Caitlyn, before her teacher could continue. "I think you want to push your ideas onto us because of your own sense of inadequacy."

"What makes you say that Caitlyn?" he asked, surprised that she would ask a question from such an astonishing place of wisdom.

"I don't know, maybe you've done some things in your life you're not proud of and you're ridden with guilt. Maybe you haven't accomplished anything that your dad is proud of, or maybe you're just a puppet, preaching the school line."

"Do you really think that?"

"We don't know you. Sure, you said this class was a special project, but teachers have been telling us shit for years. How do we know that you're not giving us more of the same? How do we know that this isn't just about finding a different way to make us behave in a certain way? Control us?"

The rest of the students looked on intently to see how their teacher was going handle this skepticism.

"Just because things have been a certain way in the past, doesn't necessarily mean they're going to be that way in the future. And just because schools have tended to operate in a certain way, doesn't mean they're not ready to change."

Caitlyn didn't respond. Instead, she just sat stone-faced, looking angrily at the front.

"You're right. You don't know me, just as I really don't know you. Which means, if we're going to make any progress, if we're going to accomplish anything this year, we need to trust each other."

"What do you mean, you need to trust me. What's there to trust? If you don't like what I'm doing or saying, you can kick me out anytime you want."

"I absolutely need to trust you, otherwise, how can I expect you to trust me?"

"I don't get it," remarked Josh, puzzled by Teach's assertion. "Why do you have to trust Caitlyn?"

"Or the rest of us for that matter," added Ryan.

"We're just a bunch of lowly insignificant peons with tiny brains who like to pee on the flowers," Josh added in jest, causing snickers from several of his amused classmates.

"I have to trust that each of you will learn when you are ready to learn. I have to trust that I can't force my ideas on you. I can only present them to you. It's up to you to decide what is right for you and if what I am saying has the potential to serve you in a manner that is in your highest good."

He then turned his attention to Caitlyn, but she looked out the window in apparent defiance. He hoped that her silence indicated that she accepted his point, but wasn't willing to acknowledge it. "I also trust that there is an innate desire in all of us to improve our lot in life. We may have to overcome our emotional woundings before we can tap into this desire, but I really believe it's there."

"Perhaps there are people who want to stay stuck in their misery," countered Tom.

"Perhaps those people have never been shown an alternative."

Tom nodded his head slowly as if to say, 'I get it.'

"Getting back to the original topic of discussion, *I believe*," the determined head of the class continued, "if *everyone* on this planet felt good about themselves, it would be an entirely different world. There would be no war, no abuse, no betrayal or any other destructive behaviours that lead to our suffering."

"If it's that simple," remarked Ryan, "why is the world in such a mess? Why haven't people figured it out?"

"Ya," added Scott, "why do people keep treating each other like crap?"

"It's mainly because of a lack of awareness. The destructive outcome of a poor self-image is not something people talk about. Day after day, people commit heinous crimes on one another, but all we talk about is retribution."

"We rarely ever consider what caused that person to get to the state that would allow them to do something so terrible, do we?" asked Jordan.

"Nor do we consider the root societal cause… poor self-image."

"So, are you saying we live in a society where nobody feels good about themselves?" inquired Matt.

"I believe the vast majority don't."

"How did it get like that?" asked Eric.

"Likely because we've never been shown an alternative. We don't talk about self-love or the devastating effects of a poor self-image. We're so focused on making money and getting ahead, that we don't seem to see anything else."

"That's true!" observed Josh. "Look at what banks and oil companies do. They don't care that people are struggling to get by. They just keep jacking up the price and making billions of dollars in profits."

"It's the same with governments," added Jordan. "They keep growing and increasing taxes. If they were really interested in serving the people, they would operate in a way that would put more money in people's pockets and less in the government's."

"And what about people who con money out of seniors? How despicable is that?" asked Tracy.

Clearly these kids were well informed and had issues on their mind. They were genuinely concerned about society's ills and John felt confident that he was on the right track with them. His initial concern about their lack of interest allayed, he continued, "Every day we witness countless examples of behaviours that reflect a society that doesn't feel good about itself."

"How do we change it?" asked Mike.

"Ya, how do we make it better for everyone?" added Eric. "Cause it sure sucks now."

"That's for sure," added Josh, who was participating in the conversation with remarkable seriousness. "It seems like there are a few people who have a lot and a lot of people who have very little."

"And everyone keeps talking about how the gap between the haves and the have nots is widening," remarked Ryan. "If this keeps up, there's gonna be a rebellion, man."

"Like everything," observed Teach, "awareness is the first step. Think about parents and the way they treat their children. Would parents spank, criticize, abuse or abandon their children if they felt good about themselves and if they really knew how much it was affecting their kids?"

"Not likely," replied Terry.

"It's appalling that parents spank their children," said Tom. "Did they forget what it felt like to be spanked themselves?"

"Spanking is not necessarily rational," added Matt, "And in many cultures and homes it's still considered an acceptable form of punishment."

"That doesn't make it right," said Stuart.

"I didn't say it was right, Stu," Matt replied.

"Maybe if someone whacked a parent over the head every time they spanked their kid, they'd stop doing it," said Scott.

"That may not be the best solution," observed Tom.

"Ya, well I'd sure like it if someone whacked my old man," countered Blair. "Maybe then, he'd leave me alone."

"Unfortunately, your father is just like all the other wounded souls on the planet, and the reality is, he's doing the best he can with what he's learned."

"That sounds like a bunch of bullshit," the angry teen retorted.

"There's no doubt that his behaviour is not appropriate, but we'll never change things if we keep blaming others and looking at things the same old way. When we look at things differently, we will begin to create change. And the first thing we need to do is bring awareness to the importance of feeling good about yourself. People talk about self-esteem, but then they turn around and do things that are completely counterproductive to building it. Parents say, 'I want you to be a good boy,' then they criticize and spank their children. Teachers expect their students to behave in a certain way and then they humiliate them in front of their classmates. Managers want their employees to be productive, but they berate them and criticize their work. We put people down economically and socially and expect them to just accept it. The list of harmful behaviours goes on and on."

"It seems that the mistreatment of others is systemic on our society," remarked Tom. "Do you really believe that simply telling people about the idea of feeling good about yourself will change things?"

"We've got to start somewhere and bringing awareness to a solution, is the best place to start. If we keep focusing on the problem, we'll just keep creating more of it."

"What do people need to know?" asked Jessica. "My parents don't know anything about feeling good about yourself, cause they sure don't talk about it, you know."

"Let's start with how we raise our children because this is where it all begins. Parents need to know that in order to raise children with a positive self-image, kids need to grow up feeling loved, wanted, accepted and appreciated, which means parents need to be there for their children. They need to be loving, nurturing, kind, encouraging, patient, understanding and forgiving. They need to allow children to express themselves... their feelings and their opinions."

"That's easy to say, but what if you're all stressed out and your kid is acting like an idiot?" asked Terry.

"Before I answer your question Terry, let's take a step back. If you have a dog, do you wait until it's one or two or three years old to start training it?"

"Of course not," replied Jordan. "You start training it right away."

"It's the same thing with children. If we want children to feel good about themselves, we need to make them feel loved, wanted, accepted and appreciated from the moment they're born."

"I guess parents find it easier to yell at their kids and spank them," remarked Scott.

"Yes, it seems they do. But I truly believe that children act out because they lack self love and if we took the time to help them feel good about themselves, we'd spend a lot less time disciplining them."

"That makes a great deal of sense," agreed Tom.

"So, if we knew that children act out because of low self esteem, we would react differently when they misbehave," Terry concluded.

"I believe we would. We'd talk to them and ask them why they did what they did. We'd have a discussion. We'd point out to them that their behaviour is inappropriate and we'd help them understand that it doesn't serve them in a positive way. Our intention would always be to leave the child feeling good about themselves."

"Yep, sometimes you don't even have to misbehave to get in trouble," said Adam.

"What do you mean by that?" John inquired.

"Basically, when I was a kid, my dad did some things that were unfair, and when I told him so, he grounded me."

"That's pretty stupid," Jessica sympathized. "Parents don't want to be told they're wrong, do they?"

"It's funny," observed Josh, "parents will tell kids to stand up for themselves, but when they stand up to their parents, they get punished. 'Now you stand up for yourself, Johnny.' 'But dad, I'm afraid of him.' Whap! 'I'll give you something to be afraid of.'"

The irony of Josh's little impromptu vignette was not lost on the students and several of them laughed out loud.

"No wonder kids are messed up!" added Eric.

"It's hard to disagree and that speaks to what I mentioned earlier. It's very important for parents to allow their children to express themselves. And not just their opinions. Children also need to be able to express their feelings and emotions, whether it's sadness, anger or whatever. When they don't express these emotions, they hold them inside and eventually they get expressed in an inappropriate way."

"We were always told that boys shouldn't cry," admitted Jordan.

"That's really stupid too," remarked Jessica. "Why should boys be treated differently than girls?"

"It has a lot to do with embarrassment," replied Tom. "Fathers get embarrassed when their sons cry."

"Ya!" agreed Mike. "They're afraid of what their buddies are gonna think."

"They are afraid of being judged."

"We could change things by following one simple rule," said Tracy, "treat others as you would have them treat you. And that goes for how parents treat their kids."

"Didn't Jesus say that?" asked Jessica. "I think he did."

"Rules are a big part of the problem," remarked Ryan. "It seems to me that parents make up all these rules, not just to keep kids safe, but to control them as well."

"That's quite true," the teacher agreed. "Quite often parents who feel disempowered will create rules out of a need to control."

"What do you mean by that?" asked Eric.

"Parents who feel inadequate or who don't feel like they're in charge of some aspect of their life make up rules to help them feel like they're in control. Of course, parents do need to establish boundaries and children do need to know that their parents are in charge. It gives them a sense of security. But these boundaries need to be based on a healthy set of values and they ideally need to come from a place of love, not the need to control."

"What do you mean by boundaries?" asked Scott. "How is that different from rules?"

Just then the bell rang. "We'll have to continue this discussion another day," John bellowed over the chatter and noise as the students closed their books and scrambled for the door.

Several students gathered outside the cafeteria after lunch. They were involved in a lively discussion about the merits of the latest teen flick. It was playing at the local theatre and a few were planning to see it.

"Why are you being so quiet?" Scott inquired looking at Josh.

Josh's mind was elsewhere and he didn't respond immediately.

"Earth to Josh," Scott added, giving him a nudge.

"What? I'm not!" Josh replied, rejoining the conversation.

"Ya!" agreed Eric. "You haven't said a word, man."

"I was just thinking about what we were talking about this morning with Teach."

"Hey, since when did you start thinking?" quipped Scott.

"Ha, ha!" Josh replied.

"Sorry man."

"Somebody told me one time that I make jokes when I shouldn't, and the reason I do, is because I have low self-esteem."

"Whoever said that is full of shit," defended Eric.

"Ya!" Scott agreed. "I like your jokes."

"Me too," said Travis. "You're funny, man."

"I think I'm funny too, but sometimes maybe I do make jokes at the wrong time."

"Why do you say that?" asked Tracy.

"Well, before, I didn't really understand what self-esteem meant. But after Teach talked about feeling good about yourself and especially about feeling inadequate, maybe I do make jokes when I shouldn't."

"Don't let that idiot mess with your head," interjected Blair, joining the conversation.

"You're not helping, Blair," countered Ryan.

"Why? You think just cause Stevens says something, it makes it right."

"It's not about right or wrong, man. It's just how I feel."

Clearly the discussion had touched a nerve with the normally comical teen and he felt the need to talk about it, but discussing his feelings wasn't something he was accustomed to.

"You need to grow some balls, man," chided Blair.

"Get lost," snarled Travis, shoving him.

The irate teen clenched his fists as if to throw a punch, but thought better of it when he spotted two teachers coming out of the cafeteria. "Later," he sneered, pointing a finger at Travis, before turning and stomping up the hallway.

"Speaking of somebody who doesn't feel good about himself," said Ryan.

"He is one angry dude!" observed Scott.

"Better keep your head up!" remarked Eric.

"I'm not afraid of that weasel."

The group watched him leave before turning their attention back to Josh. "I gotta get going," he said, losing his nerve. "Later!" he added, fist pumping the guys.

Cruising home later that day, John's favorite song came on the radio. *Layla*, by *Derek and the Dominoes*, had been his number one song since first hearing it way back in 1972. It was written by Eric Clapton after he fell in love with his best friend's wife, Patti Boyd. His best friend, of course, was George Harrison of the Beatles. The song was about the anguish Clapton was feeling, in part, over betraying his friend for having these feelings.

The hurting teacher recognized the immediate significance of the song because of the betrayal he was feeling. Not so much by Sandra, more by life itself. Like his experience with his art store, he felt as though something very precious was being taken away from him and felt powerless to stop it.

As he wheeled into the parking lot behind Sammy Wong's store, it occurred to him that a part of him wanted her to come to his rescue, save him and make him feel better. But he also knew that this wasn't possible. It wasn't Sandra's responsibility, just like it wasn't Eric Clapton's responsibility to save Patti Boyd. Unlike the famous guitarist, she wasn't buying into John's pain and wasn't about to compromise herself in order to make him feel better.

Pulling into his parking space, he brought his truck to a stop, but left the engine running in order to listen to the last part of the song. He loved the piano piece that made up the second half of *Layla*. As he listened to Bobby Whitlock's beautiful work on the keyboard, he knew in his heart that what he wanted from Sandra was coming from ego. He also realized that he needed to leave her alone for now. She needed time to make what was an extremely important decision and as painful as it was not to hear from her, he had to let her be. He needed to focus on accepting the present circumstances and living in the present moment, just like the angel said.

He thought about what he had learned since embarking on his spiritual journey; that it's okay to provide support, encouragement and comfort to others and it's okay to provide guidance when needed and advice when asked. But it's not our responsibility to save people. We are here to empathize and show compassion, not fix their problems. We are not here to take their pain away or make them feel better. That is their responsibility. By allowing people to find their own way, we empower them.

It may have felt to him like he was being betrayed, but the reality was, there was a reason for this experience. John Stevens had been so deep in victimhood that he couldn't see the purpose. But he would keep working on it, confident that the truth would be revealed.

The song ended and he slowly turned off the ignition. "I love that song!"

CHAPTER 6:
IT'S ALL ABOUT ATTITUDE

I need someone to show me
The things in life that I can't find
I can't see the things that make true happiness,
I must be blind

— Black Sabbath, *Paranoid*

As John walked briskly down the hall he recalled his visit from the angel a couple of nights earlier. He felt like he was beginning to understand his experience with Sandra. Although he was still hoping that she would stay at PLJ High, he was ready to accept what he felt was inevitable.

He was also thinking about the previous day's talk on the importance of feeling good about yourself. He felt like he'd really connected with the students and was looking forward to continuing the discussion. He was encouraged by their eager participation and their desire to understand the ideas he presented. He felt very optimistic.

Approaching the door to his classroom, he heard several raised voices that were getting louder and louder, and he walked into the room just as Tracy screamed at Blair, "You've got a lousy attitude you jerk and you deserve everything you get."

"And you need to shut up you bitch," Blair hollered back. "Nobody made you my mother."

The students saw their teacher and quickly took their seats. "Would anyone care to explain what just happened," Teach inquired.

"This is a matter Tracy and Blair need to sort out themselves," offered Tom.

"Fair enough," Teach replied, looking at the pair.

"What are you looking at me for?" pleaded Blair.

"You just don't know when to keep quiet do you?" Ryan asked of the belligerent teen.

"I was planning to continue our discussion from yesterday, about what each of us can do to feel good about ourselves, but that can wait. It seems that we have something a little more pressing to talk about.

"An important factor in how we experience life has to do with our attitude. And the fact is, each of us is responsible for our own outlook."

"Some people were born with a bad attitude," remarked Tracy, looking at her antagonist.

"Up yours," Blair snapped.

"Real mature," said Ryan shaking his head.

"Why can she say whatever she wants?"

"Why don't you two take it somewhere else so we can continue this discussion," snarled Matt, looking directly at Blair.

For a moment, there was silence.

"Let's carry on," John suggested, hoping to avert any more hostility. "Our attitude is shaped by our experiences, especially those we experience as a young child, but it also helps create our experiences and it certainly affects how we feel about them."

"I don't understand what you mean by our attitude creating our experiences," said Mike.

"If you've got a bad attitude, bad things are going to happen to you," interjected Josh.

"It's sort of like that," Teach agreed. "What goes on in our life outside of us usually mirrors what is going on inside, which means, if you are feeling anger and hostility, you will typically experience a lot of anger and hostility in your life… with your friends, your family, your work, and so on. Whereas, if you are feeling inner peace, your life will typically be more tranquil. Where I would differ with what Josh said, has to do with good and bad. Good and bad are judgments we put on things and I don't think they serve us. They tend to create unnecessary harmful feelings like shame, guilt, regret and feelings of failure."

"When life keeps dumping shit on you," Travis observed, "it tends to make you cynical… and angry."

"But is that the way you really want to live your life?" the teacher asked, looking around the class. "Does it really serve you to live that way?"

"It's the only way I know how," admitted Travis.

"Me too," agreed Scott.

"How would you like to change the way you live?"

"Depends on how it affects me," Travis replied.

"I had the pleasure recently of reading a poem Matt wrote." John's announcement created quite a reaction amongst the students and several of them began chattering simultaneously, although they were too intimidated by the big teen to come right out and say anything. "It's an excellent poem and it very much applies to this discussion. Matt, would you like to read it to the class."

"Nope, but if you want to, go right ahead."

"It would be my honour!" He ambled over and retrieved the poem, then he returned to the front of the class. "Matt's poem is called, *The Wisdom of the Night Sky*." He began reading, and as he did, he couldn't help but notice the shocked expressions on their faces.

And I stood quietly gazing up at the night sky
Awed with its magnificence, yet terrorized at its vastness
And I saw immediately the contrasts
Of the lighted stars and the darkened universe
And I saw the realness of the stars
And I saw the nothingness of the space in between
It spoke to me with great wisdom of the polarities of life
And of the polarities of the human experience
The opposing forces that are meant to bring understanding
That are meant to bring us towards peace
It told me that within these polarities
There is both contrast and sameness
It spoke to me of light and darkness

And of the light within the darkness
It spoke to me of strength and vulnerability
And of the strength within the vulnerability
It spoke to me of sensitivity and indifference
And of the sensitivity within the indifference
And it spoke of the ultimate polarity of love and fear
And of the love that is found within the fear
For it is within these polarities
That we discover who we truly are
And within these polarities
Lies the truth of our emotional pain
And the truth of our oneness
And so, when you look up into the night sky
Do so not without purpose
Just as you would not experience life itself without purpose
For when you find purpose
You will find the gifts in all of your experiences
And you will find heaven on earth
And your spirit will soar and your soul will sing

When he was finished, the room remained silent for the longest time. Tom was the first to speak. "Matt, that is an incredible poem."

"Holy shit is it ever!" agreed Mike.

"Thanks," Matt said humbly.

"How long have you been writing poetry?" Tracy asked.

"A few years."

"And everybody thinks you're just a big thug," remarked Blair.

"*Shut up!*" Jessica said. "What a stupid thing to say."

"I didn't say it!" Blair explained. "I didn't say it was true. I'm just telling you what everybody else is saying."

"I know what people have been saying about me," Matt interrupted. "People judge me because I have tattoos and I shave my head. They've heard stories about me they think are true, but they don't take the time to get to know me."

"It seems people are more interested in drama then they are in the truth," Tom observed.

"That must suck," said Jessica.

"Ya, it does."

"Well I think you're nice."

The big fella smiled.

"What are you staring at me for?" asked Jessica, realizing that everyone was looking at her.

"Moving on," Teach interjected. "It's terrific that you like the poem. What do you think it's saying?"

"It's saying that we need to look more closely at our experiences to see what the lessons are," replied Josh.

"Especially the bad… er, unpleasant ones," Ryan added.

"When we're in the midst of an unpleasant experience, we tend to fall into victimhood. We get angry and bitter. We start blaming everyone and everything, and when it continues, we start to hate life. We develop a very unhealthy attitude.

"Here's how I believe the universe works. What we feel, think, say and do creates our reality. For example, if we use the word *hate* all the time, what the universe hears is hate and so it sends more things and experiences to hate. Whereas, if we use the word *awesome* the universe will send more awesomeness."

"Is that like when people say, 'be careful what you ask for because you just might get it?'" asked Eric.

"It's sort of like that. Something I believe to be a truth is that everything we do creates an effect… it has meaning. This understanding is important because it asks us to take responsibility for what we think, say and do."

"You mean if I think something, it will happen?" asked Mike.

"It's possible. Thoughts are energy, and when you think a thought, particularly if you think it with conviction and strong feelings, that energy goes out to the universe. And what goes out must come back."

"So, if someone is feeling a lot of anger are they going to attract angry people and experiences that reflect this anger?" asked Tom.

"Yes, they likely will."

"I never thought of it that way before," remarked Ryan, "but it makes sense."

"It makes perfect sense," agreed Tom. "Think about when your parents confront you about something. If they're angry and start yelling at you, you usually get angry right back at them… or you get scared… and you deny everything. But if they're gentle and if they speak to you in a kind, loving way, you don't get angry or uptight. You feel good about it and you respond with honesty."

"That's an excellent observation," John praised.

"Wow! That's really cool. You're really smart aren't you, Tom?" blurted Jessica, bringing more snickers from the class.

"Thank you," he replied, blushing.

"What else is Matt's poem saying?" Josh asked.

"It's saying that how we react to certain situations tells us something about ourselves," offered Ryan. "If we react negatively, like with anger or frustration or fear, it tells us that we don't feel good about ourselves. Whereas, if we react positively, with patience, acceptance and understanding, it says we have a positive self-image… that we are taking responsibility for ourselves. It tells us about our attitude. And there's a word that I can't think of that describes what I'm saying."

"Perhaps the word is *consciousness*," said a very pleased Teach. "It tells us we are living in consciousness."

"Ya, that's it!" exclaimed Ryan.

"Hey, you're as smart as Tom," Jessica beamed.

"Are you trying to make me jealous?" Tom kidded.

"Oh, Tom," she said, blushing more.

As the students were bantering back and forth, John Stevens recalled what he had learned about human suffering… that it takes place in the mind… and that *suffering* is different from physical pain, and in fact, physical pain is a manifestation of our mental and emotional suffering… and the way to end suffering is to do eight things. First, *live in the present moment*. Second, *accept the present circumstances*. Third, *stop judging*. Fourth, *be grateful*. Fifth, *understand that people are doing the best they can with what they've learned*. Sixth, *find the gifts in our experiences*. Seventh, *forgive*. And eighth, *let go of the past*. He also realized that he wasn't applying this knowledge in his current experience with Sandra.

"When we are at the point where we can see the light in the darkness," Teach jumped in, "when we can have an experience, resist the impulse to judge it, simply experience it and understand its meaning… its significance… then we are well on our way to taking charge of our lives and having an attitude that works for us… not against us. When we can do this, we are on the way to ending our suffering."

"Here's a thought," observed Tom, "we can never really have a bad day."

"What do you mean by that?" asked Mike.

"When we have a bad day… I mean, a day that's not so enjoyable… it makes us really appreciate the good days… which kind of makes the bad days, good days."

"That's a great way of looking at things," Terry approved.

"I couldn't agree more," John said smiling joyfully. "And something else I've learned that might be helpful, is that we always get the experiences we need, not necessarily the ones we want."

"What do you mean by that?" asked Scott.

"If there is something that we want that is contrary to our soul's journey or contrary to a lesson we need to learn, we might not get exactly what we want. For example, if we want to be a millionaire but our soul's journey is about overcoming the belief that money represents safety, we're not likely going to live in wealth."

"But how do we know if we're not getting something we want because we need something else?" asked Jordan.

"Trust!"

"Trust?"

"We just need to trust that whatever is happening is meant to happen, because it's what we most need."

"I don't know," said Stuart, "trust isn't easy. Not when you've been kicked around all your life."

"Perhaps you need to find the light in that darkness," said Tom.

Stuart looked at Tom and nodded in agreement.

"Let's bring this conversation back to the beginning," John suggested. "We began by talking about attitude. Think about something interesting you've learned in your life? I'll bet you were fully engaged in the experience. I'll bet you gave it your full attention and you felt enthusiastic about it. I'll bet you had a really positive attitude."

"I remember when I wanted to learn to play the piano," observed Tracy. "I couldn't wait to get to my piano lessons. I could play for hours at home all by myself. My mom and dad used to talk about it all the time."

"Wouldn't it be wonderful if all of our experiences were like that?"

"But school isn't like that," said Travis. "School is shit. I had language class in elementary school and I hated it. It was stupid."

"So, you didn't have the most positive of attitudes?"

"Not a freakin' chance."

"And did you learn anything?"

"Nope."

"What have you had a good attitude about?"

"Video games."

"Have you ever enjoyed learning?"

Travis hesitated for a moment, reluctant to say anything. "Horses."

"You love horses? That's really nice," said Tracy.

"There was a horse farm near where I grew up and I used to sneak over there and pet the horses over the fence. Some days I would feed them carrots and apples."

"Did you enjoy learning about them?"

"Ya, I did. I actually went to the library and got some books about horses. I would like to raise them and train them."

"You went to the library?" exclaimed Josh. "Now that's something I wouldn't have guessed."

"That's terrific, Travis," praised his teacher. "Are you willing to do whatever is necessary to make your dream come true?"

"I sure am!"

"I used to teach a couple of girls who are avid riders. I'll talk to them and see if they can help you out."

"That would be awesome!" Travis was smiling for the first time since the beginning of the school year and John couldn't have been happier.

"Something Ryan said is really important for everyone to understand," remarked Terry. "He said that when we have a bad attitude and react negatively to things it tells us that we don't feel good about ourselves. This is true man."

"Ya," agreed Josh. "If you feel good about yourself, you likely have a pretty good attitude about stuff."

"Those are great observations," Teach praised. "How we feel about ourselves affects every aspect of our life. If you feel lovable, worthy, good enough and empowered, you're likely going to have a good attitude about things. You are likely to be more optimistic, understanding, compassionate, patient, forgiving, accepting and caring… the hallmarks of a positive attitude."

"I guess that's why it is so essential for parents to raise their children to have a positive self-image," stated Tom.

"Without a doubt."

"Mr. Stevens, you said there were some other things we needed to understand that would help us feel good about ourselves," said Jessica. "What were you talking about?"

"How we're raised is critical to having a positive self-image and so is being spiritually conscious. It helps us make sense of things, particularly when we've been raised in a home where we weren't taught to feel good about ourselves."

"Say what?" exclaimed Blair.

"Part of the reason there is so much suffering on the planet is because we don't understand the truths of our existence. We have come to believe certain things, but these beliefs are not creating peace and harmony. In fact, they're creating the exact opposite."

"What truths are you talking about?" asked Jordan.

"We would refer to these as the spiritual truths."

"Oh great, another religious fanatic!" complained Stuart.

"I'm not talking about religion here, Stuart. I'm talking about our understanding of life, and that doesn't necessarily have anything to do with religion, certainly not the religious fundamentalism that is creating so much pain and suffering."

"So what are these truths?" asked Terry.

"The first truth we need to understand is that we are not simply human beings. We are actually *spiritual* beings having a *human* experience. We are aspects of God. This is because prior to the creation of the universe, there was one-common-energy that consisted of all the same atoms that make up the physical universe we live in today. This energy could also be called the *God-energy*. Therefore, God isn't a Being who exists outside of us. *We are God*!"

The students listened intently as their teacher continued explaining the truths of life that had come to form his guideposts for living in more peace, love and joy.

"The second truth is that because we are all aspects of God, we live in *oneness*. We are all connected, *energetically*, which I just explained, and *experientially*, which I'll get to shortly. And because we are connected to everything that exists, everything we do, every thought, word and action, affects everything else.

"The third truth is that we have a life plan. Before incarnating, our souls decide the experiences we will have, the lessons we will learn, the emotional pain we will heal and the souls who will interact with us."

"I thought we had free will?" observed Ryan.

"We do. We have a life plan, but at any point in time we have free will to follow the plan or deviate from it. Whatever decision we make will simply take us down a different path."

"What if the path we take causes us not to achieve what we came here to do?" inquired Terry.

"We can always accomplish it later in life, or perhaps we will have to come back in another life."

"That's out there, but it makes sense to me," agreed Josh.

"In creating our life plan, we choose our parents…the people who will have the most significant influence on how we feel about ourselves as we grow up… and by choosing our parents, we also choose the country, culture and economic conditions in which we will live.

"The parents we choose will also determine whether we grow up feeling loved or unloved, wanted or unwanted, accepted or unaccepted and appreciated or unappreciated."

"I can see where this way of thinking… I mean, living… could be very beneficial," observed Tom.

"Beneficial indeed!"

"I still don't get this oneness thing," admitted Scott. "What exactly does it mean?"

"What don't you understand Scott?"

"Well, I can see how, if God is in everything, it would make us all connected, but so what? How does this affect us?"

"We would treat each other better," offered Ryan.

"Theoretically, we should treat each other better, but we don't seem to be doing so," remarked Tom.

"That's true," John agreed. "But there is more to it."

"Like what?" asked Travis.

"When the universe was created, Earth was created and in the process, evolution was created."

"I get that," said Scott.

"Initially, this evolutionary process was quite slow, but it has sped up over time."

"Especially since the arrival of man," suggested Ryan.

"Very true. And this evolutionary process could also be called, *the flow of life*, and everything is part of this flow, including all of us and our experiences."

"Yep, that makes sense," said Adam, looking out the window.

"So, if we have an experience, for example, going to a Bruce Springsteen concert, are we separate from this experience?"

"How can we be?" asked Matt. "We are experiencing the experience. We're part of it. So how can we be separate from it?"

All heads suddenly turned and looked at him. "That's heavy, man!" remarked Josh.

"But true," added Tom. "The *experiencer* can't be separate from the *experience*."

"So the flow of life is just an ongoing series of experiences," Teach continued. "And we are part of this flow. We are not separate from it."

"If we're all part of the flow, then this is how we're all connected, right?" asked Jordan.

"Yes, it is."

"Wait!" interrupted Stuart. "Why does this matter?"

"Cause we want to end suffering," replied Mike.

"But how does it do that?"

"If we're all connected energetically through our atoms and experientially through the flow of life, why would you want to do anything to hurt anyone?" observed Tom. "In a way, you'd just be hurting yourself."

"Right!" Stuart acknowledged.

"You've developed a good grasp of this," John praised. "But again, there is more to it."

"Like what?" asked Mike.

"What is the root cause of all suffering on the planet?"

"Greed," replied Eric.

"That's part of it."

"Hatred," added Tracy.

"That's also part of it."

"Power mongering," added Jordan.

"That too, is part of it. And what is underneath greed, hatred and power mongering?"

"Fear," replied Tom.

"Precisely! We fear poverty, so there is greed. We fear the unknown, so there is hatred. We fear powerlessness, so there is domination. We fear death, humiliation, being alone, the dark and so on."

"We fear a lot of stuff, don't we?" asked Mike.

"But why?" asked Scott. "Why is there so much fear?"

"Cause we don't know what's going on," replied Jordan.

"That's it," agreed John. "We don't understand the truths of our existence ... we don't understand the flow of life and our relationship with it ... so we're filled with this underlying fear. And this fear leads to much destructive behaviour."

"I guess if we understood these truths we would treat each other better," observed Terry.

"We certainly would!"

"Are there any other truths?" asked Jessica.

"There are many more, but there is a fourth one that applies specifically to this conversation. We are creators and co-creators of our experiences. As part of this flow of life, our life plans interact with the life plans of other souls so we can help each other learn lessons, heal and release emotional pain and evolve and grow spiritually. In certain experiences we may do something to cause pain to another person, while in other situations, other souls will cause us pain. But, because we are aspects of God co-creating in oneness, we are never *really* victims or perpetrators.

"Knowing that there is a higher purpose for our experiences gives us faith and trust. And more importantly, in the context of the discussion we've had the last two days, this awareness has the potential to lead to us feeling better about ourselves and thus have a better attitude about life."

"That's the most logical and useful thing anyone has ever said to us," remarked Tom. "We've been fed so much nonsense and told to live a certain way, mostly to serve someone else's personal agenda, that it's great to get a different take on things, something that actually makes sense and doesn't create fear."

"Thank you, Tom. As I said earlier, an awareness of these truths could go a long way towards ending our suffering."

"What about boundaries?" asked Tracy. "You said we were going to talk about boundaries today."

Just then the bell rang signaling the end of class. "We'll have to continue this discussion tomorrow, Tracy," Teach shouted above the chatter. "In the meantime, have an awesome day, everyone."

Later, a group of students were gathered in the cafeteria. "Did you hear what Matt said in class this morning?" asked Eric.

"Apparently he's got some brains, man," observed Josh.

"He blew me away," added Ryan.

"The dude's pretty sharp," agreed Eric.

"I thought he was just a punk," said Scott.

"Me too," said Eric.

"I'm still trying to get my head around his poem," Scott continued.

"Ya, man, that was amazing," agreed Ryan.

"Maybe we should cut him some slack," suggested Josh. "He might be an okay guy."

"I don't know, man, from what I heard, we should be careful," said Scott.

"Don't be a wuss," chided Josh.

"Okay, brave guy, you go for it and let us know how you make out."

"Don't worry. I will."

John was preparing to go to bed, still feeling jubilant about the day's discussion, when the phone rang. He looked at the call display… *S Connors*. As he picked up the receiver a thousand thoughts and feelings suddenly flooded into his mind and body… relief, anger, resentment, happiness, sorrow and fear. Agonizing fear of what he was about to hear… the worst. How would he react? What would he say? Would he be honest?

"Hi," he said, tentatively.

"Hi John. How are you doing?" she asked in an almost business-like manner.

"How do you think I'm doing?" he snapped back, wanting to be courteous… loving… compassionate… but not able to hold back the anger that suddenly came roaring to the surface. It seemed a foolish, inconsiderate question.

"Do you want me to call you back?"

"Pardon?"

"You seem angry."

"I haven't heard from you for two days. How did you expect me to feel?" In that moment, he forgot about the angel visit. Lost in his sudden rage, he forgot her words of wisdom.

"I didn't expect anything, John. And that's the difference. I don't expect anything."

"Then why didn't you call. Why didn't you reply to my messages?"

"I needed to be alone. I couldn't allow myself to be influenced by anything, most especially you. I care for you too much."

Her words infuriated him. They sounded rehearsed, as if she wasn't being sincere. "Care for me!" he barked. "I thought we loved each other?"

There was a momentary pause on the other end.

"Of course I love you," she replied softly, her voice trembling.

John realized he was putting her on the defensive and trying to force her to justify her actions. Deep down, he knew she did what she needed to in order to make a decision, free of his influence. He knew in his heart she was being sincere and that he had to let go of the need to control the situation in order to create the outcome he wanted.

Then as if reading his mind she said, "If you could just stop the chattering monkey in your mind, you could be more awesome than you could possibly imagine and there isn't a woman on this planet who wouldn't want to marry you."

He stood silently for a few moments, phone in hand, immobilized by her words. She was right and he knew it. His mind had been racing non-stop since she told him about the job offer. He had conjured up all kinds of thoughts and scenarios. He realized he had fallen completely out of spiritual consciousness, into victimhood. He wasn't living in the present moment and had let his egoic-mind run amok, like a wild beast raging in the forest... out of control. "You're right," he admitted, feeling the genuineness in her words.

He could see the truth. She didn't say, "*You have* to stop the chattering monkey." If she had, he might have gotten defensive. She would have been telling him what to do. Instead she said, '*If you could* stop the chattering monkey.' It put ownership of his behaviour squarely on his shoulders. It was one of the things John loved about Sandra... the language she used... always non-confrontational, never demanding or accusing; unlike his own way of communicating.

He realized that when he asked her why she didn't call, he sounded like a wounded child who was blaming someone else. The truth was that he had been triggered by her behaviour and he was having an emotional response. His reaction was his responsibility. It wasn't her fault.

It also occurred to him that he had been seeking reassurance from her that everything was going to be okay, that she loved him and that she wanted to marry him. It also occurred to him that his need for external reassurance must be coming from a deep place of lack within himself... it must be coming from the pain in his heart. He recognized that he needed to take responsibility for his reaction before he could begin healing.

"Honey, I needed to be sure that I wasn't making a decision in order to please you. If I had, it could have led to feelings of regret and I didn't want something like that to affect our relationship."

"Does that mean you've decided to take the job?"

"I called you because I wanted to come and see you. I wanted to tell you about my decision in person."

"I think it's too late for that now."

Knowing she had no choice, Sandra spoke the words John Stevens didn't want to hear. "Yes, I've decided to take the job."

"I don't know what to say."

"I'm so sorry. This decision was so hard for me."

"I don't think there is anything to be sorry for. I mean that sincerely. You had to make the decision that was the best one for you and in time, I will understand that."

"I really hope you will."

He was feeling very upset and disappointed and he needed time to allow himself to process these feelings. "I would love to see you right now, but it's best that I don't because, if I did, I would want to put my arms around you and hold you and not let you go."

"This doesn't mean our relationship has to end."

He thought about her living six hours away and in his heart he knew it wasn't practical. "I don't think it would be realistic for us to try to hold on to our relationship."

"That maybe so, but would you at least consider it."

"Sure... I will."

"John," she said.

"Yes," he answered.

"This may sound strange, but I can't help feeling that I'm doing this for you too."

He paused for a moment, thinking it was quite a strange thing to say, but then he considered the epiphanies he had experienced since she first told him of her decision and it made him wonder. It certainly reminded him of the importance of the five essentials. "Goodnight, Sandra."

"Goodnight, John. I love you!"

CHAPTER 7:
THE CHATTERING MONKEY

Now if you're feelin' kinda low 'bout the dues you've been paying
Future's coming much too slow
And you wanna run but somehow you just keep on stayin'
Can't decide on which way to go

— Boston, *Peace of Mind*

John was feeling quite foggy as he climbed out of his truck. He hadn't slept well after his difficult conversation with Sandra. Speaking to her after several days of silence had brought some relief, but he felt very distressed with her decision to accept the new teaching position.

Although he hadn't told her, he had had his heart set on marrying her someday. He wanted to spend the rest of his life with her, and with that thought, he suddenly realized that he had been unconsciously projecting, anticipating the future, rather than living in the present moment. He had created an expectation… being married to Sandra… and he had to remind himself that letting go of expectations is one of the reasons we're here on the planet. More symptoms of his ego run amok.

As he approached the main entrance to the school, he noticed Josh, Ryan, Eric and a few other students standing in a group near the front door.

"Yo, Teach!" Eric called out.

"Oh, nice, that's really polite," Josh chided.

"I wasn't being rude," Eric pleaded.

"Yes Eric," their teacher answered courteously.

"You're a big music buff, right."

"Yes, I definitely like music."

"And you know a lot about classic rock?"

"Um, yes, a little," he said cautiously, not knowing where his student was going with this.

"Well, we were just talking about the best debut album of all time and we weren't sure if Appetite for Destruction was Guns 'N Roses debut album."

"It certainly was, Eric."

"See, I told you," said Ryan.

"Ya, but I still don't think it's the best debut album. What do you think is the best of all time, Mr. Stevens?"

"Oh, boy, that's not an easy question. There have been so many good ones. I have to admit though, I really like Boston… by Boston of course."

"Ya, that had some great songs," agreed Josh, "Peace of Mind, More Than a Feeling. What an awesome album!"

John Stevens couldn't help but be marveled at how these young kids knew so much about music that was produced years before they were born and how they liked it and understood it. Tells you a lot about the quality of the music he reckoned.

"What about Bat out of Hell? It was pretty good too." observed one of the other students.

"Absolutely! That was, and still is, a great piece of music, but technically, it was Meat Loaf's second album. He had released an album a few years earlier."

"I thought you were a big Beatles fan. Why is their debut album not your favorite?" inquired Ryan.

"When I was first introduced to the Beatles they already had a huge body of work and three records, so for me, they didn't really have a single debut album. But their early music was quite extraordinary and my first favorite song came out of those albums… *You Can't Do That*!"

"What an awesome song!" agreed Eric.

"I'm afraid I don't know it," admitted Josh. "I'm gonna check it out."

"Ready for school gentlemen?"

"Yep."

"See you inside then." As John turned and opened the front door to the school, he couldn't help but feel a little relieved. He thought the students were about to test him, but it seems they just wanted to pick his brain. He had done it again... let the thoughts in his mind take control of things... negative thoughts to boot. The discussion he had planned for today was quite appropriate!

"Yesterday, we talked about the importance of attitude and how it shapes our experiences, and more importantly, our feelings about our experiences. Before that we talked about the importance of feeling good about ourselves... of having a positive self-image. Today I would like to expand on these aspects of human nature to talk about something that really gets us into trouble... the chattering monkey in our mind... and how all these things are interrelated."

His teacher's statement prompted Blair to stick his hands into his armpits while making monkey sounds.

"Is there any possibility that you will grow up some day?" chided Caitlyn.

"Why are you always so nasty to me?"

"Cause you act like an idiot."

"Mr. Stevens, did you hear what she said?"

"Blair, unfortunately, whatever comes to you, you are bringing upon yourself... and only you can change that."

With that, the misfit teen hung his head is if he was sulking.

"Did you not pay any attention to the conversation yesterday?" Tom snapped.

"Why's everybody always pickin' on me?" he asked, clearly in victimhood.

"Nobody's picking on you, buddy," comforted Stuart. "But you are making it difficult for yourself."

"Screw you all!"

"Perhaps we might continue the discussion," John interjected. "Actually, not to pick on you Blair, but your reaction to your classmates' comments provides a good illustration of what I'm talking about."

"What do you mean?" he asked, lifting his head.

"Most of us are constantly lost in our thoughts... thoughts that quite often have nothing to do with what we are doing in that moment. Frequently, these thoughts are working against us because they are negative. They keep us from living in joy. They cause us to suffer. We spend much of our time fretting about the past... living in shame, guilt, regret, resentment and bitterness... or worrying about the future."

"I know what you mean," agreed Tracy. "My mom drives me crazy worrying about her job and how much money we have."

"My mom hates my dad... wherever he is," added Travis. "She's so bitter."

"Why is that?" asked Mike.

At first, Travis appeared not to want to answer the question. "Well, I guess cause he took off after he found out she was pregnant. She was a teenager and he was twenty-one."

"Have you ever met your dad?" asked Josh.

"Nope... and I hope I never do."

"Why?" asked Eric.

"Cause I might kill him."

"Whoa, that's heavy."

"I'm serious man. He really messed with my mom's head, the bastard. He took off and left her to raise me by herself. She didn't get to go to school because of him."

John wanted to say something to Travis, but he realized that he needed to be very gentle because it was evident he was feeling emotional. "What if there was another way of looking at this experience that could change the way you feel about it?"

"What do you mean?"

"What if there was a way to look at it that would take away the anger and bitterness and hatred?"

"What, you want me to like him?" he asked with pure venom in his eyes.

"No, you don't have to like him, just let go of the negative emotions that you and your mom are feeling."

"I'm not sure I'd know how, I've been angry all my life."

"Perhaps that's because up until now you didn't realize that you had a choice."

"What's my choice?" he asked looking very puzzled.

"Let's say that the route you took to school every day was fraught with danger… vicious dogs, muggers, and so on. Each day you were terrified, but you managed to get to and from school without incident. What would you do?"

"That's rather obvious," observed Tom. "I'd look for a different route."

"But it's the only route you know of."

"I don't care, I'd still find a different way to get to school."

"You'd look for something safer… more joyful?"

"Absolutely!" said Jordan.

"Doesn't the same apply to your life situation? If you are living in unhappiness… be it bitterness, anger, resentment or hatred… doesn't it make sense to look for an alternative?"

"I guess."

"Where does all living take place?"

"What do you mean by that?" asked Terry.

"Do we live in the past, the future or the present?"

"We live in the present," replied Ryan.

"That's right. We don't live in the past. We can think about the past, but we don't live in it. Similarly, we can imagine the future, but we don't live in it. And in this moment, right here and now, is there anything to regret?"

"I guess not," replied Josh.

"Is there anything to fear?"

"Ya," said Blair, "Final exams."

"Don't be stupid, Blair," scolded Tom.

"I'm not being stupid. I hate exams."

"Are you writing final exams right at this moment?" asked Teach.

"Well, no, but it scares me to think about it."

"Then why think about it?"

"Cause I can't help it."

"But you can help it, because you have a choice…"

"To live in the present moment," Travis smiled, finishing his teacher's statement.

"Precisely. You have a choice. You can spend your time thinking, fretting and worrying about the past and the future, or you can focus your energy on the now."

"I know what you mean," agreed Tracy. "When I'm playing the piano I don't think about anything else."

"And how do you feel?"

"Great!"

"Euphoric?"

"Yes, euphoric!"

"That's exactly how you feel when you live in the moment… because there is nothing else to feel. There is no worry or regret or anger or hatred."

"That's messed up," said Travis. "My mom and I have been wasting so much time being angry over something that happened years ago. I guess we've missed out on being happy all this time."

"But isn't it okay to think about the past?" asked Stuart.

"It's okay if you are thinking about something that can assist you in the present moment."

"What if it's a happy memory?" asked Jessica.

"Again, that's okay. But remember, each moment you spend thinking about the past distracts you from experiencing the euphoria of living in the present."

"What about planning for the future? Aren't we supposed to do that?"

"Definitely. Plan, yes, but worry about things that may or may not happen… no. Living in fear does not serve us in any way."

"What if we're out in the jungle and we're confronted by a lion?" asked Eric. "Are we not supposed to have fear then?"

"What would you be afraid of?"

"Dying… obviously."

"Again, that's projecting. You are experiencing fear over something that *might* happen."

"What do you mean, might happen?" asked Mike, looking at Teach as if he was an idiot.

"What if the lion had just finished eating, perceived you as no threat and had no desire to eat you or defend its territory?"

"What are the chances of that happening?"

"I don't know. Anything is possible. But wouldn't it make more sense to devote your energy, in that moment, to taking action. After all, if it's inevitable that you're going to die, what's there to be afraid of?"

"Good point," agreed Tom.

"Yes! And the real point is that we have a choice on how we use our minds. We can take charge of our minds or we can allow them to run amok. We can continue to think about the past and the future or we can live in the here and now. We can suffer or we can live in joy. The choice is ours."

"How do we do it then?" asked Travis. "How do we live in the present moment? I've never thought about how my mind works."

"Make each moment like the moments Tracy experiences when she's playing the piano. Focus totally on what you are doing in that moment, whether you are getting dressed, watching television or simply washing your hands.

"Let's try an experiment. On the count of three everyone take a deep breath in and then breathe out. Make a noise when you do, like this." John demonstrated how to do it.

"Now. One, two, three."

All of the students took a deep breath.

When they were finished, he asked them a question. "What were you thinking of while you were inhaling and exhaling?"

The students sat silently for a moment. Tom was the first to speak. "I wasn't thinking about anything. I was just thinking about breathing. My mind was blank."

"Awesome! That's exactly what happens. Was anybody thinking about anything during the exercise?"

"Not me," replied Josh, as all the students shook their heads. "Although, I had the urge to shout out Namaste!," he added to the amusement of his classmates.

"That's a simple exercise on how you can bring yourself into the now."

"Is that why people tell you to take a deep breath when you are feeling nervous?" asked Jessica. "My mom always tells me to take a deep breath."

"That is precisely the reason."

"How easy was it for you to learn to be present?" asked Jordan.

"It took a lot of practice and I still have to remind myself. I'm still learning." He wanted to share his recent experience with Sandra to illustrate how he had to be reminded of the importance of staying present and not letting your mind run loose, but given that she had not informed Principal Clark of her decision to leave the school, he thought better of it.

"Another way you can train yourself is to say, *I am now placing my mind in the present moment.* Then just look around and observe. Don't judge or attempt to analyze what you see. Just observe it. Buddhists use a similar technique when they meditate."

"Do you really believe this could make a difference in our lives?" asked Stuart.

"Yes, I really do."

Just then, the bell rang, signaling the end of class. "Have a great day everyone!"

After packing up his briefcase at the end of the day, John took a few moments to consider what to have for dinner. In the midst of his mental planning, Ryan walked into the classroom.

"Hi, Ryan," he said cheerily.

"Hi, Mr. Stevens."

"How was your day?"

"It was good. Could I talk to you about something?"

"Certainly."

"I'm afraid to go home."

"Really! Why is that?"

"Well… um… I hope you don't think this is weird, but I see ghosts."

"I don't think that is weird at all," John said reassuringly. "A lot of people have the ability to see spirits."

"They do?" Ryan said, somewhat relieved.

"Absolutely. One of my nephews can see spirits."

"Oh, that's cool, man. I thought I was the only one."

"How long have you had this ability?"

"For as long as I can remember. When I was little, I used to think they were real. I would talk to them and they would talk to me."

"And why are you afraid of them? Have you ever had a bad experience?"

"No, it just freaks me out."

"Have you seen the movie, *A Sixth Sense?*"

"Yes, it was really good."

"And did that help?"

"It helped for a little while, but then I started getting scared again."

"What scares you?"

"I don't know… the unknown maybe. I guess I'm afraid they're gonna hurt me or possess me."

"Have these spirits done anything in the past to suggest that they might want to harm you?"

"No."

"Then why do you think you are holding on to this belief?"

"Maybe because I've seen too many movies."

"That is certainly a distinct possibility. Do your parents know about this?"

"When I was little, my father heard me talking in my room one day, so he came into the room and asked me who I was talking to. I told him I was talking to my friend, Tommy. He asked who Tommy was and I told him it was the boy sitting on my bed. Then dad yelled at me to clean my room and stop making up stories. After that, I figured it was better if I didn't say anything."

"What about your friends?"

"Are you kidding? If I told them, I'd never hear the end of it. They'd make fun of me."

"How do you know that? Maybe some of them can see spirits."

"I don't know, Mr. Stevens. I think they'd laugh at me."

"I can understand your concern. Ryan, it would be helpful if you put into practice what we talked about today."

"You mean living in the present moment?"

"Yes! It seems that part of what is going on is the negative thoughts you are having… you are worrying about what might happen. You are projecting into the future."

"Ya! That makes sense."

"It would also be a good idea for you to do some research on Indigo and Crystal children."

"What children?"

"Indigo and Crystal children."

"Who the hell are they... oops... sorry."

"No need to apologize. It's funny that we make a swear word out of an imaginary place."

"What do you mean?"

"Contrary to popular belief, hell isn't a real place. But that's another conversation. Crystal and Indigo children are children who have come to the planet with special gifts. They are very sensitive beings and one of their abilities includes being able to see spirits."

"Cool. Is that why I can't drink milk or eat wheat... cause I'm sensitive?"

"Yes! It is!"

"So you think I might be one of these children?"

"Yes, I believe you are."

"So it's okay that I can see spirits? I'm not weird or nuts?"

"Not at all. In fact, what you have is very special."

Ryan gave John a big smile of relief. "Why is this happening? Why are these children like this?"

"They are coming onto the planet to help bring change to the way we live and to the systems and institutions that don't serve us anymore."

"Like the education system?"

"Definitely. And this includes all the children who have been told they have ADHD, autism and Asperger's syndrome."

"Really? I thought those kids were just stupid or retarded?"

"Not at all. Like your ability to see spirits, these children... these people... are quite gifted. Other people just haven't been able to see it."

"But I don't get it. How can they be gifted?"

"They have abilities the rest of us don't have and I believe they are here to serve a higher purpose."

"Now I really don't get it."

Just then, there was a commotion out in the hall and several students came charging into the classroom, playfully pushing and shoving one another.

"There you are," said a tall, long-haired teen, sporting an AC/DC t-shirt. "We've been looking all over for you, man."

"I guess I gotta go," Ryan said turning to look at his teacher.

"Very good. Perhaps we can finish this discussion another time."

"Cool," said the relieved student nodding in approval.

He turned and headed out the door with his buddies. "What was that all about?" one of the boys asked. "What were you doing talking to him?"

"It was nothing," Ryan replied.

On the drive home, it suddenly struck John that he had managed to get through the day without obsessing over Sandra. In fact, he hadn't really even thought about her at all. Strange! Perhaps knowing about her decision had helped him find a small measure of peace. Perhaps he had been putting into practice what he had been teaching the students about quieting the chattering monkey. Either way, he felt better than he had in days. He was looking forward to seeing her, although, it would certainly feel strange.

For a moment, he thought it peculiar how his life had unraveled so suddenly. One second he was deeply in love with this amazing woman and in the next, she was leaving his life, voluntarily. They hadn't had a fight or any type of disagreement. At the moment he didn't fully understand why this was happening, but he accepted her assertion that he would benefit from this experience. He was also sure that she still loved him.

CHAPTER 8:
COMPASSION

Sitting on a park bench
Eyeing little girls with bad intent
Snot is running down his nose
Greasy fingers smelling shabby clothes

— Jethro Tull, *Aqualung*

Elijah peered out through the dusty front window of his shop and watched with curiosity as the old man passed unhurriedly by. He appeared to be walking aimlessly up the street, something he had been doing each day since Elijah's eyes first settled upon him. Although he had seen him quite often, the shop owner had never shared a word with him.

There appeared to be no purpose to his daily treks through the village and although he kept to himself and seemed to pose no threat, the villagers were suspicious. They didn't trust him. He seemed peculiar. Odd perhaps.

The stranger had drifted in to town several months earlier and no one knew from where he originated or how he had arrived at their peaceful little village. He mumbled to himself as he wandered each day throughout the streets. His clothes, although ragged, were of fine quality. Perhaps the man at some point in his life had enjoyed wealth or possibly the clothes had been given to him long after their original owner had found them useful. The origin of his clothing, clearly a mystery to the villagers, created more suspicion. He might have killed a gentleman in order to procure such a fine suit, reasoned some. Elijah thought it preposterous, but he did not like to cause trouble, so he kept silent.

A short while after the old man had passed by, David and Matthew burst into the shop. Elijah had grown up with the pair. They were the best of friends. "Little Patricia from Wind Swept Farm has disappeared," exclaimed Matthew, visibly upset.

"Disappeared during the night," added David, panting heavily.

"What do you mean, disappeared?" asked Elijah.

"She is nowhere to be found."

"Her parents are terribly distraught. Her fine mother was heard screaming quite hysterically outside their humble farmhouse."

"Oh my," Elijah exclaimed, quite shocked by the news.

"A search party is being formed. You must close your shop and join us."

"Most certainly," said the shop owner, removing his apron.

The three friends made their way out into the street amidst chaos and pandemonium. People were shouting and running in all directions. A group had formed in front of the barber shop and the trio hurried to join them.

The village's mayor was standing on a raised platform addressing the crowd. "We must find little Patricia without delay," he urged them, his fist pumping in the air. "She has been out quite possibly all night and her parents are panic stricken. Why her poor mother is about ready to lose her mind. We must act quickly."

"Our great mayor has spoken," a tall man near the front yelled. "Let us proceed with great haste."

The crowd quickly dispersed in all directions. It seemed an unorganized search, but Elijah and his friends nonetheless joined in. They thought it best to head in the direction of the farm from which little Patricia had disappeared. At her tender age they reasoned, she couldn't have gone far.

It was towards twilight, exhausted, their search having taken them to the forest west of the farm, when they got word that little Patricia's body had been discovered under a large evergreen tree north of the village. She was found as it turned out quite a distance from her home. By the time the three men returned to the village, most of the townsfolk had gathered in front of the esteemed home of the county doctor, where the little girl's lifeless body had been taken. It was a somber mood that greeted the three friends as they approached. They stood quietly with the others waiting for word from inside.

A short while later the front door flew open and the sheriff marched out onto the porch. "The little girl has been murdered," he announced to the stunned crowd. "We must go now and find her killer. Look not among you for the culprit, for we are all friends. Instead look for the stranger who lurks among us, for it is surely him, with dirt on his hands, who is responsible for taking the life of this precious angel."

The crowd knew that of which the mayor spoke and they scattered quickly in search of the old man. Elijah thought it odd their assumption that he was responsible for the taking of little Patricia's life. Observing his daily treks up the street, he appeared quite harmless, incapable of such a heinous act. Besides, surely he would not have made an appearance in the village earlier that day had he harmed the little girl. Indeed he would have made his escape forthwith.

Though filled with doubt, Elijah joined the others and began scouring the area. Finding the old man required considerably less time than it took to locate little Patricia. A mere ten minutes into the search, he was discovered at the village well quietly filling his tattered pouch. The irate crowd quickly seized him and dragged him to the same platform from which the mayor had addressed them earlier. The old man spoke not a word, but stood quietly, head bowed, as if awaiting his inevitable fate. The mob seemed particularly proud of themselves as the mayor and sheriff hurried up the street to join them. Men were slapping one another on the back, offering congratulations for a job well done, although they had done very little. It was clear to the humble shopkeeper that the old man had made no attempt to hide and must either be innocent or mad.

The mayor and sheriff quickly worked their way to the center of the throng. While the sheriff's look was dour, the mayor seemed particularly delighted with the results of crowd's fine effort. He shook the hands of several men. "A first-rate job indeed!" he said, smiling broadly.

The sheriff wasted no time in interrogating the old man. "What do you have to say for yourself in the death of dear little Patricia," he bellowed, violently shaking the poor fellow.

"But I have harmed not a soul," he responded softly.

"Be not a liar and speak only the truth," countered the sheriff. "You are undoubtedly responsible for the taking the life of this beloved child."

"Is that so," said the stranger.

The sheriff looked with disgust at the wretched old soul. "Your deceitful ways will not save you from a just fate. Take him to the tall oak beside the blacksmith's shed," he directed the crowd. "The limbs there are thick with age and will provide ample support for the task at hand."

Elijah was about to raise his hand in protest when the mob suddenly surged forward in the direction of the great tree. He was bumped and jostled as he stood helplessly, unable to comprehend the actions of his friends and neighbours. He did not follow them for he was aghast at their behaviour. Instead, he bowed his head in shame, turned and trudged off home.

Several days after the hanging, two elegantly dressed gentlemen drove in to town on a magnificently crafted horse drawn buggy. Elijah was closing the front door at the end of the day when they pulled up in front of his shop.

"Good day, fine sir," said the man holding the reins.

"Good day," was the polite response. "May I be of assistance to you?"

"Indeed you may," said the second man.

"We are searching for our father. He disappeared quite suddenly several months ago and we have been scouring the countryside for him. We were told by the friendly citizens of the village beyond the far ridge that he may be here. Perhaps you have seen him."

"Would you be so kind as to tell me of his appearance?"

"He is an elderly gentleman. In his sixties," said the first man.

"And well groomed," added the second.

"Yes, well groomed," agreed the first.

"He is a fine man, our father. Both kind and gentle. Would never harm even the tiniest of creatures. He is a caring soul indeed."

"And he is a fine husband and friend to all those who know him."

"What was the cause of his disappearance," Elijah inquired, trying to hide his guilt.

"He has not been right since being kicked in the head by an untamed horse."

"Yes, he began talking to himself and wandering aimlessly about our estate."

"We kept constant vigilance on him, but regrettably he disappeared late one evening after the family had turned in."

"We must find him. Winter is approaching and the nights are getting much cooler."

"I am most sorry," the shopkeeper offered, trying to sound sincere. "For the man you describe has not set foot in this fine village and I've not chanced upon him. I am familiar with all those who inhabit here and the countryside that surrounds us and I can assure you that he has not been in these parts."

"Well then," said the first man. "We must be on our way."

"Yes," agreed the second. "We shall not be of further bother to you."

"Thank you kind sir for your time."

Elijah nodded his head as the driver pulled the reins to the right, urging the horses onwards as they drove out of the village from the direction in which they had come. Both men smiled and waved as they rounded the corner and were quickly out of sight. He simply nodded and offered a faint smile in return. As they drove away, Elijah was overcome with guilt. He felt enormous shame and hung his head in silence.

"You did the right thing," said Jacob, who had quietly witnessed the entire exchange from his shop next door.

"Of that I am not so sure, friend."

"We have no way of knowing if the old man was their father."

"We could have retrieved his coffin from the ground in which it rests."

"What purpose could that possibly have served the fine people of this village?"

Looking at Jacob, the words he sought to express his outrage would not come, and so he hung his head once more and sadly headed home.

John was startled awake by the sound of traffic on the street below. It was early morning. Quickly his mind returned to the dream and for a few moments he considered its message. It had seemed so real, so profound. How sad he thought of the fate of that old man. How quickly the villagers were to judge and condemn him, simply because he was different. How little compassion they showed. The dream mirrored very intensely life on the planet… far too much fear and judgment and far too little compassion. He realized that it also spoke of the polarities of human behaviour, particularly of kindness versus unkindness, and how fear quite often impels us to the dark side of the polarity; for example, why so many people are drawn to greed rather than generosity. He immediately understood its significance and the need to speak to the students about this destructive aspect of human nature.

John also realized that he had slept well for the first time since Sandra told him about her job offer. They had spoken briefly on the phone the night before. Despite the distance that had so quickly come between them, he still felt a strong connection. Heck, he was still in love and that wasn't something that one easily released. They agreed to meet for dinner and John Stevens reckoned that he would have a difficult time focusing today.

The students' eyes were immediately drawn to the blackboard as they strolled into the classroom. It had been separated into two halves. On the left side was written words that represented our ideal way of living… words such as love, peace, happiness, compassion, acceptance, forgiveness, nurturing, gratitude, patience, harmony, tolerance, abundance, generosity, optimism, co-creation, trust and faith. On the right side were words that represented the contrary… chaos, anger, hatred, resentment, bitterness, jealousy, regret, frustration, intolerance, greed, anguish, despair, judgment, competition, lack, pessimism and fear.

"What's that stuff on the board all about?" asked Blair.

"What do the words mean to you?" John replied.

"Bullshit!"

"Why do you say that?"

"Cause school is bullshit."

John Stevens sensed that something was bothering his student and it had nothing to do with the words on the blackboard.

"Is there something you would like to talk about?"

Blair sat quietly for a few moments. "I hate being here."

"Why do you hate being here?"

"Because it doesn't make any sense to me."

"And why is that?"

"My dad was giving my mom a hard time again last night. He's such an asshole."

"Would you like to talk about what happened?"

"My mom and dad don't sleep together. My dad's bedroom is in the basement. It's where he spends all his time… watching TV. He's such a loser. My mom spends all her time upstairs. My parents hate each other, but neither one of them will move out. They never talk and when they do, it's always a fight. Last night my mom asked my dad to fix the washing machine. He told her to f-off."

"Why did he say that?"

"Cause he was watching the game and his team was losing, so he was pissed."

"What did your mom say?" asked Tracy.

"She didn't say anything. She just got mad and left the house. So I fixed it."

"Why do your parents stay together?" asked Josh. "If they're so unhappy, why doesn't one of them move out?"

"She can't afford to and my dad's too stubborn. Besides, if dad moved out, mom would have to sell the house cause she couldn't afford to pay for it."

"Regrettably, it seems that many very unhappy couples stay together for financial reasons," lamented John.

"Or for their kids," added Eric.

"Ya, but the problem is, that they just create an unhappy, toxic environment and their kids suffer because of it," said Ryan

"Worse still," added Terry, "they set a bad example. They show their kids that it's okay to live like that… but it's not okay."

"Blair's situation at home illustrates a predicament many kids find themselves in," observed Tom. "They have absolutely horrible home lives and yet are expected to come here to school to learn stuff that seems insignificant under the circumstances."

"Ya, what's the point, Teach?" asked Stuart.

"The point is that an education can give us the tools we need to rise above our present circumstances. It exposes us to things we might not otherwise be aware of. It gives us alternatives to consider."

"Not if we have no interest in what we're learning," responded Ryan.

"The challenge for the education system is to help you discover it."

"Ya, but schools don't do it. They just stick to the curriculum and most of the time it is irrelevant."

"Well, I can't argue with that."

"Do you know who Loreena McKennitt is?" asked Tracy.

"I certainly do. She's the Celtic singer who wrote the Mummer's Dance and Dante's Prayer among other great songs."

"Ya, she's awesome!" agreed Jessica. "My mom and I listen to her all the time. My dad even likes her."

"Well," interrupted Tracy, before Jessica could go on. "She grew up planning to be a veterinarian, but then she became a musician. She said that music found her. She didn't have to go to school to figure it out."

"Indeed that can happen. But we need a foundation to build on before Providence can set in."

"Say what?" asked Scott.

"Providence. Divine intervention."

"Oh, I get it."

"And we need to be exposed to many different things, whether through school or extra-curricular activities, in order to discover what interests us."

"And to find out what we're good at," added Josh.

"Absolutely! Actually, that ties in quite nicely with what I wanted to discuss today. If I could ask you to return your attention to the words I've written on the board, I would like to ask you about their significance. Let's begin with the words on the right. What do they represent to you?"

"They seem to characterize much of life here on the planet," said Ryan.

"And how we treat one another," added Scott.

"And how people are feeling," said Jordan.

"They represent all the suffering that exists in our society," observed Matt.

"Those are all good points," praised John. "Do they represent how we would like to live?"

"Certainly not," replied Tom. "Clearly the words on the left side represent how we really want to live."

"Then why do we choose to live otherwise? Why is there so much negativity and suffering on the planet?"

"Because Adam couldn't keep his hands off that apple," grinned Tom, causing a few snickers.

"Or Eve," added Josh, as the class to burst into laughter.

"And we've been paying for it ever since," laughed Matt.

"I suppose there's some truth to that," smiled Teach. "The story of Adam and Eve is of course a metaphorical story with an important message. It seems that the Garden of Eden represents the planet Earth, while Adam and Eve represent the masculine and feminine energy, which must be in balance in order for there to be harmony. Unfortunately, somewhere along the line, things got out of equilibrium."

"Perhaps when we began submitting to temptation in order to procure things for our own *selfish* enjoyment even when those things didn't serve us individually or collectively," said Tom.

"Like eating chocolate cake to satisfy our sweet tooth, knowing that it is not good for our bodies," said Tracy.

"And hoarding things out of fear, while others do without," added Eric.

"Yes, these are all good examples of how we do things that don't serve us."

"So why do we behave this way?" asked Mike.

"It's human nature," replied Terry.

"But why is it human nature? Why do we do things that don't serve us?"

"Because we don't understand our purpose... who we really are and why we're really here on the planet," replied their very enthusiastic teacher. "We don't know we are aspects of God... that we are in fact, God... living in oneness, connected to all that exists. And we don't know that we are here to remember who we are, to experience everything, to let go of emotional pain, to gain wisdom and be good stewards of the planet, rather than to become rich, powerful and famous. It's because we live in fear that there won't be enough and because we don't understand the significance and importance of feeling good about ourselves. It's also because we're not taught about love, compassion, acceptance, kindness and all the other things that are written on the left side of the board."

"What is compassion?" asked Jessica. "I don't understand it."

"Compassion means being able to observe and understand the suffering of others, to empathize with them and to have the desire to assist them without treating them as a victim or identifying with their suffering."

"So does that mean we're supposed to have compassion for rapists, child molesters, murderers and suicide bombers?" asked Blair.

"It does. People who commit heinous acts against other beings must reach a certain state of mind in order to do so and something has caused them to be that way."

"Yep, people don't become killers for the heck of it," added Adam. "Something caused them to get like that."

"I guess if we can eliminate the things that cause people to become murderers we will eliminate murder," observed Travis.

"And by extension, we can eliminate all forms of behaviour that don't serve mankind," added Tom.

"That's right," praised John, thrilled at how the students grasped these ideas.

"At the beginning of class," noted Matt, "Blair talked about the stuff that is happening in his home. Perhaps there is another important lesson for us to learn from the unhappiness of our parents. Maybe their suffering shows us how we don't want to live and therefore inspires us to find an alternative. Perhaps our parents are giving us a gift."

"Yes," agreed Jordan. "And our challenge is to step out of our own misery to see it."

"Those are excellent observations. That is the purpose of all forms suffering. It motivates us to change."

"Why doesn't society… families, schools, athletic teams, businesses, governments, police and the penal system… operate with compassion?" asked Travis.

"Because they're stuck in their ways," replied Matt. "They haven't taken the time to consider that there might be an alternative."

"Something more fulfilling," added Jordan.

"Exactly! Nobody talks about the significance of feeling good about yourself and how our collective negative self-image is at the root of so much suffering."

"Most people aren't aware of the concept," remarked Tom. "They don't understand where it fits in as it relates to human behaviour."

"There is a tremendous lack of awareness," agreed John.

"I guess this is why they don't teach these ideas in school," suggested Terry. "People don't understand how important it is."

"They're not aware of it period," remarked Ryan.

"That's a good point," Teach agreed. "Perhaps we need to begin creating this awareness."

"It seems essential to our survival," Tom observed.

At that moment, the bell rang signaling the end of class.

"That was an awesome discussion," Jessica beamed. "The best one I've ever had at school."

"You know," said Blair, smiling uncharacteristically at Jessica. "For once I might have to agree with you."

"Oh Blair," she smiled, slapping him playfully on the shoulder, her face a crimson red.

"Travis, do you have a second?" John asked as he was passing by his desk.

"Certainly, Teach!"

"I spoke to the girls I told you about and as it turns out there is a job available at the stable where they ride. It involves cleaning the stalls."

"That's awesome!" the grateful student exclaimed.

"They gave me a number to call," Teach said, handing him a piece of paper. "The lady's name is Joan Cornell."

"I don't know what to say," he said, taking the paper, his hand shaking. "Thank you so much!"

"My pleasure. The girls said it's a very good stable with lots to do. It's a good start."

"Wow! This so awesome!" Travis beamed reaching out shake hands.

"I'm glad you're happy. You'll do great!"

The future horseman looked at the paper, then wheeled and practically sprinted out the door, while his teacher looked on gleefully.

"It's quite alright, I'll see myself in," Ken Clark heard an unfamiliar voice say to his admin support.

"Please sir, let me make sure he is free," Karen pleaded as the man barged through the doorway, with her in hot pursuit.

"It's okay," Clark assured her, recognizing the intruder. "Let me introduce you to our new Director of Education, Jonathan Fox."

Fox offered his hand and at first Karen refused to shake it. She was a stickler for protocol and in her mind, Fox had deliberately circumvented it.

After a rather uncomfortable pause, she finally shook his hand.

"So sorry to have ignored you," he said smoothly. "Perhaps next time I will follow the rules."

Perhaps there won't be a next time, she thought, immediately distrusting him. "Would you like me to close the door?" she asked, looking at the Principal.

"Please," he replied.

Without saying another word, she wheeled and marched back to her desk, closing the door behind her.

"Sorry for the unannounced visit," Fox said. "Just doing the rounds with all the schools in my district."

"We are accustomed to a call in advance whenever someone from the Board pays us a visit."

"Yes, well, it's the way I like to do things. Keeps everyone on their toes."

"Fair enough, then," said Clark. He thought it a peculiar way to build trust, but decided it best to let it go for the time being. "What can I do for you?"

"Oh, nothing in particular, although I understand you have a teacher who may be resigning."

"Has resigned. She informed me this morning."

"I see," said the new Director, a slight smile washing over his face. "That's too bad," he added, nonchalantly.

"It's a big loss for us," added Clark, puzzled by Fox's expression and interest.

"I'm sure you'll find a suitable replacement."

"I'm sure we will!"

On the drive home, John Steven's mind was drawn back to the discussion about the chaos and turmoil that the human race is experiencing. Blair's admission about his parents' toxic relationship provided some valuable insights into his behaviour and the anger that was at the root of it. John couldn't help but wonder about all the families who were living under similar conditions because the parents were too fearful or stubborn to let go and move on.

He realized that anger, bitterness and resentment characterize many marital relationships and is greatly affecting the emotional health of their children. Worse still, this is what too many children are learning and people who are taught violence, anger and hatred enact this on other people. It's why there is so much bullying and abuse in our society.

With some awareness it could all change. If people only knew how much happier they could be and how much better it would be for their children, if they would examine their own unhappiness. If they felt good about themselves and acted with kindness and love they could let go of their misery.

Then his mind was drawn to Sandra and his own sense of grief. Clearly, he needed to let her go, although it would not be easy for him. He was deeply in love with her and the thought of her leaving left a huge hole in his heart. He knew that trust would help him through this crisis and time would help him heal this wound, but for now, he was very sad. He needed to give himself time to process this experience. He couldn't force himself to let go. It needed to come naturally and he was confident that it would.

John's hand was trembling as his index finger pressed the doorbell. He shuffled nervously, still unsure as to what he would say. So many thoughts were flooding his mind. Then, a few seconds later, the door swung open and she was there. For a brief moment they stood in silence, looking into each other's eyes. Sandra smiled and stepped through the doorway. She threw her arms around him in a deep embrace. They remained there for several moments, afraid to let go.

John held her. She felt warm. Comfortable.

"I'm so glad to see you," she said.

He wasn't quite sure how to respond, given that she had been avoiding him for several days. "I've missed you," he replied finally, wanting to speak the truth.

"I'm sorry, very sorry for what I've put you through."

He still held a glimmer of hope that she would change her mind and he chose his words carefully. "I know you are. It couldn't have been easy."

They held each other for a few minutes longer, each awash in a sea of emotions. Clearly, they were still in love.

"Shall we go," he said stepping away from her.

"Certainly," she smiled.

The maitre de placed their menus on the table and informed them that their server would arrive shortly.

They took their seats and John Stevens shifted nervously, not quite sure how to begin the conversation.

"I told Principal Clark today that I would be leaving the school," she began.

"How did he react?"

"He was quite disappointed."

"I'm not surprised."

"I had actually told him about the offer the day after I told you."

Just then, the waiter arrived at the table, introduced himself and took their drink order. They sat quietly for a few moments.

"How are you doing?" she asked, genuinely concerned.

"The last few days have not been easy. If someone had told me before the start of the school year that this was going to happen I would have thought them crazy." Crazy is an understatement he thought, considering the turmoil of the last few days. His world had been turned upside down and he was still reeling with the emotional upheaval.

"I hope you understand that this is the most difficult decision I have ever had to make. I love you deeply and didn't want to do anything to hurt you, but I just felt that I could not turn down this opportunity. I didn't want to face the day when I might resent you for not taking the job."

He was somewhat taken aback by what she said. She was projecting into the future about something that might happen, but he understood her concern.

"I know we're not supposed to project," she said, as if reading his thoughts, "but that's where I saw it heading. I've wanted a job like this all my life and I didn't want to put myself in a position where I might resent you. I couldn't bear the thought."

"How were you able to come to a decision?"

"I spoke to my mom and my sister, but mostly I just meditated."

"What did your mom say?"

"She told me to follow my heart."

"That's the type of advice I would have expected your mom to give you. She's very wise."

"And caring. She was very concerned for you."

John smiled. He had grown very close to Sandra's family. They were all very wonderful. "I love your mom," he smiled.

They spent the rest of the evening talking about what seemed like a million things... her new job, the student's reaction, who would replace her, when she would be leaving, selling her home... and later, they drove home in silence, each immersed in their thoughts.

When they arrived at her house, he climbed reluctantly out of the truck, walked around to the passenger side and opened her door. He held her hand as she stepped gracefully out onto the driveway.

"Would you like to come in," she asked as they walked up onto the front porch.

"It would be best if I didn't," he replied.

"I had a wonderful evening."

"I did as well."

Sandra looked at him, leaned up and kissed him on the lips.

For a moment, he wanted to accept her offer. He wanted to go inside, take her upstairs and make love to her. But the uncertainty of their future brought him quickly back to reality.

"I don't want to give up on you and me. I hope you will consider us staying together."

This was a conversation he was hoping to avoid. He just didn't see the point. He didn't see how it was feasible and he didn't want to try to hold onto something that was going to prolong the hurt. "I don't think it's very realistic. I love what I'm doing here and I don't see myself moving in the near future."

"Would you please consider it? We could find something for you."

"I know what you're saying, but right now, my life is here and if we try to keep this relationship alive, we'll only see each other from time to time and eventually it will fall apart. One of us will meet someone and the other will get hurt and I don't want that to happen."

"I know what you're saying makes sense, but I'm not ready to give up yet."

"I understand, but I've had to focus hard on letting go of you and I need you to do the same."

She put her arms around his waist and rested her head on his chest. "I know you're right, but I'm not ready yet."

He held her tightly. She was the love-of-his-life. He didn't want to say it out loud, but the thought of her leaving broke his heart and he could not hold back the tears.

They held each other for several minutes. He did not want her to see him crying. She was already having a difficult time with this. As he stepped away, he could see that she too had tears.

"Will I see you before I go?" she asked, her voice trembling.

"Of course, sweetie," he replied softly

He reached out and took her hand, held it for a few moments, then silently turned and walked back to his truck.

CHAPTER 9:
LETTING GO

So never mind the darkness
We still can find a way
Nothin' lasts forever
Even cold November rain

— Guns N' Roses, *November Rain*

Sir William, Lord of Barrington, dismounted and handed the reins of his steed to the diminutive stable boy. "Walk him for several minutes before you water him," he instructed.

"Yes, m'Lord," the boy responded, bowing.

"And only the best of oats, lad," he added.

"Yes, m'Lord."

Sir William treasured the big black stallion, as majestic and powerful a horse as he had ever ridden. It was a recent purchase having come into his possession a mere two months prior, but the pair had become quite attached in that short period. He patted his mount on the rump as the stable boy led him away snorting, proud of his stature.

The handsome gentleman from Barrington had just come from the county magistrate's office where he had only today completed another significant land acquisition. He was now the largest property owner in the county with territory stretching from east to west and having arrived at the estate of Lady Marion he felt certain she would now accept his offer of marriage.

He strode confidently up to the front door where the delightfully familiar doorman, Edward, had been awaiting his arrival.

"Good evening, sir," Edward said, guiding him courteously into the elegantly adorned front reception.

"Good evening my good man," the land baron responded, graciously turning his back so the elderly fellow could remove his topcoat. He then handed him his tunic and whip.

Sir William held Edward in high esteem and was prepared to take him on as a valued employee after he and Lady Marion were wed. He knew this would please her very much and he smiled at the thought.

"Lady Marion awaits you in the parlor, sir."

"Thank you, Edward. No need to direct me. I am quite capable of finding my way."

"As you wish, sir."

William turned and marched down the long candlelit hallway to the stately parlor room, where his beloved Lady would soon be in his arms. As he made his way towards her he thought about how the county's noble elite would now see him differently. With vast land holdings and the beautiful Marion on his arm, no longer would he be looked down upon, shunned, left out of their assemblies and social gatherings. Yes, it was his time to take his rightful place among them.

Seeing him enter the room, a flurry of attendees quickly scurried away through the archway directly behind her. She looked beautiful in her lavender evening gown.

"Sir William, how nice to see you," she smiled, hesitantly.

"The pleasure is all mine," he said, taking her hand. "I have been anticipating this day immensely and it is with high hopes that I have come to you."

"You have news?"

"I do m'Lady and it is my deepest wish that you will make me an enormously happy man."

"I cannot make promises, but I will hear you out."

"My dear Marion, I believe I have made my wishes very clear to you. I dearly long for you to be my wife, to live with me at Barrington, to bear my children and to enjoy with me the fortune I have amassed. Until now, I felt that I was not worthy of your love and companionship. You have spurned my every advance on the assertion that I could not provide for you. But now, with the acreage I have just this day procured, perhaps that has changed."

"It seems you believe that it is wealth and privilege that I seek, but this I already have and it gives me little pleasure. I have all that I need materially. It is fulfillment that I lack and that for which I yearn."

"Am I not to understand that it was your wish for me to provide for you? I have servants to tend to your every need and money to grant your every wish," he replied curtly, feeling slightly agitated.

"Servants and money will not fill the emptiness in my heart." she said disconsolately, head bowed. "They will not grant me the peace of mind that I so desperately desire, nor will they restore the joy that has been missing from my life."

"Lady Marion, such are the fanciful wishes of dreamers."

"But I am not content. My heart yearns."

"Then let me provide for you."

"Contrary to your assertion, I do not wish to be provided for. I wish for simplicity and enlightenment."

"But I will provide that for you."

"And how do you propose to do that when I cannot do it for myself."

"In this moment, I have no answer, but you must at least let me try," pleaded William, feeling his anxiety rising.

"I see no possibility. I am certain this was not meant to be," she said determinedly.

The agitated gentleman's anxiety quickly turned to anger with her last words. "You are being unreasonable, a foolish, insolent child."

"Say what you like. I have made up my mind."

Sir William was furious. He had waited too long for this. He was certain that he would have Marion's hand and he did not intend to leave here without it. In a rage he grabbed her by the shoulders, lifted her out of the chair and shook her violently. "You must come to your senses," he bellowed.

In a desperate struggle to free herself, she slipped and fell, smashing the back of her neck against the stone hearth, dying instantly. Her lifeless body lay motionless on the floor as the bewildered courter looked on in shock. Uncertain about what to do, he stood completely immobilized. "My God, what have I done," he cried.

He could have tended to Lady Marion. He could have held her. He could even have called out for help. But he did none of these. He simply stood there, wracked with grief, paralyzed by shame. "How can I ever forgive myself?"

When John awoke, the dream was still fresh in his mind and as he lay quietly, he began to understand the fullness of its meaning. It was partly about the need to let go... of everything... projections, expectations, attachment, ownership and judgment. Sir William was determined to have Lady Marion's hand, just as he was determined to have Sandra's and he needed to let her go.

He also surmised that her decision to leave him at this time was to some extent about clearing karmic debt. John was certain that Sandra was Lady Marion in that lifetime and he was Sir William. In a fit of rage, he had ended her life and he now understood that he had come into this life to seek atonement... to heal the emotional woundings between them, particularly that of grief and shame. He understood that he needed to release this emotional pain before he would be able to have a joyful, long-lasting relationship.

It was also another reminder about the importance of self-image. Clearly Sir William's definition of self-image had to do with material wealth, a mindset that is pervasive in our society. This preoccupation undoubtedly reflected his sense of inadequacy. If William had felt good about himself, he would have realized that he didn't need vast land holdings in order to impress Lady Marion, he just needed to be himself. Evidently, John's guides didn't want him to forget or neglect this aspect of our experience.

Most importantly, the dream spoke about the need for forgiveness, something he was not particularly good at. In the past, he had tended to hold onto resentment and he knew in his heart that he had to learn how to forgive in order to have peace of mind. He now understood that his inability to forgive others was due to his inability to forgive himself. There were so many things he had done in this life for which he had not yet absolved himself. There was much self loathing that he carried.

He looked at the clock and saw that he was running late. He would have to deal with this later.

As he climbed out of bed, he thought about Sandra. She was right. Her decision to take this new job was as much for him as it was for her. This dream had given him new insights and he wanted to talk to her about it. He wanted her to leave with no regrets.

Like wildfires sweeping across the plains, rumour mills are very active in schools. They move quickly and consume everything in their path. PLJ High had a very lively rumour mill and it wasn't long before news spread that Sandra Connors was leaving. When Teach walked into the classroom, most of the students were already present and they wasted no time in peppering him with questions.

"Is it true that Ms. Connors is leaving the school?" asked Tracy.

"Yes, she is," he replied.

"See, I told you," exclaimed Stuart, punching Blair in the shoulder.

"Who cares?" Blair snapped.

"Oh, that's really mature," Tracy chided, eyeing her adversary.

"That must really suck?" smiled Caitlyn, her voice dripping with sarcasm.

John looked at her, but didn't reply. He knew that her comment was born out of unhappiness and he chose not to engage her.

"We're all quite surprised," remarked Tom. "Ms. Connors is well respected around this school."

"She's an awesome teacher," added Jessica. "I had her two years ago and she was great. She was really patient with me and she didn't seem to mind that I like to talk a lot. You must be really sad. She was your girlfriend, wasn't she?"

"Yes, she is, and yes, I am very sad, Jessica."

Leave it to Jessica to bring things out in the open. Sometimes, her lack of filters could be a blessing. John hadn't talked to anyone about his feelings and perhaps this was his opportunity to do so. Maybe sharing his feelings would help some of the students to open up about their own issues.

"It's never easy to lose someone you're close to and that is especially true of romantic relationships."

"So, she dumped you," remarked Caitlyn, coldly.

Several of the students were surprised at their classmate's lack of compassion, but they knew better than to say anything. She relished conflict and would not hesitate to unleash her rage on them. She could be downright nasty.

She had put her teacher in a bit of a pickle. He felt that sharing his feelings about this experience could be beneficial to the students, but he didn't want to divulge anything that would betray his and Sandra's privacy.

"I'm very much in love with Sandra," he admitted, "and I believe she is in love with me. But she has been given a wonderful teaching opportunity that has been her lifelong ambition and as painful as it has been for both of us, she has decided to follow her dream."

"Wow! I'm sorry, Teach," sympathized Josh, being uncharacteristically serious. "That's gotta hurt."

"It hasn't been easy." For a moment, he felt very vulnerable standing there before the class. He was not accustomed to sharing his feelings, let alone doing it in public, but he felt it necessary for himself and the students.

"I grew up feeling very unloved and even though I know now that my parents loved me, it doesn't change how I felt as a child and it hasn't necessarily allowed me to let go of those feelings."

"You must feel like you've been kicked in the teeth," observed Terry.

"More like in the heart, Terry. An experience like this is a way of allowing us to see if we are holding on to emotional pain, so from that perspective, it's a very important experience."

"So, are you?" Caitlyn prodded.

"It's been a difficult experience, so yes, I guess I am."

"I guess you're not the guru everyone says you are."

"I never professed to be a guru, Caitlyn. I'm not sure that we're ever free of emotional pain. In my experience, letting go of it can be a life-long process."

"Well, you're not talking like Ms. Connors' leaving the school is upsetting you. You sound very matter of fact, like you're a doctor giving us a diagnosis. Are you upset about it or aren't you?"

John's eyes suddenly welled up and his throat constricted. His stomach was tangled in knots and his legs began to tremble. Slowly, he took his seat. He sat silently for several minutes, the class looking on with both concern and curiosity. Tears were rolling down his cheeks as he began to speak. "I am very much in love with Ms. Connors and the pain of her leaving has been almost unbearable. I've never felt a love like this before and the ache in my heart has been enormous. This isn't something I would wish on anyone.

"It's like when you're given this kind of love for the first time in your life, you suddenly have feelings that you've never felt before and a happiness that you just can't believe. They are foreign to you at first and they feel so good you never want to let them go. You want to hang on for dear life."

It took all the courage he could muster to pour out his feelings, but as he did, he could feel something beginning to shift within himself.

"You know," observed Tom, "it strikes me that you are allowing all of your happiness to come from outside you. Maybe that's partly why Ms. Connors is leaving."

"Ya," added Ryan. "Maybe you're supposed to figure out that true joy and happiness come from within, as you've said before, from knowing who you are and being connected to all that is."

Teach was stunned by his students' observations. They were right. He realized that much of the happiness he had been experiencing was largely due to his relationship with Sandra and that if he had stayed with her, it is conceivable that she would have continued to be the source of his happiness. She was right in her assertion that she was doing this for him and suddenly he felt more at peace.

He looked at Tom and Ryan and smiled. "Thank you," he said gratefully. "Every experience is meant to be a gift and that includes the painful ones. But the gift isn't always apparent. It's not always easy to see, especially when we're in the middle of it. I'm still feeling a great deal of sadness, but after what was just said, I'm also feeling a little better because I understand part of what this is all about. Thank you, gentlemen," he repeated.

They smiled in return.

John couldn't help but be marveled by his students. He was blown away by their wisdom. They saw something very clearly that he hadn't been able to see for himself and he could only shake his head. They had displayed an amazing intelligence since the beginning of the school year. How is it he wondered that they haven't been able to cope and why are they in this class when they have so much to offer? He thought about how we judge and label things. If somebody doesn't fit into our idea of the world, we dismiss them. We don't see their beauty or potential.

"Looking at our experiences this way takes us out of victimhood and empowers us, which in turn helps us feel good about ourselves," he continued.

"You mean it raises our self-image?" asked Eric.

"Yes, it does."

"A few days ago you said there were things we could do to make sure we're doing our part to feel good about ourselves," remarked Jordan. "What things were you talking about?"

"The single most important thing we can do is become spiritually conscious. It is to understand who we really are and why we're really here on the planet."

"You mean like the other day when you told us that we are actually spiritual beings?" asked Josh.

"And that we are not separate from each other or God?" added Ryan.

"Yes! This is an important first step because when you understand this truth, then you know that it is unconscious people ... including parents ... who do things and say things that cause people ... especially children ... to not feel good about themselves."

"Because if we're all spiritual aspects of God," added Tom, "then we're all equal and there is no reason for anybody to think or act like they are better or worse than anyone else."

"Precisely!"

"That's awesome!" exclaimed Jessica grinning from ear to ear, looking around the classroom.

"It certainly is," echoed an ecstatic teacher.

"So if parents were conscious and felt good about themselves they would raise their children to be conscious and feel good about themselves and in a generation, the world's problems could be solved," observed Jordan.

"That's being quite optimistic," snorted Caitlyn.

"Beats being a pessimist," Jordan replied, to which she huffed and looked out the window.

"You said there were several things we could do," said Terry. "What else is there?"

"First, we can be kind. You cannot possibly feel good about yourself if you mistreat another being."

"I like that," agreed Jessica. "Sometimes people aren't very kind to me because I talk a lot and they think I'm weird. I wish everyone would be kind."

"You are weird!" snarled Blair.

"Shut up, big mouth!" Jessica yelled. "You're the worst!"

"One of these days, man, somebody's gonna fill you in!" snapped Travis.

"Any time!" the combative teen replied.

"You people are missing Teach's point," Ryan interrupted, silencing the group.

John waited a moment for calm, before continuing. "When you mistreat somebody, and that includes speaking unkindly to them, quite often we feel guilt. Perhaps not right away, but soon enough."

"What about gangsters and psychopaths?" asked Terry. "Do they feel guilt?"

"Some people are so unconscious and have done such an efficient job of shutting down their sensitivity and their ability to feel that they can mistreat others without feeling any emotion, at least on the surface."

"What else can we do?" asked Josh.

"Related to being kind is treating people with respect and never allowing anyone to treat you with disrespect."

"But what do you do if somebody disrespects you?" asked Scott.

"Punch them in the face," Stuart joked.

"*Stuart!*" John replied. "It would be more beneficial if we all made meaningful contributions to the discussion."

"Sorry."

"There are a couple of things we can do, Scott. First, we can ignore them. If you ignore somebody long enough, eventually they will lose interest.

"Second, and perhaps a better response would be to say calmly, 'that's not an appropriate way to speak to me, so please don't do it.'"

"I like to say, 'did I do anything or say anything to lead you to believe that it is okay to talk to me that way?'" added Tom.

"What if they say, 'ya, you're an idiot?'" Stuart inquired.

"Simply respond with, 'Is that so!'"

The class sat silently considering his words.

After a few moments, Mike picked up the conversation. "That's a great idea, Teach, cause what do you say after that? 'Oh ya!' You'd just sound like an idiot!"

"Speaking up for yourself in any situation is very empowering, whether you are expressing your feelings or beliefs, or simply standing up for yourself."

"I get that," agreed Jordan.

"The next thing we can do is to be honest. Again, you cannot possibly feel good about yourself if you lie, cheat or steal. If you do any of these things, it immediately puts you in a state of fear of being caught and this is disempowering."

Many of the students nodded their heads.

"What about integrity?" asked Ryan.

"That's the fourth thing."

"What exactly is integrity?" asked Scott.

"It's doing the right thing even when no one is watching."

"I get it. It's like seeing someone drop some money out of their pocket without knowing it and you pick it up and give it to them."

"That's a great example."

The grin on Scott's face suggested he was feeling very proud of himself.

"Some other things we can do are to live in gratitude, be forgiving, be thankful, focus on doing your best, treat your body like a temple, stop judging, be genuine, do things you love to do and never, ever criticize… especially yourself."

"My mother is always criticizing herself," remarked Travis. "It drives me nuts."

"Always keep this in mind. No matter how it may appear, everyone is doing the best they can with what they've learned… and that goes for each of you and for your mom, Travis."

"Yep, that's a pretty good way of looking at things," agreed Adam.

"And related to that, I urge you to take a different view of mistakes and failures. Rather than looking at them in this manner, consider them lessons or an opportunity to learn something, because the reality is, that's what they are. We call them mistakes and failures because of our need to judge."

"It seems like there are a lot of things we do to bring suffering onto ourselves that could change with a little awareness?" observed Jordan.

"That's quite true and one of them is the five essentials."

"The what?" asked Eric.

Just then, the bell rang. "You may have questions about some of the things we discussed today, and if you do, we'll hopefully have time to address them tomorrow."

"I'd like to know more about the five essentials," remarked Tom.

"Well, we just talked about two of them and with any luck, we'll get to the rest tomorrow."

CHAPTER 10:
VALUES AND BOUNDARIES

Say that you're leaving
Well that comes as no surprise
Still I kind of like this feeling
Of being left behind

— Blue Rodeo, *Hasn't Hit Me Yet*

As John exited the school, he was met by brilliant sunshine. He quickly slid his sunglasses down from the top of his head to cover his squinting eyes before continuing on to his truck. Pulling the keys out of his pocket, he noticed Tracy hurriedly walking toward him. "Mr. Stevens," she called out, "Could I talk to you?"

"Certainly!" he replied. As she came closer, it was apparent from her expression that she was feeling distressed.

"There's something that has been bothering me… a lot… and I thought maybe you could help me figure it out."

"I would be happy to listen and assist any way I can."

"Great! I'm on my way to my friend's house. Her name is Lisa. We get together twice a week to play piano and most of the time we go to her place. My piano's not as good as hers and I don't think she enjoys playing it, although she's never come out and said so. She just makes up excuses for why she wants to play at her house."

John nodded in acknowledgement.

"I like going to her place, she's got a great piano and I really enjoy playing with her. The problem is her mom is constantly interrupting us to see what we're doing or to tell us to play quieter because her brother is doing homework."

"So you don't have a lot of privacy?"

"No, we don't. And it bothers me."

"Why does it bother you?"

"I go there to play piano, but we don't get to play as much as I would like."

"And Lisa doesn't want to go to your place because your piano's not as good."

"I think so."

"Have you told her how you feel?"

"No, I'm afraid she'll be upset."

"But you're upset and she doesn't even know it."

"Yes! I guess that's right."

"Sounds like it's making you feel powerless."

"That's exactly what it feels like!"

"Let's consider each of the aspects of this situation. First, would you have more privacy if you practiced at your house?"

"Yes we would. Nobody's home."

"And would you be happier practicing at your place, even on an inferior piano?"

"I would be, but I'm not so sure about Lisa."

"But can you say with absolute certainty that she wouldn't and that she'll be upset if you tell her how you're feeling?"

"No, not for sure."

"And if she does react negatively, are you responsible for her feelings?"

"No."

"And I'm guessing you don't want to continue feeling the way you feel?"

"Definitely not."

"So, you're in a bit of a pickle. If you don't say anything, chances are you're going to continue to be unhappy, and in all likelihood, at some point, you'll explode and perhaps say something in anger that will really damage your relationship. Or you'll develop so much resentment towards the situation, you might eventually turn that resentment towards Lisa and perhaps end the friendship."

"I don't want that to happen."

"On the other hand, if you tell her how you're feeling, she might get angry with you and not want to be your friend. Can you see how a situation like this can make you feel powerless?"

"For sure. But what can I do about it?"

"It's always best to speak our truth, to say what's in our heart and to take action that empowers us. How do you think your friend would feel if she knew how unhappy you are right now?"

"She'd be upset."

"That's quite likely. And what would your ideal practicing arrangement look like?"

"I would like to play once a week at her place and once at mine."

"That sounds fair. And what would work best for you when you're at her place?"

"I would like her to tell her mom to not disrupt us when we're practicing. We can talk to her when we're finished. And I would like her to ask her brother to do his homework in his bedroom, or another part of the house where we won't disturb him."

"If you tell her that, she might get upset because she may feel that you are telling her what to do. Perhaps you could begin by telling her what is going on and how it makes you feel. Tell her that you really value her friendship. See how she reacts to that. If she reacts favourably, then tell her what you would like; first, that you alternate between your place and hers, and second, when you're at her house, that you are able to play uninterrupted. Perhaps Lisa will figure out a solution on her own, which will make her feel better about it, or perhaps she will ask you what to do."

"That would be great."

"Keep an open mind though. She may have some fears of her own. She may be afraid to speak to her mother and brother."

"In which case, maybe she'd okay with practicing at my house both days."

"She might."

"What if she doesn't want to talk to her mom or come to my place once a week?"

"Then perhaps you will need to play on your own. Would you be okay with that?"

"I would miss playing with her, but at least I wouldn't be unhappy."

"Yes! And you might need to be prepared to tell her that."

"I'm feeling a little nervous about talking to her."

"That's quite understandable, but sometimes we have to face our fears. It's the only way to overcome them. We may not always get the outcome we want, but if we speak our truth, it usually works out okay. At the very least, we feel more empowered."

"Thank you, Mr. Stevens. I'm gonna do it."

"Awesome, Tracy! Good luck!"

"There she is now," she said, looking back towards the school.

The elated teacher smiled, as his apprehensive student turned and headed off to meet her friend. How often, he mused, do we allow our fears to stop us from doing the things we want to do and how often do we compromise our values in order not to offend someone?

"Understanding our values and establishing boundaries that are aligned with our values is an important part of the human experience," Teach began, standing beside his desk at the front of the class. "Quite often, we suffer when we don't understand our values, or when we compromise them, or when we don't establish and honour our boundaries."

"Do you mean like when you let somebody push you around?" asked Scott.

"Absolutely! In that instance, what value would you not be honouring?"

"Not being pushed around," answered Mike.

"Duh!" said Blair.

"What's another way of looking at that or phrasing it differently?" John continued, smiling at Blair.

"Being treated with respect," replied Matt.

"That's right. What you value, is respect, and your boundary would be never allowing anyone to treat you with disrespect."

"Yep. What are your values?" asked Adam.

"Some of the things I really value are family, simplicity, order, fun, learning, compassion, effort, authenticity, independence, freedom, wisdom and spirituality."

"Cool!" remarked Josh, "I never thought about something like values before."

"It's important to understand your values. They serve as guideposts and they help you understand when and why things are out of alignment in your life, particularly if you're feeling stressed about something."

"I value power," bragged Blair.

"That is evident in the way you bully younger students," remarked Tom.

"Somebody's got to show them who the boss is."

"Why don't you pick a fight with Matt?" asked Mike

"What, are you stupid?"

"Gentlemen, is this relevant to our discussion?" their teacher asked, looking at the pair of combatants.

"Not really," Mike admitted.

"The type of power you value Blair comes from a sense of disempowerment. It's not really a value. It's more of a need to make up for a sense of lack."

"So, how are we supposed to know what our values are?" inquired Jordan.

"One place to start is to simply ask, 'what is important to me?' Is freedom important, or respect or family or honour or patience or being physically fit?"

John held up a piece of paper. "This sheet contains a list of the things people commonly value. What I would like you to do is go through the list and pick out ten that are meaningful to you. Then, go through that list and pick out the top three."

"That's not going to be easy," remarked Josh.

"Here's a simple tip you can use to help you determine your core values. Imagine you are travelling to a new planet and you are only allowed to share the three things you value most with its inhabitants."

"That's an interesting idea," remarked Scott.

Teach walked around the class handing out a sheet to each of the students. "Keep this list," he encouraged them. "You can refer to it from time to time to see what has changed."

The students spent the rest of the class creating their lists. When the bell rang, most of them were still at it and they agreed to complete the assignment prior to tomorrow's class so they could discuss it then.

After the rest of the students had left, Tracy approached his desk. "I took your advice and spoke to Lisa yesterday," she smiled.

"That's terrific."

"Ya, I thought I should do it right away, before I forgot what you said."

"How did it go?"

"Way better than I thought. She actually said that her mom drives her nuts, interrupting us all the time, but she hasn't had the courage to say anything. I told her what you said and she was going talk to her mother after I left."

"Awesome!"

"Ya! I even talked to her about playing at my place and she confessed that she prefers her piano. But she also admitted that it wasn't fair to me, so we agreed to play at my place once a week."

"That's wonderful! How did you feel during your conversation?"

"Nervous at first, but when I realized she wasn't going to freak out on me, I felt okay."

She looked up at the clock behind her teacher's desk. "I better get going or I'll be late for my next class."

"I'm very proud of you, Tracy."

"Thanks Mr. Stevens. I'm very proud of myself. I really feel great about it."

"And empowered, I bet."

"Very empowered!" she agreed, looking over her shoulder as she headed off to her next class.

As John pulled out of the parking garage at the airport, his stomach was still in knots and tears were running down his cheeks. It had been an emotional farewell. Saying goodbye to Sandra, knowing that he might never see her again. It was quite possibly the most difficult thing he had done in his life.

Her brother was going to pick her up at the airport upon her arrival at the other end and she would be staying with him until she found a place of her own. Knowing she had a familiar place to stay helped put his mind at ease.

As he made his way out of the maze of roadways that connected the airport to the main highway, his thoughts were drawn to his experiences with this wonderful woman… the day he met her in the lunch room, their many excursions to Henderson Lake and their first night together. These were magical moments that lightened his mood.

He vowed that in order to get through this, he would stay in the moment, focus on understanding the higher spiritual purpose of her departure and put his energies towards his students. He also promised that he would allow himself to grieve in those moments when he needed to. Grieving is an important part of the healing process when there is loss and he needed to grieve.

Driving back into town, he found himself behind a car that was travelling well under the speed limit. Lost in his thoughts, he didn't realize it at first, but when he noticed how slow the other car was traveling, he immediately felt irritated. "What is this guy doing?" he muttered. The longer he followed the slow moving vehicle, the angrier he got and when he was unable to pass on a long straight-away, he lost it. "What the fuck are you doing, you idiot!" he screamed, pounding the steering wheel. "Get the hell out of my way, God-damn-it!"

John Stevens was taken aback by his outburst. Looking in the mirror, he couldn't believe what had just occurred. Then suddenly it struck him and in dismay, he spoke the words out loud, "My God, I'm still full of anger!"

CHAPTER 11:
GOOD HEALTH

Some things take so long
But how do I explain
When not too many people
Can see we're all the same

— George Harrison, *Isn't It A Pity*

John eased his truck into the last parking space, threw the gearshift into park and climbed out of the driver's side door. The sun was high in the eastern sky, patiently making its way westward, as he walked easily across the parking lot towards the front door of the school. It had been a few weeks since Sandra's departure and despite his heavy heart, he was feeling upbeat about the day's topic. He felt that a discussion about the education system would spark the student's interest. It was a hot topic and it seemed everyone had an opinion. He also wanted to finish their conversation about values and boundaries because he felt this understanding was significant for the students' personal growth.

Entering the classroom, he was immediately bombarded with questions. There were so many coming at once, he couldn't think straight. "Hold on a second," he pleaded. "One at a time, please."

"It's coming up to the anniversary of George Harrison's death," Josh began. "And we want to know why so many people keep dying from cancer."

"Yep, basically it's crazy," added Adam.

"Well, that's not exactly what I had in mind for today's discussion, but why not?" their adaptable leader replied.

"It's an important issue," stated Tom.

"I couldn't agree more."

"Cancer is one of the leading causes of death in developed countries," said Eric.

"It's one of the leading causes of death, period," added Ryan.

"The music industry has lost quite a few great musicians to cancer," observed Terry. "Bob Marley, Bobby Hatfield, David Bowie and Carl Wilson, to name a few."

"And the sad part is that it doesn't have to be this way."

"It doesn't?" asked Ryan. "What do you mean by that?"

"Ya," added Josh. "Don't you think if there was a cure, they would have discovered it by now?"

"The problem is that we spend too much time focusing on the effect and not enough time on the cause."

"Say what?" exclaimed Stuart.

"Perhaps you could explain that statement," suggested Tom.

"Ya," agreed Scott. "What about all the money that is being spent on research and treatment?"

"Again, we are focusing much of our energy on the effect, because that is where all the money is."

"Are you a conspiracy theorist?" asked Caitlyn.

"Not at all, although, the reality is that there is a lot of money to be made from the treatment of cancer. It's an entire industry in itself and millions of people would be out of work if a *miracle* cure was found. It's sad that so much of our energy is focused on what to do after we develop cancer, when the truth is, the best way to cure it is to prevent it in the first place."

"You mean, by not smoking and things like that?" asked Eric.

"George Harrison smoked, didn't he?" asked Mike.

"Yes, he did, but I'm afraid there's more to it than that."

"There must be," observed Tracy. "I'm sure smoking doesn't cause breast cancer or colon cancer."

"And what about prostate cancer?" added Terry. "It's one of the leading causes of cancer death among men."

"Then how do we stop it?" asked Jordan. "It seems to strike randomly."

"Perhaps we could begin by asking ourselves a couple of questions. Is it a coincidence that a disease that eats away at the physical body is killing millions of people each year around the world at a time when the human race is incredibly stressed and overwhelmed with anger, shame, guilt, grief, resentment, bitterness and hatred... feelings that are eating away at us emotionally?"

"Hey man, I never looked at it that way before," said Josh.

"And is it a coincidence that this planet is rife with sexual shame while prostate cancer and breast cancer are killing men and women in record numbers?"

"Maybe that's why there's so much colon cancer," remarked Ryan. "Maybe it's because we're so full of toxic emotional energy."

"You're very smart, aren't you, Ryan?" enthused Jessica admiringly. "I don't think I could have figured that out."

"It's not likely that you can prove all this," said Tom.

"Perhaps we can't prove it, but aren't we foolish to ignore it?"

"I suppose we are."

"So, if we heal our emotional pain, will that end cancer?" asked Josh.

"That sounds rather simplistic," countered Tom. "What about all the pollution and chemicals in the air we breathe and the water we drink?"

"And what about the crappy food we eat?" added Mike. "Don't these things cause cancer?"

"Yes, on a physical level, they certainly are a factor. But if they were the sole cause, why doesn't everyone develop cancer?"

The class sat quietly, contemplating their teacher's last point. He had given them pause to think, to go beyond the rhetoric that was so often put forward by the *establishment*.

"It's not so simple or straightforward. There are a number of factors that must be considered and our emotional state is a critical one."

"If I understand you correctly," said Tom. "You are saying that how we feel leaves our bodies susceptible to disease."

"Without a doubt! Our emotional state sets forth physiological changes in our body that weakens our cell tissues and compromises our immune systems. And it's our immune system that largely determines the state of our health."

"You mean if our immune system is functioning properly, then we'll be healthy?" asked Scott.

"Essentially, yes. The sole function of the immune system is to keep the body healthy, but when faced with overwhelming stress, it breaks down."

"So what can we do?" asked Jordan.

"There are several things. First, as we've been discussing, we need to heal our emotional pain. Each of us needs to find a way to let go of all the anger, shame, guilt, grief, resentment and fear we're holding on to. These emotions are being held in our physical bodies… in our limbic brain and cell memory… and they are helping to create a toxic environment in our cell tissues. They are making our bodies acidic."

"So how can we heal our emotional pain?" asked Tracy.

"I'll get to that, Tracy, but first I'd like to review all the factors that weaken our immune system."

"Okay."

"Next, we need to eat healthier foods."

"You mean I have to give up junk food?" asked Blair.

"Ideally."

"Not a chance."

"Well, I guess that's your choice."

"Do we really have to give up everything?" asked Jessica. "I kinda like eating junk food too."

"Ideally, yes. The more unnatural foods you put into your body… sugar, processed foods, junk food, soft drinks, meat from animals raised on factory farms, pasteurized milk and juices and artificial sweeteners… the more you compromise your immune system, making it more difficult to keep your body healthy."

"What about eating things in moderation?" inquired Ryan.

"Certainly, that would be a start."

"There are people who have healed cancer by going on organic diets," added Tracy.

"Yes, there are many cases and I truly believe it's possible to prevent and overcome cancer with a healthy diet. And again, what have you got to lose by eating healthy."

"A lot of enjoyment," remarked Stuart.

"Yes, but at your peril," countered Tom.

"I have to admit," remarked Eric, "that I really don't understand how junk food affects your body. Is it just because it doesn't have any nutrients?"

"That's a big part of it. Most people's diets are lacking in nutrients, but of equal importance is that the consumption of these foods can turn a perfectly healthy alkaline body into one that is acidic."

"Hey, go easy on me," joked Mike. "I flunked chemistry."

"Perhaps if you'd attended class you might have passed!" observed Tom.

"Ouch," said Eric, smiling. "Nice one, Tom."

"Guilty as charged," Mike admitted.

"The human body is healthiest with a pH level in the 7.0 to 7.4 range. Water has a pH value of 7.0 and remember, our bodies are about 75% water. Anything below 7.0 is acidic and above 7.0 is alkaline, so our bodies do best when they are slightly alkaline."

"Do fruits and vegetables help keep our bodies alkaline?" asked Jessica.

"Yes, especially raw organic fruits and vegetables... the greener, the better. Almonds, beans, legumes and brown rice also help to keep the body alkaline."

"Does that mean everything else acidifies the body?" asked Tracy.

"Pretty much... to varying degrees."

"Does that include coffee?" asked Stuart.

"Definitely."

"Eliminating coffee could kill me!"

"Again, what you eat and how you treat your body is your choice."

"Aren't our foods also laced with chemicals?" asked Terry.

"They certainly are. Most of the foods we eat are grown on soil that has been fertilized with chemical fertilizers and sprayed with chemical pesticides, not to mention all the chemicals and additives that are added during the production process."

"Yep, and everything grown outside is acid-rained on too," added Adam.

"It's scary, isn't it?" observed Jordan.

"It certainly is, because most people have no idea what's really in their food. What is worse, though, is that these unhealthy foods we eat really compromise our immune systems, because 80% of our immune system lies in our gastro-intestinal tract."

"Wow, I didn't know that," admitted Scott.

"I think it's safe to say that most people don't."

"So eating crappy foods is like dumping a bunch of garbage and sewage in the school every day and then asking the maintenance workers to keep the school clean," suggested Ryan. "Eventually they're not going to be able to keep up and the school is going to start breaking down."

"Not to mention the affect it's going to have on the poor maintenance workers," added Josh.

"That's an excellent analogy," John praised.

"Are there other things we can do to prevent cancer?" asked Jessica.

"Yes, there are. The third thing we need to do is bring more joy into our lives and one of the best ways to do that is through laughter. Laughter, like raw organic diets, helps to alkaline the body."

"Laughter also causes the release of endorphins," added Ryan.

"Laughter boosts the immune system, reduces stress hormones, relaxes the body and helps strengthen the heart."

"It's hard to have a bad attitude when you're laughing, isn't it?" inquired Mike.

"Yes! And a bad attitude is a real killer. If you walk around all day in a negative thought pattern, angry at the world, you're creating an acidic body and setting yourself up eventually for disease."

"I've been laughing a lot more since I discovered *The Rick Mercer Report* on Youtube," said Josh.

"I really like Stephen Colbert," added Mike.

"Singing, dancing, spending time in nature and doing what we love are other ways to bring joy into our lives," Teach continued.

"That makes a lot of sense," agreed Eric. "I'm happiest when I'm playing baseball. I love it, and I don't care if we win or lose. I just like playing it."

"I guess exercise is also important," commented Jordan.

"Exercise is critical for keeping the body strong and healthy. A good balance of cardiovascular, strengthening and stretching exercises is important, and again, we need to do it properly, with a relaxed attitude and for the pure joy of it... not to prove anything to anybody or to win at all costs if we're playing a competitive sport."

"What about our environment?" asked Eric. "All the polluted air we breathe and water we drink. That has to be a factor."

"It's a huge issue. Anything unnatural that goes into our body, be it the pollutants and chemicals in the air and water or the chemicals in the cosmetics we put on our bodies, affects us adversely. They all help to acidify our bodies, stress our internal organs... especially our livers... cause a build-up of toxins in our colon and damage our body cell tissues."

"I read that John Wayne filmed a movie in the desert in Utah where some nuclear testing took place and then he and other cast members died from cancer," said Matt.

"Yes, that's true. And although nothing could be proven conclusively... even Wayne himself blamed his cancer on his cigarette smoking habit... almost fifty percent of the cast and crew of that movie developed cancer."

"That's ridiculous man!"

"What kind of cancer did he die from?" asked Jessica.

"Stomach cancer."

"What does that have to do with smoking cigarettes?" asked Scott.

"I'm not sure that there is a connection. Wayne did overcome lung cancer earlier in his life, but he died from stomach cancer."

"Crazy!" added Josh.

"It seems that when you factor in unresolved emotional pain, with bad attitudes, poor diets, lots of day-to-day stress, unhealthy lifestyles, over exposure to chemicals and polluted air and water, we've created a very lethal cocktail for ourselves," remarked Tom.

"We certainly have," agreed John.

"What about chemotherapy, radiation and other forms of conventional cancer treatment?" asked Matt. "Isn't there a place for them?"

"The medical profession clearly supports the use of these forms of treatment and drug companies make a lot of money from their use. But they are incredibly hard on the body and again, you have to ask yourself, if they are so good, why do so many people continue die from cancer?"

"Doesn't chemotherapy actually impair the immune system?" asked Tom.

"Yes! In the process of destroying the cancer cells, it also destroys our immune system."

"So we actually wipe out the very thing that we need to fight the cancer and keep us healthy," observed Eric.

"Basically, that's stupid," remarked Adam, looking out the window.

"What a pity," added Josh.

"Is that supposed to be a pun?" asked Ryan

"What do you mean?"

"George Harrison wrote a song called *Isn't it a Pity*."

"He did?"

"Yep!"

"Ya, that was a great song," added Mike.

"It certainly was," agreed John. "It is definitely a pity that millions of people continue to die from cancer and other diseases, when for the most part, they could be eliminated."

"Hold on! Hold on! You mean I made a joke without realizing it?" asked Josh.

"It appears you did," replied Tom.

"I'm either really good or I'm losing it then," Josh sighed, causing snickers amongst his classmates.

"No, you've still got it," praised Terry, patting him on the shoulder.

"What can we do about pollution and all the toxins in our environment?" asked Scott.

"Lobby government and boycott the companies that pollute and produce these chemicals," answered Matt. "The companies that make this shit do it for money. They don't give a rats-ass about you or your health."

"The same goes for genetically modified foods," added Ryan. "We need to stop eating this crap and boycott the companies that produce them."

"Ya," agreed Josh. "I found out not too long ago, that the corn we eat is genetically modified, so the corn plant doesn't die when it is sprayed with the pesticide that kills corn borers. Unfortunately, the pesticide also kills honeybees."

"I wonder what it's doing to us?" asked Travis.

"That's stupid," said an outraged Eric. "Why isn't the government stopping them?"

"Like Matt said," observed Ryan, "It's all about money."

"That's bullshit," said Stuart. "What about our health?"

"I guess this is why people who seem happy and who live healthy lifestyles still get cancer?" remarked Adam, turning his attention to the front of the room.

"There might also be stuff going on in their lives that you don't know about," said Travis.

"That's possible," agreed John. "And maybe it also has something to do with clearing karmic debt."

"Pardon?" said a puzzled Ryan.

Just then, the bell rang.

"We'll have to get to that another day."

"Mr. Stevens?" asked Tracy. "You mentioned something about healing our emotional pain in order to prevent cancer. How do we do that?"

"We'll have to get to that another day as well. It's an extremely important part of the process and well worth reviewing. I also want to finish our discussion about values and boundaries. In the meantime, have an awesome day everyone."

"You too, Teach."

Driving home later that day, John Steven's mind was drawn back to the discussion about cancer. He couldn't help but be marveled by the participation of all the students. This was a group of kids considered unruly, disrespectful and unreachable, and yet nothing could be further from the truth. It was they who had initiated the discussion and who had willingly participated in it… even Blair.

John was convinced that the main reason kids lose interest in school is because what they're being taught is not relevant to them, particularly for those with learning challenges. Yes, many kids have problems at home that affects their interest level, but he was convinced the main issue was the relevancy of the curriculum.

Caitlyn was still a bit of a concern. She had only made one comment during the discussion, although she also didn't do anything to disrupt the class. No acts of rebellion, thankfully. Perhaps this could be considered a good sign. Matt's participation was also encouraging. Looking in the rearview mirror, he realized he was smiling.

Then it occurred to him that he still hadn't discussed the five essentials of health and happiness. Today would have been an ideal time to introduce it. Oh well, there is always tomorrow.

The guest waited for the door to close before beginning the conversation. "As you are aware, Jonathan, Ms. Connors has accepted the position at the arts school."

"Yes, I spoke with Principal Clark yesterday."

"It seems that she had a price after all."

"Everybody has their price."

"She was no easy sell. Clearly, she is in love with our nemesis."

"Money trumps love every time."

"I like your attitude."

Jonathan Fox smiled at the compliment.

"Are you ready then to execute the rest of the plan?"

"I certainly am."

"I must reiterate that he must not succeed."

"I understand completely."

"Then I will leave you to it."

The two men stood and shook hands, satisfied that everything was in order.

CHAPTER 12:
FORGIVENESS

Stand up beside the fireplace
Take that look from off your face
Cause you ain't never gonna burn my heart out

— Oasis, *Don't Look Back in Anger*

It was raining and miserably cold on this day, impossible to escape the dampness and even more challenging to stay warm. Machai tugged on the drawstrings of his jacket in a vain effort to stop the rain from dripping down his frozen back. But it was no use. It assaulted him relentlessly, like a raging waterfall. It seemed as though Mother Nature had chosen him personally to unleash the torrent of her anger against humankind and he had no choice but to endure it.

"Get back to work you useless little man!" Tyzhe bellowed. "Do you think this rice will harvest itself?"

The exhausted, half frozen worker lifted his head as if to say something, but thought better of it. He did not wish to feel the sharp sting of his tormenter's leather whip on his wet skin. Not on this bitter day. He did not want to be humiliated once again, so he bit his tongue, just as he had every day since coming to work for this vile, insensitive man.

Tyzhe reminded Machai of his father. Demanding. Impossible to please. Quick to strike out when he was unhappy.

Machai hated his employer. He worked long hard hours for little pay and no appreciation. Not once in two years had this contemptuous tyrant complimented him for his effort. Not once had he smiled, asked him about his family or invited him into his home.

The young man seethed with anger. He wanted desperately to quit, but couldn't. There was little work in the area and he had a wife and child to support. He wouldn't dare let them down. They depended on him. He felt such overwhelming bitterness.

He was an honourable man. His father would have nothing less. He had been taught the role of a man. To provide for his family. To father a son in order to carry on the family name. He was determined to show his father that he was a capable worker. That he was an able husband and father.

His life was filled with accomplishments. High marks in school... the top of his class. Success in sports... always the best player on the team. A talented horseman... able to outride all comers. An expert marksman... he could put an arrow through the centre of an apple at 100 yards. None of which seemed to please his father. Whatever he did was never good enough.

But on this day, none of his successes mattered. It only mattered that he was here in this rice paddy, working for this wretched man, providing for his family, enduring the rain and the cruel taunts.

Startled from his thoughts, he suddenly realized that he had to urinate. His bladder was bursting. He put down his sickle and turned to face the man he so despised.

"Why are you stopping?"

"I need to relieve myself," he replied, head hung sullenly, like a shamed child standing before a domineering parent.

"You are a weak man. Why, I can work all day without relieving myself."

He looked at the man with contempt, but dare not move without permission.

"Go if you must, but you'd better not pee in my rice paddy. I don't need you to contaminate my rice."

Machai thought it a silly thing to say given that birds and animals regularly defecated in the paddies. But he would never express disagreement, for the punishment would be harsh.

He turned abruptly and hurried over to the bushes. As he was relieving himself, he noticed that he was being watched. "Hurry up now. Don't be wasting time over there."

He wanted to scream and stand up to his abuser. But he just couldn't muster up the courage to do it. He was paralyzed by fear and he couldn't risk losing this job.

He suffered through the rain and cold the rest of the day. Only when the job was done and darkness fell was he allowed to go home.

"Don't be late tomorrow," Tyzhe sneered as he trudged off down the path.

Too tired to acknowledge his tormentor, he simply put his head down and continued on.

When he stepped sullenly through the door of his hut, Gaia was there to greet him. She did so every evening. Always smiling, ready and willing to take care of her man. On this occasion, he brushed by her too exhausted to talk, too angry to be with anyone.

"Are you okay my husband?" she asked with great concern.

"Leave me be," he replied harshly.

Gaia looked at him, confused by his outburst. "Did I displease you," she inquired softly.

"You did nothing," he screamed, feeling the aggression well up inside. "Can't you see that I'm tired? Are you too blind to see that I want quiet?"

His humble wife bowed her head, shamed that she had angered him.

Suddenly, his rage came boiling to the surface. He screamed at her, raising his hand as if to strike her. But something caused him to pause. He couldn't bring himself to hit this wonderful woman who loved him so much.

Overwhelmed with shame, he bolted from the hut and ran full out until he could run no more. How symbolic was his attempt to flee…to run from his pain… the agony that assaulted his self-image like an endless barrage of cannon fire. But there was nowhere to escape these feelings.

In total despair, he collapsed to the ground and sobbed. As he lay there weeping he felt a gentle hand on his shoulder. He looked up to see Gaia. "I love you," she said softly, trying to comfort him.

Machai could see the love in her eyes, like a mother comforting her newborn baby. He wrapped his arms around her and held her tightly. He felt safe.

John was awakened by the sound of his cell phone alarm. It was dark and the birds were not yet singing. *Odd*, he thought. *I'm usually awake before the alarm. Right. I set it early to go for a walk.*

His eyes were blurry, not yet ready to be awake. As he tried to bring his vision into focus, he slowly began recounting the dream. It seemed a pretty direct reflection of his life. It provided clues to his challenges ... why so many things had gone wrong. His unconscious need to hold onto bitterness and resentment. His inability to forgive, especially himself.

As he continued to reflect on the dream, he suddenly felt a familiar presence enter the room, filling it with a blanket of loving energy. In his mind's eye, he envisioned dolphins swimming joyfully through the waters of a silent blue ocean. Blinking until his vision was clear, his attention was drawn to the corner of the room. There, hovering peacefully was the angel. He had seen her many times before, enough to know that he was safe and so he felt at ease. All the tension he had been feeling slowly dissipated from his body. He gazed into her eyes and was overwhelmed by the love she was emanating.

John Stevens was transfixed by the softness of her voice and the wisdom of her words. He lay still waiting for her to speak.

> "You are being asked at this time to bring your attention into the realm of forgiveness. For it is forgiveness that will free you from the shackles you have placed upon yourself. Those that have burdened you so heavily. It is forgiveness that will release you from anger and it is forgiveness that will open the door to happiness and the peace of mind you so greatly cherish.

"Forgiveness is liberation from suffering. It is a signal to the body…to your very soul…that healing has begun. It is an elixir, like the kiss of a dove.

"Quite often there are steps that must be taken before we are ready to let go and forgive. Guilt and shame, like resentment and bitterness, often tastes like a fine wine. They become more potent over time. They stoke the fires of our inferior self-image and imprison us in a dreadful state of misery.

"In the beginning we may find ourselves unable to absolve because we are mired in victimhood and we find it easier to blame. This is what we have been so effectively taught. How often have we been punished for our misdeeds? How often have we felt the sting of the whip or the pain and humiliation of cruel words? Seldom are we taught the art of forgiveness and compassion. Never are we taught how to let go.

"And so we hold onto the feelings that are familiar to us. Like the baby that clings to its mother's bosom, we hold tight. Though they may be toxic, we understand them. They are familiar to us. They are like a loyal companion and they nourish our need to seek revenge. They stoke the fires of negativity that are so powerful an instrument of conflict and destruction."

John listened quietly, captivated by her words. He felt their power and he began to understand their significance. He had spent so much of his life being angry, unable to let go of the resentment and bitterness that boiled below the surface of his otherwise joyful demeanour. It affected his relationships. The power of this unconscious toxic energy sometimes frightened people away, like a deer fleeing from the ravenous wolf pack. Clearly it was still a big part of his life given his outburst on the way home from the airport. He wanted to know more.

"Forgiveness begins with a desire for peace and this is the challenge. For we must overcome our pain and we must have a willingness to step out of our familiar patterns of suffering. This requires courage.

"Forgiveness also asks us to examine closely who it is we really need to set free, and that is first and foremost, ourselves. We cannot begin to absolve others until we have bathed in self-forgiveness. This is where it begins.

"Forgiveness beseeches us to let go of our victim roles… our need to blame others. It reaches out to us and begs us to take responsibility, for it is we who are the architects of our experiences. And this requires honesty.

"And so, once we understand the importance of forgiveness and have made the decision to forgive, the question becomes, how do we do so?"

John most certainly wanted to forgive and he was eager to understand how to do it. He was tired of being angry and he was tired of being tired. Such a burden this anger he carried, like an oxen dragging a plough through frozen soil. He had wrestled in the past with the idea of forgiveness, but the process had eluded him. Simply uttering the words, *I forgive*, does not necessarily bring forgiveness, at least it certainly hadn't for him. It hadn't lessened the anger.

"The path of forgiveness may guide us to tranquility, but finding the willingness to forgive can be quite challenging. It seems much easier to hold onto resentment, anger, bitterness and hatred, and so it requires us to let go of old habits and familiar patterns and step into the unknown. It commands us to trust.

"The first step is something you are already aware of, and that is to know that everything that is happening in your life is happening as it was meant to... everything! It is part of your life plan. For one reason or another, you have made decisions that have led you to this particular experience and every other experience before it. It is both your destiny and your free will. And it is essential that you understand that every experience is a message from God... a spiritual lesson. On a soul level, you have chosen a particular path in order to release old patterns and embedded emotional energy in order to achieve spiritual growth. This knowledge that you are, in a way, responsible, is integral to forgiving. It is empowering.

"The second step asks for your awareness that only spiritually *unconscious* people ... those who are unaware of truths of who they really are and why they're really on the planet ... behave inappropriately. Only those who are ignorant of their true, divine nature create negativity and suffering.

"The third step too, is a reminder of what is already known, and that is, it is people who don't feel good about themselves who mistreat others. When you feel unlovable, unworthy, inadequate and powerless, you enact these feelings on others in a misguided attempt to make them feel the same way, while falsely strengthening your sense of self-worth.

"The fourth step requires you to look deeply, most importantly at yourself, and remember that everyone is doing the best they can with what they've learned. When you grow up with abuse and fear, that becomes the template for your behaviour. When you grow up with love, you become love. And so, armed with this knowledge, you are able to look past each person's behaviour, particularly those you perceive to have wronged you, to see the emotional pain that is at the root of their behaviour and thus you let go of judgment and the need for retribution. This is empathy. This is compassion.

"With the awareness of these four steps, in reality, there is nothing to forgive, for if you know that everything is happening for a reason and if you know that it is those who are spiritually unconscious and don't feel good about themselves who mistreat others and if you know that everyone is doing the best they can with what they've learned, then you have understanding, and thus, forgiveness is natural.

"So, you have a choice, in every moment and every situation, you can choose to blame. You can hold on to resentment, anger and hatred, instruments of the ego, or you can to let go. You can choose to forgive through comprehension.

"Continue this dialogue until all is well. In the beginning, you will resist. Your ego wants to be in charge. It wants to feel pain. It relishes suffering. Stay with it. Trust. Do it over and over until it becomes the familiar… the comfortable reaction. This is liberation.

"Finally, focus on love… become love. Stand before a mirror, naked and see your true beauty… your inner beauty. See your God-like nature. Close your eyes and feel the love emanating from your heart, out to the universe. Do this often. Like the determined violinist practicing his craft you will create beautiful music in your life. This is divinity."

This was John's *aha* moment. A simple process. Understanding and liberation. *Fantastic*, he smiled knowingly to himself.

"In time, it is possible that your society will learn to circumvent those experiences that require forgiveness. When you learn to let go of that which leads to victimhood, blame and emotional suffering… projections, expectations, attachment and judgment… and when you truly understand the truths of human existence, when you feel these truths to the depths of your soul, and all human beings feel good about themselves, you will set yourself free and the need for forgiveness will no longer exist.

"As you step into this new way of being, we ask for your patience. The universe understands your intent… your desire for change… but not all beings share this desire. And so, you will be tested, like the baby bird who dares to look out over the edge of the nest to face the world below. You will be faced with challenges, and your reaction, your willingness to forgive and eventually your unconditional acceptance of all experiences devoid of any negative response will be the measure of your growth. Remember, forgiveness is freedom. Forgiveness is love. Flap your wings and let love be your guide. And that is all."

Slowly, the angel dissipated until she was gone. John lay in stillness. The angel visits were very comforting to him, like a gentle nurturing hug from a caring mother. As much as they brought him guidance, they also brought reassurance that despite his travails, all was well.
    She had shown him how to forgive … in fact, how to bypass forgiveness through understanding. He understood it and a confident smile slowly crept over his face.
    The birds had begun chirping and the first signs of light were beginning to creep through the window. Time to go for that walk.

The voice at the other end of the line was eager to hear the news. "So, you're making good progress on this issue?"
    "We certainly are," replied the middleman. "The obstacle has been removed."
    "That's terrific! The people I represent will be elated."
    "You can assure them that all is well."
    "You are ready then to proceed?"

"We are."

"Excellent! There is a great deal at stake here and we can have no mistakes."

"I understand."

"Keep me apprised."

"I will," he assured the middleman, hanging up the phone.

CHAPTER 13:
PEOPLE PLEASING

But it's all right now
I learned my lesson well
You see you can't please everyone
So you got to please yourself

— Rick Nelson, *Garden Party*

John was erasing the blackboard at the end of the day, still feeling quite jubilant after his angel visit. It had been a pleasant day and he was feeling the vibe, like a violinist mastering a complex concerto. Just then, Mike walked in. "Forget something?" the teacher inquired amiably.

"No," he hesitated. "I, um, there is something I want to talk to you about."

"Certainly," John replied, putting the eraser down. "Let's have a seat."

"I have a hard time talking to people, Teach."

"In what way, Mike?"

"I have a hard time telling people off."

"You mean, you have a hard time speaking your mind?"

"Ya, that's it! You told us that it's important for us to speak up for ourselves, but I can't do it."

"What makes it difficult for you?"

"I don't know."

"What are you afraid would happen if you spoke up for yourself?"

"People would get angry at me and I might get beat up."

"What makes you think that?"

"I don't know. It's just the way I feel."

Given John's experience, he had a pretty idea what was at the root of Mike's reluctance to express himself. "Did you ever stand up to your mom and dad?"

"Are you kidding, I'd get the shit beat out of me. Oops, sorry, didn't mean to swear."

"No worries. I understand what you're saying."

"Do you think that might have something to do with it?"

"It has everything to do with it. How can you possibly feel confident in speaking up for yourself when your experience has been to be punished when you do?"

"Ya, I guess you're right. So what can I do?"

"What's your relationship like with your parents now? Do you talk to them about how you feel about things, especially how you feel about them?"

"Nope. No way I'd do that. We don't talk about stuff."

"It's really important for us to learn to speak to the people who have done things that have hurt us. Many people talk to others about it, but that's sort of like gossiping and it doesn't really help you feel better."

"Like backstabbing, right?"

"Yes! It takes a lot of courage to speak directly to the person who has hurt us, but it's the best way to overcome our fear and let go of whatever emotional pain we might need to resolve."

"Ya, I guess you're right."

"There are a couple of things you can do that would be helpful. First, it would be a good idea for you to talk to your parents and tell them how you feel about the way they punished you, particularly those times when you were simply speaking up for yourself."

"But I don't want to make my parents feel bad."

"I understand that, but the main thing that prevents us from speaking up for ourselves is our fear of how the other person is going to react. Are they going to be angry or sad or embarrassed? The truth is we have no control over how someone else is going to feel."

"But what if they feel guilty?"

"It's the same thing. It's not about making them feel guilty... although it's quite possible they will... it's about you expressing yourself so that you can overcome the fear of doing so. Keep that as your intention and however they react is up to them."

"Okay, I can do that."

"The second thing you can do is to express yourself whenever you have the chance. Start by doing it in small ways and start with positive stuff. Express gratitude. Tell people when you think they've done a good job. Thank your friends for being good friends. Tell them how you feel about them. Start with people you feel comfortable with and then do it with people who will put you a little outside your comfort zone. That will make it easier to start expressing yourself when you feel hurt or troubled or angry.

"When somebody expresses an opinion that you disagree with, express your opinion. You don't have to tell them they're wrong. Just say you see it differently."

"I wish I was more like my sister. She can stand up to my parents. She's not afraid of them like I am."

"We all have different personalities, different paths to travel and different lessons to learn."

"She doesn't seem to care if anyone gets angry with her, especially my old man."

"Sounds like she's not a people pleaser."

"She sure isn't. She'll yell at anybody."

"Perhaps your parents weren't quite so harsh on her."

"That's true, they weren't. They never spanked her, because she was a girl. My dad seemed to spoil her. Me, I got punished all the time."

"Sometimes parents see things in their children that reflect the things they don't like about themselves and so they unwittingly take it out on that child. And the next thing you know, the child is doing everything he or she can to please their mom and dad, including not speaking up for themselves, because they don't want to feel the sting of their parent's harsh words or the pain of their rejection. And this becomes a pattern in the child's behaviour."

"I get that you know. I had a girlfriend last year and I did everything she wanted me to, cause I didn't want her to get upset. But the more I did for her, the more she wanted. Then she got mad and broke up with me."

"People who want to be pleased have a never ending list of needs."

"That's for sure."

"What's worse though, is that people pleasers get taken advantage of and they do things they don't want to do, like compromise their values, and they end up hating themselves."

"I sure was angry with myself. I did everything for her. I'm such an idiot."

"Mike, I'm sorry, but I don't tolerate self-criticisms. They are extremely damaging to our self-image."

"Ya, I guess that was a stupid... I mean, not a good thing to say."

"Not really. You were just expressing how you felt. But there is a different way of looking at this that will help you feel better about the whole experience and more importantly, better about yourself."

"Oh ya, what's that?"

"What if, like we talked about recently in class, you knew that prior to being born, your soul planned out your life journey and the lessons you were going to learn?"

"You mean my lesson might be to learn to speak up for myself?"

"That could certainly be part of it. I think there might be a bigger lesson to learn though."

The eager student sat looking at his teacher with a puzzled expression.

"There is a purpose for everything that happens in our lives. There has to be, otherwise, what's the point of our being here on the planet. And the main purpose of our existence is to learn the truth of who we really are. It is to awaken spiritually. We just have different experiences that bring us to this awakening."

Mike was still looking very puzzled.

"What do children want most from their parents?"

"Love, I guess."

"You're right. And if it isn't forthcoming, a child will do everything it can to receive that love."

"They do everything they can to please their parents," Mike echoed with a smile.

"Yes, they do. And when they don't receive the love they crave, they grow up feeling empty, and so they try to find love in their relationships."

"From their boyfriends and girlfriends."

"Yes! And as they get older, from their husbands and wives. And usually they choose partners who are like their parents, and so the cycle of trying to please repeats itself."

"Until they get the lesson!" The teen's eyes lit up, indicating that he understood what Teach was saying.

"Yes! And the ultimate truth we are here to learn is that *we are love*. We are aspects of God. We are God. God is love and that makes us love. And because we are love, we don't have to please anyone to receive their love. It's not our job to please others. It's only our job to be kind and compassionate and do our best. We're not here to mistreat others, but we're not here to compromise ourselves in order to please them so that we can receive their love."

"But isn't it okay to do things for other people."

"Absolutely! It's okay to be helpful, supportive, loving and caring, but not so others will love us, just because it's the right thing to do. And when we know this truth about love, we also know that it's okay for us to stand up for ourselves. It's okay to express our opinions and feelings without fear of reprisal or loss of love. Because the reality is, we can't really hurt anybody."

"Wow, that's heavy stuff, but I get it."

"That's awesome! Speaking up for yourself and learning that you don't have to please people is very empowering."

"Ya, I can see that."

"There's one other thing that will help you feel differently about this experience, especially about your parents and your ex-girlfriend."

"What's that?"

"Looking at every experience as a gift."

"Like from God."

"That's a good way to look at it. If we're here to learn lessons and grow spiritually, we need other souls… people… to help us on our journey.

So we pick parents and boyfriends and girlfriends who will behave in certain ways."

"So that we get hurt, because if we didn't get hurt we'd never learn the lesson, right."

"That's it!"

"In other words, my parents and my ex helped me learn that I don't have to please people to be loved."

"And to help you understand the truth of who you are."

"Cool," Mike smiled. Then suddenly his smile turned to a puzzled expression. "Tom has always treated me really well. He's always been nice to me. I wonder what his role is in my life."

"Perhaps it's just to remind you that you're a good person."

His smile got bigger. "I like that."

"Terrific," John grinned in return, holding up his hand for a high-five.

"Thank you, Teach," Mike beamed, slapping his hand.

"My pleasure. Glad I could help."

He hopped out of his seat and strode purposely towards the door. Before leaving, he turned to address his teacher. "I'm going home to talk to my parents," he stated confidently.

"That's awesome!" John felt enormous pride as he watched the likeable young man exit the classroom. *I love my life*, he thought.

Later, on the drive home, his mind wandered back to his conversation with Mike and about the faulty relationships parents quite often have with their children that cause suffering… relationships that are abusive, highly critical, demanding, meddling, controlling, alcoholic, drug addicted and abandoning. He thought about how destructive these relationships are and how this could be rectified with a fresh understanding. If we only knew that we choose our parents and our relationships with them are meant to serve a purpose. They are a necessary part of our spiritual growth.

Looking at himself in the rearview mirror, he said, "Now try to remember that!"

Two men dressed in dark clothing moved quickly. The night cleaning staff had just left and they only had two hours before the day staff would arrive. They easily picked the lock on the side entrance door and as there was no alarm system, were able to enter the building and walk unconcerned down the hallway. So as not to alert passersby with flashlights, they wore night-vision goggles.

The job was simple. Place two hidden cameras in classroom 21. They didn't know the name of the teacher. Heck, they didn't know the name of the client or the reason for the job. They didn't need to know. The less information, the better ... less trouble to deal with if things went south.

Moving swiftly they located the designated room and after a brief scan, determined the ideal spots to place the cameras; one in the front left corner, so as to be able see people entering and exiting, and one at the rear, directly in the center.

The miniature cameras were highly sophisticated, custom built for the job. Whatever their intent, the first intruder thought, they'll do the trick.

Within minutes, the cameras were installed, tested and the pair were safely out of the building. As they drove down the street, the first man's cell phone rang. He checked the call display before answering. He nodded his head several times before hitting the *end* button and placing the phone in the center console. "The client is happy," he said, looking straight ahead.

"Excellent," the second man stated, without expression.

The two men drove silently out of town.

CHAPTER 14:
SELF-IMAGE

He'd soar like an eagle on the hill
Where he went when he ran from the raging storm
He couldn't think at school he couldn't take the pain
He cried out for love but no one came

— Payolas, *Where is This Love*

It was early morning and the sun was shining brightly, having just risen in the eastern sky. The dew was still quite heavy in the grass and it glistened under the sun's intense glare. Manuel turned and waved to Maria. Standing at the front door, her beautiful smile lit up the day. Waving back, she shouted her familiar words of encouragement, "Good luck my love. You will do well."

Although Maria was smiling, secretly she was apprehensive that Manuel was going to be mistreated again. It seemed he was always allowing himself to compromise what he valued; mostly integrity and respect. He was constantly doing things he didn't want to and being taken advantage of because he was afraid to take a stand. When he gave his word, he kept it, but he rarely received the same courtesy from others. Consequently, he was frequently unhappy. She hoped things would be better this time.

Manuel, his confidence brimming, continued joyfully down the laneway on his way to his new dream job. He had worked hard all his life in menial, unfulfilling positions, certain that someday good fortune would come his way. And surely it had. A few months earlier, friends had told him of a vacant teaching position in a nearby village. It was perfect for him and after several interviews he secured the job. And so today he was heading off for his first day of work.

At the end of the laneway, he turned left and headed west toward his village. There, he would catch the carriage to Pamplona and his new place of employment.

The school was an impressive eight-room structure with capacity for over one hundred students. It was by far, the largest in the area. Although he knew nothing of the school beyond its outward appearance, he had been told by acquaintances that similar institutions in other villages were well run and offered excellent wages and rewarding teaching experiences.

Manuel considered it a great honour to teach at this school, although he would surely miss Maria. Because it was quite a distance away, he would stay in Pamplona during the week and return home each weekend. It meant spending a great deal of time away from his beautiful wife, but she had agreed enthusiastically when he told her of the arrangement.

Upon arriving at the school, the eager new teacher was met by the headmaster's assistant. He explained that the headmaster was engaged in other matters and would not be available until much later. He coldly directed Manuel to his classroom without providing any instruction. Upon inquiring about a curriculum, the assistant curtly said that one was not available, but it was expected that he would know what to do. Manuel Fuentes was perplexed, but eager to get started, so he thanked the assistant and headed off to his classroom brimming with anticipation.

Upon entering the room, his enthusiasm was quickly dashed. He was met by a group of unruly and uncooperative children who seemed to have no interest in learning. They were very disrespectful, evening refusing to give their names. They were also quite needy, as it seemed Manuel was tending to one tantrum after another. Although his first day was not quite as he had hoped, he made the best of it and resolved that things would get better.

The school had arranged a place for him to stay at a local rooming house and he was excited to see his temporary accommodations. He was, according to the school headmaster, to have an upstairs room overlooking the river. But upon arriving he was quite disappointed to learn that his room was in the cellar. Despite assurances from the school to the contrary, he was told by the proprietor that there was no space on the second floor.

He trudged awkwardly down the stairs requiring considerable effort to squeeze his bags down the narrow stairwell. His room was damp and smelly. After depositing his bags on the tiny dresser in the corner, Manuel sat dejectedly on the edge of the bed. He considered speaking to the headmaster in the morning, but then thought better of it. He was certain the headmaster's assistant would not offer any support. After considering his situation, he resolved to make the best of it.

Each day went the same as the day before and by the end of the week, the new teacher was feeling frustrated and weary. Before leaving the school to return home, he visited the headmaster's office to pick up his weekly wages. "You will have to wait until next week!" the assistant informed him. "I have not yet received your pay from the headmaster."

"But that was not our agreement," Manuel stated.

"Yes, but there is nothing I can do about it. You will have to wait."

He left the headmaster's office feeling quite dejected. He had been looking forward to receiving his pay so he could buy a gift for Maria on the trip home. What would he say to her? It was a long gloomy ride back to his village, but he resolved that next week would be better.

When questioned by his adoring wife about his first week at the school, "It went well," was all he said. Puzzled by his response, she asked no more questions.

Later, when asked by his children about his new school, Manuel struck his eldest son, Rafael, on the cheek and scolded him never to ask such a question again. When his son asked why he had hit him, the angry papa screamed, "That was nothing compared to what my father would do to me if I had been so foolish." The son hung his head, humiliated and heartbroken having so disappointed his father.

Hopping up the front steps of the school, Manuel was looking forward to the new week. Surely he would be remunerated accordingly, but more importantly, he was to begin coaching kickball, for which he would receive an additional fee.

Kickball was popular among the children and matches between schools were heralded as major social events in the villages. He was excited about the prospect of directing the school's team and the privileged stature that would be bestowed upon him.

As he reached the top step, he slipped and his foot gave way. He crashed down hard in excruciating pain. Laying helpless, his ankle throbbed intensely. After several minutes, he was able to make it to his feet. Without putting any pressure on the injured foot, he hobbled awkwardly to the front door and made his way slowly down to the headmaster's office.

"You are being paid to teach and so you will teach," the assistant scolded after Manuel had explained his misfortune. "It is your clumsiness that is at fault and the children will not suffer as a result."

"But ..."

"I will not hear of it. Now be off to your classroom."

Dejected, he hung his head and limped away. He spent the day in great pain, having again to deal with very unruly and undisciplined children.

Despite his difficulties in the classroom, he was buoyed by the thoughts of coaching kickball, and so, at the end of the school day, with considerable difficulty, he made his way back to the headmaster's office to inquire about getting started.

"You will not be required to lead the students in kickball this week," the assistant informed him. "You must be able to run with the team and clearly that is not possible. We will see next week if your health has improved."

"But it is part of the agreement."

"You are clearly not able to fulfill your end of the arrangement," he countered. "If you continue to complain we can discontinue the position permanently."

"Are you able to pay me today?"

"I have not yet received your wages from the headmaster and under the circumstances, I am surprised you would ask."

Manuel realized there was no point in continuing the discussion. Sadly, he turned and limped out of the school.

Later, he slumped despondently on to his bed looking sullenly into the corner of the room. He noticed something on the floor and upon closer examination realized that it was rat droppings. With great difficulty, he made his way back up the stairs to the clerk's office to inform him of his discovery, hoping to be moved to a new room. Instead, the clerk reached under the counter and presented him with a large rat trap. Too stunned to say anything, he simply took the trap and hobbled miserably back down to his room. At the end of each day, Manuel returned to the headmaster's office to inquire about his wages and each day he was met with the same harsh response. When he left at the end of the week to return home, he was utterly crestfallen, and when Maria inquired about his week, "Not very good," was his only response.

Alone with his children, he yelled at them constantly. He spanked his eldest son several times, sending them all to their rooms at the slightest provocation. Later in the evening, he was wracked with guilt as he had promised himself that he would never do to his children what had been done to him.

When he returned to the school the following week, he was informed that he would not be coaching kickball. The substitute coach had performed magnificently and had been taken on as a fulltime replacement. What was worse, Manuel only received half of his first week's salary. Clearly, this job was not turning out as he had anticipated.

This pattern went on week after week. Each Monday morning he would go to the headmaster's office to inquire about his pay only to be told that he would receive it at the end of the week. At the end of the week he would receive only a portion of his pay with a promise that the balance would be dispensed the following week. Each week he got further and further behind. Each week he promised himself that this would be the last. But on and on it went.

Several weeks later, when asked by Maria about his week at the school, "I will not be returning," was his only response.

John Stevens slowly opened his eyes, awaking from his dream. Drenched in sweat from the intensity of it, he sat up and swung his legs over the side of the bed. The floor felt cold under foot and he reflexively clenched his toes.

The dream, he realized was bringing him a number of messages. First, it was a reminder of the importance of feeling good about oneself. Clearly, his dream experience was about feeling unworthy and the consequences of this faulty belief.

He could see how it played a role in each of Manuel's disappointing experiences. First, he was given this magnificent opportunity to teach at what he believed to be a prestigious school. But his self-belief that he was unworthy manifested when he was hired by a school that didn't treat him well.

Then he was promised a second floor room overlooking the river, but instead he found himself in a damp, smelly, rat infested room in the cellar.

Next, he was looking forward to coaching kickball, but then he injured his ankle and was unable to coach. Worse still, he was replaced by a substitute.

In each of these situations, Manuel felt powerless to do anything about it. He simply accepted what was and eventually quit rather than standing up for himself.

The dream reminded John of the importance of understanding how our faulty beliefs and negative self-image… for example, that we are unworthy and powerless… undermines our goals and sabotages our happiness. More importantly, it was meant to serve as a reminder that when our best intentions are not being realized, we need to identify the faulty beliefs that are at the root of this discord.

Clearly the dream was also about values and boundaries. Manuel valued integrity and respect, but he allowed others to treat him with dishonesty and contempt, another indicator of an inferior self-image. He didn't hold others to the same standards for which he held himself and as a result was constantly being mistreated.

It was also apparent that the dream was meant to bring his attention to our need to resolve the emotional turmoil from our experiences with our parents and our children. He could see how these woundings were tearing at him from both sides… the grief, disappointment and resentment he felt from growing up feeling unwanted and unimportant, and the guilt, shame and self-loathing he felt from the harsh discipline he sometimes meted out on his own children. It was evident how these woundings shape our feelings of self-worth. He could see clearly how his children's neediness mirrored his own and how he unleashed the anger he felt towards his parents, for not meeting his needs, on his own children. It was like he was saying, 'how dare you want something from me, when my own needs went unmet.'

The last message contained in the dream, he suspected, had to do with clearing karmic debt. He had learned about it several years earlier and it seemed that the poor treatment Manuel received was meant to serve as a reminder to examine the role of this important aspect of healing whenever we are in the midst of an unpleasant experience.

Before John could begin, Scott raised his hand. "Yes Scott?"

"What do you do when somebody goes back on a promise?" he inquired.

"What do you mean?" Teach asked respectfully, as the other students looked on intently.

"A couple of months ago my boss promised me a new job and a pay raise, but when I asked him about it the other day, he said he couldn't give it to me yet."

"Did he say why?"

"He just mumbled something about not talking to his bookkeeper, then walked away."

"Did you say anything to him?"

"Naw! I figured, what's the use. He's just gonna blow me off like he always does."

"He's done this before?"

"Yep, I've asked him a couple of times about the new job."

"Scott works his ass off and the guy treats him like shit," offered Josh in support.

John thought about his dream and realized Scott's situation was eerily similar. He quickly concluded that it was a message from his guides telling him that he needed to finish the discussion on values and boundaries.

"The guy yells at him all the time too," offered Eric.

"Is this true?"

"Ya, he's a prick."

"Why do you continue working for him?"

"Cause I need the money."

"Aren't there other jobs?"

"I've been looking, but I haven't found one yet."

"Did he ever tell you why he offered you a new job and a pay raise?"

"Cause Scott's a good worker and the guy doesn't want to lose him," said Terry, joining in the conversation. "He's just jerking him around."

It seemed that everyone was aware of their classmate's predicament.

"That's not fair," objected Jessica. "If he promised you something, then he has to give it to you. I would just quit."

"I would quit," Scott explained, "but my old man says you don't quit a job unless you've got another one lined up."

"That might be okay if you're being treated fairly, but when you're being mistreated or deceived, that's a different story," John observed.

"What should I do?"

"We need to look at this in terms of values and boundaries. Let's say we value integrity and respect and we have established boundaries that are in alignment with these values. We have promised ourselves that we will never allow ourselves to be mistreated or lied to without taking action. When we encounter someone who lies to us or treats us disrespectfully, what do we do?"

"It depends on who they are and what they've done," replied Matt. "Sometimes it's best just to ignore people."

"Yes, that can work in certain situations."

"You could tell them what they've said or done is not acceptable," replied Tom.

"And what if they continue doing it?"

"Tell them in no uncertain terms that if they do it again, this is what I'm going to do," said Ryan.

"Like what, punch them in the face?" asked Stuart.

"Perhaps your reaction need not be quite that extreme," Tom countered.

"If it was a friend, you could tell them that you will no longer be their friend," suggested Eric.

"And I guess if it's your boss, you could tell them that you're going to quit," Scott added.

"That is a great idea, buddy," added Josh. "Take this job and shove it, man!"

"Yep. And don't tell him to shove the job," added Adam. "That's disrespectful."

"I was just kidding," Josh said, knowing that Adam took things literally.

"When you stay in a situation that is contrary to your values, especially when you're being mistreated, you are in effect saying to yourself and telling the universe, I'm not worthy, which affects how you feel about yourself."

"That can't be good," remarked Jordan.

"It certainly isn't. What is more, when you want to quit something, but say I can't for this reason or that, you are rendering yourself powerless. You're saying something beyond your control is in charge."

"Why don't people know about values? It's something parents should teach their kids or it's something we need to learn in school," suggested Travis.

"That would be ideal," agreed Tom.

"As a society, we don't seem to recognize the significance of values and boundaries. Hence we don't teach it. Some people intuitively know what they value and establish boundaries accordingly. The better you feel about yourself the more likely you are to know your values, establish your boundaries and not allow them to be crossed.

"Recently, I asked you to make a list of your own values and then narrow that list down to your top three. How did everyone make out?"

"I had trouble figuring out my three core values," admitted Josh.

"So did I," added Jordan. "It wasn't as easy as I thought it would be."

"Would anyone care to share your list with the rest of the class?"

"I will," offered Jessica. "I value happiness, peace and good manners."

Her list caused a few snickers from some of the guys. "Speaking of good manners," admonished Tracy, glaring at the culprits.

"I don't care what they think," Jessica growled. "They're just immature."

"Remember!" said John, "All judgment comes from self judgment and when you laugh at others for what you perceive to be their shortcomings, you are reflecting this judgment of yourself and you are also reflecting a less than positive self-image."

"Sorry," Eric offered. "I wasn't really laughing at you, it just sounded kind of funny."

"Thank you," she replied. "I know sometimes I say things you guys think are funny, but it hurts my feelings."

"I'm sorry too," added Stuart.

"What do you want us to do with our list?" Tracy asked, thankfully changing the subject.

"Let them be your guideposts. When you find yourself in a situation that makes you feel uncomfortable or unhappy, relate it back to what you value. That will help you decide what action to take."

"Like if someone is getting me into trouble?" asked Stuart, glancing at Blair.

"Yes, that would certainly be one way to apply it."

"Actually, I already applied it!" said Eric.

"Would you like to tell us about it?"

"Sure. My older brother always borrows my stuff and most of the time he doesn't return it. So I have to go and get it and it pisses me off."

"That's rude," said Jessica, visibly perturbed. "Why don't you tell him he can't borrow your stuff? That's what I'd do."

"He doesn't do it on purpose. He just forgets. But it still makes me angry, so I told him the next time he borrows something and doesn't return it, I'm not going to let him borrow anything, anymore."

"What did he say?"

"He already borrowed something and forgot to give it back, so I told him no more."

"What did your brother say?" Jessica asked.

"He actually apologized and said no worries. He wouldn't ask."

"That's great. And how do you feel about it."

"I feel really good. Empowered!"

Just then the bell rang. "I hope you found this discussion helpful!" Teach offered.

"At the risk of sounding like I'm sucking up to you," replied Tom. "I thought it was very good."

"So did I," echoed Terry.

"Have a fantastic day everyone!"

A very powerful man busied himself in his office at the end of the day, while waiting patiently for the phone to ring. He had demanded daily updates until the situation was resolved. There was too much at stake too much money at risk too many powerful people involved and he felt it necessary to be well informed.

He looked at his watch. Seven-fifteen.

A few moments later, the phone rang. He waited a few seconds not wanting to appear too anxious. Picking it up, he hit the green button and held it up to his ear. "Yes. I see. Nothing today. Okay. Well, stay on it. I want to know the moment you have something. Goodbye."

Placing the phone on the desk, he was satisfied with the update. He knew this might take time, although he would convey urgency. A sense of urgency, in his experience, tended to encourage faster results.

CHAPTER 15:
LOSS OF HOPE

At home
Drawing pictures
Of mountain tops
With him on top

— Pearl Jam, *Jeremy*

John surveyed the class and noticed on empty seat. "Does anybody know where Terry is?" he inquired before getting started with the day's lesson.

"He's not here," Jordan replied curtly, without giving an explanation.

"Fine. Thank you, Jordan," he said courteously, puzzled at the normally cordial student's abrupt response.

"Okay, then, let's get started. Please open your books to page thirty-eight."

The students took their time opening their books and John Stevens sensed that something was amiss. "Is everyone okay this morning?" he asked.

After an excruciating period of silence, Jessica spoke up. "Terry's brother committed suicide last night and we're all pretty upset about it. It's really a terrible thing."

"I'm sorry to hear that. Would someone tell me what happened?"

"He started using cocaine and he got into some trouble with some bad dudes," said Mike.

"What do you mean trouble?"

"He owed them money... a lot of money."

"It's pretty sad," Jessica offered. "Terry was very happy that his brother was doing good. He was off coke and he had been looking for a job."

"How's everybody feeling about this?" a concerned teacher inquired.

"Well," Jessica replied, taking on the unusual role as spokesperson for the class, "like I said, we're pretty bummed out about it. It makes me so sad and I want to cry."

"Really pissed is more like it," Jordan interjected. "The guys that got Anthony back into this shit need their heads kicked in."

"Do you think that would really solve things?" John asked carefully.

"You're fuckin' right it would. Those guys took advantage of him. They exploited him. They need to pay for it."

It was evident that Jordan was seething with anger and needed to be handled gently. "I understand your anger. Would you be okay to tell me more about what happened?"

"Anthony was a small kid and he got bullied a lot in school. He was a couple of years older than Terry. In order to stop him from being bullied, their mom sent him to live with his grandparents."

"What about their father?"

"Ya, right," scoffed Jordan. "He's a bigger scumbag than the guys who got Anthony into drugs. Terry hasn't seen him for years. When he was around, he used to beat them."

"That's very unfortunate. It sounds like they've had some significant challenges in their lives."

"I don't understand how parents can be so mean to their children," observed Jessica. "It's so sad."

"It's because they don't feel good about themselves."

"Well, it's not right," added Travis.

"It sounds like you're all feeling Terry's loss."

"Yes, we are," agreed Josh. "We like him."

"That means you are showing empathy, which is important."

"It doesn't make me feel any better," said Mike.

"Unfortunately, life isn't always about feeling good. Remember, life is in part about polarities. We are going to have unpleasant experiences, just as much as we're going to have joyful ones. The challenge is not to judge them or fall victim to them."

"Why not?" asked Eric.

"All experiences are part of the flow of life. We have to be able to feel everything, pleasant and unpleasant. When you can experience the *bad* experiences without judgment, they're no longer *bad* experiences. When you can allow yourself to feel emotional pain, such as grief, without judgment and without projecting it… without attaching to it and falling into victimhood… then you can truly experience happiness and joy."

"You've got to be serious," snarled Caitlyn. "Terry's brother commits suicide and you're trying to put a hairy-fairy spiritual experience spin on it. Get real!"

"I really believe that understanding the truth of our experience is the only way to bring change. Otherwise, we just keep repeating our suffering."

"But haven't you been telling us that we're here to create heaven on earth… that we're here to live in peace, love and joy?" asked Stuart.

"Ya, I don't get it," said Jessica. "I thought you wanted us all to be happy."

It was evident that the *spiritual* concepts he had been discussing with the students were lost on them at the moment, clouded in their grief and anger over what had happened to Anthony. "Perhaps we can put a different perspective on this."

"What do you mean?"

"Remember some of the things we've been talking about over the past few weeks. First, that our souls map out a plan for us before we incarnate, and as such, each of us comes into life with a purpose."

"Yes, we all understand that… at least intellectually," said Tom.

"And second, that there are no victims or perpetrators, only co-creators of experiences. On a soul level, we're all in this to help one another on our spiritual journeys."

"We get that too," agreed Ryan.

"Third, that we're all connected… we live on oneness… and therefore our thoughts, feelings and experiences affect everyone around us… some directly, some indirectly."

"We understand that too," said Tracy.

"So if Anthony had a life plan and if we think of him as a co-creator rather than a victim, and if his experience was intended to affect all the people around him, why do you think he would take his own life?"

"Basically, it's cause there is a lesson we need to learn?" Adam replied with uncharacteristic confidence.

"And what do you think the lesson might be?"

"Perhaps this is a test for us," replied Jordan. "Perhaps this is meant to test our spiritual beliefs… to see if we really understand what you have been teaching us."

"That's definitely part of it. Those who live in conscious awareness of the truths of our existence will constantly be tested."

"I think we're all feeling like victims right now," added Tom, "and we're looking at Anthony and Terry as victims, so perhaps this is an opportunity for us to see if we can change our perspective."

"Yes, when you step out of victimhood and stop blaming, you are taking responsibility for your experiences, and this is amazingly empowering. It shows that you are in charge and that you know it."

"But why suicide? Why would somebody want to take their own life and why is suicide part of the human experience?" asked Tracy.

"Do you think someone who feels good about themselves and who is living in conscious awareness would take their own life?"

"It seems unlikely," replied Tom.

"What causes someone to *commit* suicide?"

"When they're depressed," said Stuart.

"And why do people get depressed?"

"Because they lose hope," replied Josh.

"When they're in despair," added Ryan.

"Yes! And aren't these real human emotions just like joy and bliss?"

"Yes, they are!" agreed Jordan. "So I guess the point is, how can we experience bliss if we don't understand what bliss is, and in order to fully understand it, we need to understand the opposite?"

"Precisely! And does each of us need to experience despair in order to understand it, or is it possible for us to gain this perspective through someone else's experience."

"Wow!" exclaimed Josh. "Now I get it."

"So, are you saying that Anthony *chose* this experience *on a soul level* in order to help everyone connected to him achieve some level of understanding of bliss?" inquired Tom.

"Yes, by understanding the despair he was experiencing each of us has the opportunity to gain a better understanding of bliss."

"Think about this," mused Ryan, "if everyone on the planet lived in conscious awareness there would be no more suicide."

"Yes, because we wouldn't need to experience despair in order to understand bliss," added Jessica proudly.

"You got it girl," said Mike, as he high-fived her.

"I think there might be another lesson in this," noted John.

"What's that?" asked Scott.

"What have we learned about who we really are?"

"We're *spiritual* beings having a *human* experience," replied Tracy.

"Yep, we are God… and God is us," added Adam, "because God is all that exists."

"And we live many lives," said Ryan.

"And we each have our own journeys," added Scott.

"We are all part of the flow of life," remarked Eric.

"We aren't just having an experience," observed Tom. "We are experience itself."

"If we are truly spiritual beings that exist in perpetuity, do we ever really die?"

"I guess not," replied Tom after a few moments of consideration. "We just change form."

"Yes," agreed Ryan. "Part of the time we're in human form and part of the time we're in spirit."

"And when do we experience grief?"

"When someone dies," replied Mike.

"When we experience loss," added Matt, finally joining the conversation.

"You're mother died when you were really young, didn't she?" asked Jessica.

"Shut up, stupid," snarled Blair.

Matt turned and glared at Jessica's antagonist. "Sorry," Blair said sheepishly, hanging his head towards the floor.

"Yes, I did lose my mom and I was never allowed to grieve her. I was seven years old when she died. When my father told me, I cried, so he slapped me across the face and told me to be a man. He told me mom would be ashamed of me if she saw me crying. But it was my dad who was embarrassed. I never got over that incident and I guess it was why I grew up with so much anger."

For a moment, the class sat in a stunned silence, surprised at their classmate's difficult confession.

"There are a couple of elements to this experience of loss that we need to examine," John continued, diverting attention from the big teen. "First and foremost is our misunderstanding of death and our belief that death is final, when the reality is, as Tom and Ryan pointed out, that we are just changing form. The true essence of us… our soul… never dies."

"Even knowing this, the idea of someone close to you *dying* is very heartbreaking," noted Ryan.

"Yes, it certainly is. And it's important to understand that it's okay to grieve. It's okay to mourn the loss of a family member, friend, pet or anything that is important to us."

"You mean like a toy?" asked Mike.

"Absolutely! Anything that is meaningful."

"Like a job," noted Scott.

"Definitely. We need to honour our feelings of loss because they're very real. But at the same time, if we understand the truth about *death* and that we never really *lose* anything, we don't fall into victimhood. We can grieve without falling into depression or despair. And this is critical."

"That makes a lot of sense," agreed Travis.

"Another thing that helps us deal more effectively with loss and grief has to do with understanding the truth of ownership. We all believe that we own everything we are in possession of, be it our children, our house, our car, our money… our whatever. But the reality is, we *own* nothing."

"I don't understand that," said Jordan, looking very puzzled. "If I buy something with money, don't I *own* it?"

"Yes, and if I have a child, isn't the child mine?" asked Tracy.

"No," said Tom, looking very excited. "Think about it. We don't come into this world with anything and when we leave we take nothing with us. So technically speaking, anything we *own* is just temporary."

"So, if we're not owners of the things we're in possession of, what does that make us?" asked Eric, looking confused.

"Sort of like, renters," suggested Scott.

"How about, stewards?" proposed Tom.

"I like that," said Josh. "That would eliminate a lot of worry."

"Yes, think about it," said John. "If each of us has our own life journey, and if, as souls, we choose our parents, do they really *own* us?"

"I guess not," replied Tracy.

"And if we don't *own* the money in our possession, it seems to take a lot of pressure off," noted Josh.

"Ya, that's true," agreed Stuart. "When I think about being a steward of money I don't feel so much fear about losing it."

"I guess a different perspective could eliminate all the fear we experience around death too, couldn't it," said Tom.

"Certainly," Teach agreed. "The fear of death, particularly as we get older, is very debilitating."

"Isn't it stupid," said Jessica. "We have so much fear about dying, even though we're going to die anyway."

"Speaking of…" Blair stopped short as Matt and several other students glared at him. He quickly turned his head and looked out the window.

"If we understand that we don't really own anything then we have nothing to lose, and if we don't have anything to lose, then we really have nothing to fear."

"It might take awhile before I can make that understanding part of my life," observed Ryan.

"That's okay, these things take time."

"I'm sorry for what I said about your mom," Jessica apologized, looking at Matt.

"It's okay. I know you didn't mean anything by it. I loved my mom," he said with a rare smile. "She was very understanding and she was a lot of fun…"

Matt suddenly stopped in mid-sentence. He sat silently for a moment, then without warning, pounded his desk with a mighty fist and screamed, "WHY? WHY DID SHE DO IT?"

His outburst startled everyone, causing several students to jump in their seats.

John waited a few moments for everyone to regain their composure. "What is it Matt?" he asked softly.

With the rest of the class looking on in stunned silence, he sat quietly for a few minutes before speaking. "My mom committed suicide," he whispered.

"My God, I'm so sorry," Jessica blurted. "I didn't mean to…"

"It's okay. You didn't know," Matt trembled. "Nobody ever told me how my mom died. Just after it happened, I heard my dad telling somebody that she killed herself. There was so much shame in my family. After her funeral, we moved to a new town. Here I was, this skinny little kid, living in a new place, without my mother. I was so scared the first day I went to my new school. Two kids started bullying me that day."

"That must have been awful," said Jessica.

"It was. I had nobody to talk to about it. My dad was a mess, so I just suffered in silence."

"You've sure changed," said Ryan, acknowledging Matt's muscled body and menacing look.

"I had to or I wouldn't have survived."

John could feel the compassion in the room as the students reached out to comfort their classmate. He was grateful that he now understood his story… why Matt had become the person he had. We do what we have to, to protect ourselves… our physical self and more importantly, our emotional self.

Just then, the bell rang. The students quietly got up and filed off to their next class, several stopping to pat Matt on the shoulder and offer him their encouragement and support.

Caitlyn was the last to leave. Except for challenging John about his take on Anthony's death, she hadn't said a word the entire class. She stopped in front of Matt, looked at him for a moment, and then simply said, "I know how you feel." Without explaining, she turned and walked out of the room.

After Caitlyn left, John turned to him. "If you ever want to talk about it, I would be pleased to listen."

"Thank you, Mr. Stevens. I would appreciate that. For now though, I just want to go somewhere to be alone… and cry. I couldn't do it in front of them."

"I understand. I'll let the office know that you've gone home for the day. Will you be okay?"

"Yes. Talking about my mom's death was a relief. I don't feel so much shame or anger anymore."

"That's good. Really good. And there is one other thing that would help you understand this experience."

"Yes, I need to know what happened to my mom."

"I think it would very helpful."

"Thank you," he said, as he turned and walked out the door.

As he left, Teach felt enormous admiration for the young man.

Blair was waiting outside the classroom when Matt walked out. "Can I talk to you?" he asked.

"Sure."

As they walked down the hallway, Matt noticed several of the students eyeing Blair. "You terrorize a lot of kids don't you?" he asked.

"Ya, I guess I do," Blair answered sheepishly.

"Why do you do that?"

"I don't know. Makes me feel tough, I guess."

"Why don't you go after guys like me?"

"That would be crazy. You'd kick my ass."

"And how do you think they feel," Matt said, nodding his head towards a group of younger kids.

"I mostly do it just for fun."

"Do you think it's fun for them?"

"I get your point."

"You don't have to act like an idiot all your life, man."

"Ya, I know."

"So, what did you want to talk to me about?"
"You're not like everyone said you are."
"What do mean?"
"Everyone thinks you're a criminal."
"People can say whatever they want. It means nothing."
"Why don't you say something?"
"They've got to figure it out for themselves."
"Don't you worry about what they say?"
"I can't do anything about what other people say and I don't want to fight anymore."
"You used to fight?"
Matt hesitated for a second. "Ya, I did. And I hated it. I hated fighting."
"Then why did you do it?"
"Cause I didn't have a choice."
"Some of the stuff Mr. Stevens talks about has made me think about things," Blair admitted.
"Like what?"
"Like feeling good about yourself. I guess I do the things I do cause I don't feel good about myself. I guess I have low self-worth."
"You can change it, you know."
"How?"
"Start being kind to people."
"I don't know if I know how to be nice to people."
"You're doing it now."
"What do you mean?"
"You're talking to me. Do you know how many people talk to me?"
"I guess, not many."
They walked in silence for a few seconds.
"I guess I can figure out how to be nice to people."
"Just treat everyone like you treat Stuart."
"Ya, I could do that. Thanks man," Blair said, holding up his hand for a high-five.
"No problem," Matt replied slapping his hand.
Blair smiled and headed off to his next class.

As Matt watched him saunter off down the hallway, it suddenly occurred to him that Blair was actually not a bad guy. Like himself, he had a lot of challenges, mostly due to anger, and he was simply handling them the best way he knew how. He had never been shown another way. All he needed was some proper guidance. If Matt could turn his life around, Blair certainly could. He decided he would try to help him as best he could.

Caitlyn saw Jessie waving at her from the other side of the schoolyard, hurrying in her direction. She raised her hand slightly as if to return the wave.

"Why are you still at school?" her friend inquired as she crossed through the smoking area, looking disdainfully over her shoulder at two boys who appeared far too young to be there.

"Got some stuff to think about."

"Still worried about Rick?"

"Ya. He's not doing very well."

"Has he done anything lately?"

"No. He just sits in his room all day doing nothing. Some days he doesn't even want to talk."

"Is he taking his medication?"

"Yes, but he hates it almost as much as he hates being sick."

"I feel for you girl."

"He's my only brother and I don't know how to help him."

The pair stood silently for a few moments while Caitlyn puffed anxiously on her cigarette.

"I have an idea," Jessie offered hesitantly.

"Ya, what's that?"

"Why don't you talk to Mr. Stevens?"

"About Rick?"

"Yes."

"Not a chance."

"Why not?"

"It's none of his business."

"I've heard that he's really good at helping people solve problems. What have you got to lose?"

"I don't really like him."

"This isn't about you."

"I know it's not. Besides, what does he know about schizophrenia? Just cause he's helped a few high school students doesn't qualify him to help someone who's mentally ill."

"You won't know until you talk to him."

If anybody else spoke to Caitlyn this way, they would risk a verbal tirade, perhaps even the threat of physical harm, but Jessie had a way with her. "Okay, I'll think about it."

"That's awesome!"

Two men sat in a room observing the video feed. "Nothing," the first one said, exasperated.

"This guy's as clean as a whistle," remarked the second one.

"We got squat on him so far."

"Ya, what are we gonna do?"

"Call it in."

"He's gonna be pissed again."

"What can we do? It's not our fault."

"Don't matter."

"Actually, I think what this teacher is saying makes a lot of sense."

"What?"

"Ya, man. I like what he's saying!"

"Have you lost your fucking head? We got a job to do, man. Just watch the video and don't get any stupid ideas."

"I'm just sayin', man."

"You heard me. We don't need to mess this up."

"Ya."

CHAPTER 16:
WITHDRAWING

Nowhere man please listen
You don't know what you're missing
Nowhere man the world is at your command

— The Beatles, *Nowhere Man*

John sensed that he was hovering high in the air in the dimly lit room, it's only light, a candle in the far corner. A frail young woman lay on a bed, her back to him, sobbing quietly.

There was a light knock on the door. "May I come in?" a male voice asked timidly from outside.

The woman did not respond.

The door opened a crack and the man leaned partway through. "May I come in?" the bearded face repeated.

Again, silence.

"You must try to understand," he pleaded softly, stepping fully through the doorway.

"The woman lifted her head partially off the bed. "*Get out!*" she snapped.

"But I am worried about you."

"You should have thought about that before you decided to get me pregnant," she screamed.

"But you agreed."

He tried to sit on the bed beside her, but she pushed him away. "Don't ever touch me again."

"Can't you be happy?" he asked, trying to be cheerful.

"No! I don't want it. It was stupid and selfish of you to ask me to bare another child and I am foolish for letting you do so. I will never forgive you."

Several months earlier the man had persuaded his wife to have a baby, even though she had recently given birth to their second child. They needed another pair of hands he said, to do the chores.

She never wanted to be a mother in the first place. She was young and wanted to experience life. There was so much she desired to see and do. But she was careless and she had gotten pregnant

"Let's wait," she had begged him. "I need time to rest and adjust. I am not yet accustomed to having one child, let alone two or even three."

But he was persistent and one night in a state of intoxication, she had relented. She let him take her.

The woman shrieked as the contractions began again, this time, more intensely. Suddenly a nurse rushed into the room. "You must leave at once," she commanded, pushing the man towards the door.

He looked solemnly at the woman on the bed before exiting quietly.

"Your water has broken," said the nurse, after examining the young woman. "Your baby will arrive soon."

"Don't ever say that again," she shrieked. "It is not my baby. It is his and his alone."

"Surely you don't mean that," replied the nurse sadly.

"How can you possibly understand? You know nothing."

The woman screamed as she was again overcome by the contractions. They wracked her body as if she was being mauled by a starving tiger. The pain was at times unbearable. She was full of anger and hatred towards the baby and him for doing this to her.

"You must push now," directed the nurse. "Your baby is coming."

The young woman attempted to scream at the nurse. She wanted to tell her again, "I told you, this is not my baby." But the overwhelmingly intense pain would not allow her to speak. And so, she held the pain inside and in that moment, that anger and fear and hatred was passed on to the child. And he would mirror her agony.

The nurse cut the baby's umbilical cord, wrapped him in warm cloth and held him out to the young mother. But she would not have him.

"Take him," implored the nurse. "He is beautiful. You will love him."

The mother turned her head away. "I will never love this baby," she cried, refusing to hold him.

John knocked softly on the door and waited for a response.

"Come in," said a gentle voice from the other side.

He quietly opened the door and stepped into the room. It was dimly lit and sparse. The blinds had been pulled down, shielding the room from the golden sunlight outside.

The young man was sitting in a chair beside the bed, staring blankly into hands that twitched nervously in his lap. He motioned the newcomer to take a seat on the edge of the bed.

John walked over and held out his hand. The young man reached out and gently shook it. "My name is John," he said. "Your sister, Caitlyn, asked me to come and speak with you."

Sitting on the bed, he took note of the can of cola and the open bag of potato chips on the nightstand. He also spotted the empty milk container and chocolate bar wrappers in the waste can.

"I know. She told me you were coming. She's always trying to look after me. She said you are a nice person and you could help me."

"Well, I sure hope I can," he replied taking a seat.

"What if I don't want to be helped?"

"Then I'll leave. It's your choice."

"You'd give up that easily?"

"I wouldn't be giving up, just honouring your wishes... although I might ask you why you don't want to be helped."

Rick glanced briefly at his sister's teacher. "And what if I can't be helped?"

"At least we'd know we tried."

The young man sat quietly.

"Do you want to be helped?"

"I hate being on these pills and I hate being cooped up in this room."
"I can understand that."
"I hate the pills but they help control the voices."
"What voices?"
"The voices in my head. They're always tormenting me. Yelling at me. Telling me bad things."
"What bad things do they tell you?"
"That life is stupid. That we're all going to die. That I'm stupid and useless. That people are out to get me. That I'm gonna get beat up."
"And how do these voices make you feel."
"They terrify me, even more than the things I see."
"What is it you see?"
"Illusions."
"How do you know you see illusions?"
"Cause I know what's real and what isn't."
"I don't mean to sound silly, but am I real?"
"Yes, I know you're real. I can tell the difference. I just can't stop the illusions from coming."
"How often do you see these illusions and hear the voices?"
"Every day."
"And they scare you?"
"Ya, they do."
"They would scare me too," John empathized. "Especially if I didn't know what was causing them. Where do you think they are coming from?"
"My mind."
"Why would your mind create such a thing?"
"I don't know."
"If you had to take a guess, what do you think it would be?"
"Because I'm bad."
"Why do you think you're bad?"
"I don't know. I just think that is why I would be doing it?"
"Sometimes we think we are bad because other people have done something or said something to make us feel this way. Has anybody done this to you?"
"My dad used to tell me I was bad."

"Why did he say that?"

"Because I caused a lot of trouble?"

"Sometimes we create suffering for ourselves because we put judgment on things. We say this is good or this is bad, and our feelings, especially how we feel about ourselves, is affected by these judgments. If parents took a different viewpoint it could really change things."

"I don't understand what you are saying."

"If parents understood that children act out… do *bad* things… because they don't feel good about themselves, it might change the way they raise their children."

"Is that because parents cause children not to feel good about themselves?"

"Most of the time, yes! It is the result of the way parents raise their children. They yell at them, chastise them, criticize and harshly punish them. They don't allow their children to express themselves. They don't let their children know that they are important to them, or wanted or accepted or appreciated. And often, they don't nurture them, hug them or tell them they love them."

"Our parents never hugged us and my dad thought I was a weakling. He used to call me a coward and a sissy."

"And did he also tell you that you were stupid and useless?"

"Yes he did," Rick exclaimed, understanding John's point. "These voices I'm hearing are just repeating what my dad used to say."

"Yes, they are. When you were a child, do you remember repeating the things your dad said?"

"Yes, I did. I remember sitting in my room chastising myself by saying exactly what he said."

They both sat quietly for a few moments.

"Why did my dad say such cruel things to me? Why did he think I was a weakling?"

"I guess he didn't understand your sensitive nature."

"My mom said I was a very sensitive boy," Rick said, smiling for the first time. "She used to tell me that I needed to watch out though, because other kids would pick on me. That's why she didn't want to baby me. She didn't want me to get beat up."

"I'm afraid sensitive children quite often become the target of bullies."

"I did. I got teased and beat up a lot."

"I got beat up too, Rick."

"You did?" he asked, his smile even broader.

"I certainly did. I was very sensitive too."

"What did you do?"

"I learned to hide it… and to fight back."

"You liked to fight."

"I hated fighting. I was always afraid that I would get beat up. But when I had to, I fought."

"I never learned to fight. Caitlyn is the fighter in our family."

"I can see that," John said, returning his smile.

"I love Caitlyn. I don't know what I'd do without her."

John felt that he had connected with this troubled young man. He had found some common ground and Rick knew that his visitor understood him. "You mentioned that your mom didn't want to baby you, did she hug you very much?"

"Never. I don't remember her ever hugging me or cuddling me or telling me that she loved me."

"Do you think that she loved you?"

"Now, I think she does, but I sure didn't think so when I was growing up?"

"And how did that make you feel?"

"I was sad. I wanted to run away."

"I can imagine. Unfortunately, there are a lot of children who grow up feeling the same way. There might be a way out of this, though."

"What do you mean?"

"You said before that these illusions and voices you are hearing were coming from your mind."

"Uhuh."

"So, if they're coming from your mind, who do you think created them?"

"I guess I did."

"It would have to be you because no one else is in charge of your mind."

"That makes sense."

"And if you were going to create illusions and voices in your mind, why would you create things that would scare you?"

"I'm not sure."

"Again, if you had to take a guess, what would you say?"

"Fear."

"Fear of what?"

"Fear that I'm bad."

"It would have to come from some negative belief about yourself."

"You mean I'm punishing myself cause I don't feel good about myself?"

"Yes! If you felt good about yourself… if you thought you were a good person… isn't it more likely that these illusions and voices would make you happy."

"Ya, I guess they would." Rick sat quietly for a few moments. "I think God is punishing me too," he whispered softly, looking at John for the first time.

"What makes you say that?"

"I believe that God created everything and I believe God wants me to be sick. He wants to punish me."

"I'm not so sure that God wants to punish you. I don't believe God punishes anyone."

"Well that's what the church says."

"Perhaps there is a different way of looking at this that might help you feel differently about it."

"What do you mean?"

"If you were to describe God to someone who didn't know anything about God, what would you say?"

"I would say that God is the great creator of the universe, capable of moving mountains. God is a wise, loving being … an amazing beam of light. He is omnipotent and can see everything. He is everywhere and all knowing. God is pure love."

"I think most people would describe God in a similar way. Now what if I told you that you are God?"

"What? No way, man!"

"Why do you say that?"

"Cause I'm not God. That's bullshit."

"Again, there is a different way of looking at this... a different belief system... that could help you overcome this condition you're experiencing."

"Ya?"

"The common belief among Western religious orders is that God is a being that exists outside of us, up in heaven perhaps, and that this Being controls our lives. They believe this God judges us, condemns us and punishes us for our behaviour."

"Ya, that's right."

"And how has this belief served humanity?"

"It makes us behave."

"But have we behaved? Has it stopped us from murdering, raping, abusing, torturing, persecuting, robbing, swindling and mistreating one another?"

"No, I guess it hasn't."

"So would you say that it hasn't really served us?"

The young man nodded his head.

"Well, there is another growing awareness that is different and that might serve humankind better. This awareness says that we are one with God. That everything was created from one-common-energy... the universal God energy."

"Oh ya?"

"Yes. And if this was true, how would you then describe yourself?"

"What do you mean?"

"A few minutes ago, you provided an eloquent description of God. You said God was a powerful, loving being. If you knew that you too were God, how would you describe yourself?"

"The same way," Rick said, his smile returning.

"And do you think this loving being who we call God would punish his or her self?"

"I don't think so. But we punish ourselves cause we don't know any better, don't we?"

"It appears we do."

"I guess believing that we are God, whether it is true or not, serves us better, doesn't it?"

"It certainly does."

"But how does knowing this help me stop the voices and illusions?"

"You've already begun. By knowing that you created them from fear, false beliefs and self loathing, you can tell yourself when you hear them that they're not real. In essence, you can retrain yourself. With practice and persistence, over time, I am confident that they will stop."

"Is that all I have to do? That seems too simple."

"There are three other things that are really important. The first has to do with understanding and overcoming fear."

"What do you mean?"

"Where does fear come from?"

"I'm not sure."

"What are we afraid of?"

"That something bad is going to happen to us."

"Right. And more importantly, it comes from the belief that we won't be able to handle whatever happens to us. It comes from a lack of trust."

"Ya, I get that."

"If we trusted that everything is happening as it is meant to and if we had faith that no matter what happens we will be okay, we would have nothing to fear."

"That sounds kinda simple, but I understand it."

"Sometimes we have a tendency to discount things that seem simple."

"That's for sure. My dad never used to acknowledge the things I did, because he thought they were easy."

"How did that make you feel?"

"Worthless!"

"That is at the root of much of our inability to trust. We lose our ability to trust when we are betrayed and the most significant betrayal we experience is the loss of the love of a parent. As a child, we take it as a given that our parents will love us. When they don't show us this love... in fact when they show us the exact opposite with criticism, abuse, lack of acknowledgement, excessive demands and harsh punishment... we feel betrayed."

"I understand that."

"And when we lose trust, we also to a degree lose hope. We fall into despair."

"That's sad, but it makes sense." Rick sat silently for a few minutes absorbing this new information. "You said there were three things. What's the second one?"

"You also need to heal the emotional pain that is in your heart."

"You mean the sadness?"

"The sadness, anger, grief, shame, guilt, resentment, hatred, hopelessness and any other emotional pain that you are holding on to... actually, more like the wounded inner child inside you is holding on to. It is an important part of the healing process."

"What do you mean, wounded inner child?"

"Quite often, we have traumatic experiences in childhood that we're not able to or allowed to express our feelings about. When this happens, we sometimes stay stuck in the experience. So in essence, we have a wounded child inside of us."

"Is that why people, especially men, are so immature?"

"It's part of it."

"What's the third thing?"

"Live in the present moment!"

"Pardon?" said Rick looking very puzzled.

"To help you understand, let me ask you some questions. First, do we live in the past?"

"No, we just think about it."

"And what about the future?"

"Same thing."

"That's right. We don't live in the past or the future, we only think about them. We only live in the present."

"What about when we're daydreaming or fantasizing?"

"When we're doing this, again, it usually has to do with some future event or reshaping a past memory."

"I can see that. And hey, what's getting me into trouble are my thoughts, so if I stop thinking, I'll get better!"

"Exactly!"

"How do I live in the moment?" he inquired.

"There are a few things you can do. You can focus on your breath. Or you can observe the things around you. Or you can focus totally on what you're doing, like washing your hands."

"Yes! I can do that."

"Awesome!

"So you think you can help me heal this?"

"Yes! I do! And I would love to help you."

"Could we do it another day? I'm feeling tired and this is a lot for me to take in."

"I can come back whenever you're ready. Before I leave though, there is a simple technique I'd like to teach you to help you get started. It's intended to reprogram your brain by changing your thought patterns. It's very effective."

"That would be okay."

"All you have to do is this, just tap the karate chop part of your hand while repeating positive affirmations, such as, 'I love and accept myself the way I am,'" John said, demonstrating the technique. "Tapping on this part of your hand, which is an energy meridian point, sends an electrical impulse to the brain. It helps to ingrain the positive affirmations."

"I've heard about energy meridians and it seems simple enough," observed Rick, as he repeated the tapping technique.

"Do it every day. It will really help. And say any positive affirmation that comes to mind."

"I will."

"There is one other thing that I am confident will help restore your health."

"Oh ya, what's that?"

"I'd like to talk to you about your diet."

"I guess the pop and junk food aren't really helping me are they?"

"Unfortunately, they're not. There is a lot of evidence to suggest that an improper diet plays a significant role in the development of mental illness, just like it plays a role in all other health conditions."

"I guess that makes sense, so ya, we can talk about it."

"Awesome! Hippocrates said, *All illness begins in the gut*, and that's where healing begins."

"Thank you. I really appreciate this. Maybe I can start to get my life back," Rick said, as he stood up and gave John a big hug.

As he drove away from the group home, John Stevens felt both encouraged and overwhelmed. There was nothing quite like the experience of touching the heart of a wounded soul… nothing like helping someone find light in the darkness… and so he felt optimistic about his ability to help Caitlyn's brother recover. But at the same time, he felt a little beleaguered with the knowledge that so many people are stuck in childhood traumas too emotionally shattered to move forward. The thought of it was very distressing.

He also recalled something he learned several years earlier. The shaman who taught him about tapping told him that we are all here to learn certain lessons relating to living in trust and oneness, and living in love and knowing that we are pure love. He also told him we will have experiences that are meant to teach us that we are in charge of our lives, that we are good enough to do anything we want to do and that we are worthy of receiving and enjoying everything life has to offer. The shaman told him that these lessons come to people in different ways and that part of the lesson is experiencing the opposite first. Before we can learn to live in trust, sometimes we need to understand fear, which means we will very likely experience fear. Similarly, part of learning to live with love, first involves knowing hatred, especially self-hatred.

The shaman told him that our parents are quite often involved in helping us learn these lessons by giving us experiences that teach us the opposite. For example, if we need to learn about love, it is possible that we will have experiences with one or both of our parents that will cause us to feel unloved, and by extension, to feel self loathing. It seems that this is an important part of the process.

These experiences with our parents program our brain to think in a certain way… they condition us… and quite often they cause us to develop negative thought patterns and negative beliefs about ourselves. Tapping is one way to reprogram our brains. It reconditions us. When we do this in conjunction with therapies that help us release unresolved emotional pain, it is very powerful.

He would have to tell Caitlyn about his session with Rick. He knew she would be excited to hear about it.

Jonathan Fox hit the *end call* button and slammed his cell phone in the center console of his sporty Nissan. This was not the news he wanted to hear. It had been two weeks and still nothing that could be used to discredit John Stevens. He was furious. Perhaps Stevens was in fact as honest and genuine as Fox had been told. Maybe he wasn't going to trip himself up. Not without some help.

Fox was prepared for this. He didn't get to where he was without being a meticulous planner. He had an ace up his sleeve and that ace was a kid with a criminal record.

CHAPTER 17:
HAPPINESS

Feels like the things that I've wanted
The most in this life I can't have
So you see
I've been damning the world
Before it damns me

— Holly Cole, *Onion Girl*

Rounding the corner towards his classroom, John spotted Caitlyn at the far end of the hallway. She was sitting alone on the bottom step of the stairway leading to the second floor. Noticing her teacher, she quickly closed the book she was reading and stood up, ready to bolt up the stairs.

"Caitlyn," he called out. "May I speak with you?"

"I guess," she responded coldly, stopping half turned, ready to flee at any moment.

"I spoke with your brother yesterday."

"Oh ya. How did it go?" she said sharply.

"It went very well. He is quite a bright young man."

"He was gifted in school," she added, softening her stance.

"I don't doubt it."

"Can you help him?"

"Yes, I'm confident I can."

"He had so much potential. And then he got sick and everything changed. It infuriates me."

"Caitlyn, I understand that you want your brother to be well. You want him to be the way he used to be. We all want our family members to be healthy. But why does it make you so angry?"

"Are you serious? Wouldn't it make you angry if it happened to somebody in your family?" Knowing that she was feeling very emotional about her brother's condition and her volatility could send her off at any moment, he chose his words carefully, "There is a way of looking at this that will help lessen the anger."

"And just what is that supposed to mean?"

"When we understand the truths of our existence, it helps us to cope with experiences like this."

"That sounds like bullshit."

"Yes, I suppose it does, but would you mind sitting for a few minutes while I explain?"

"I guess," she said, reluctantly taking a seat on the stairs.

"It's okay when we get angry about things," he continued, sitting down beside her. "It's a natural emotion and a normal part of being human. But when we hold on to this anger, it works against us and it seriously affects our health."

"But he's the only brother I have and the only one in my family I could talk to. When we were growing up, we were very close. I miss him and I just want him to be normal again," she said, softening a little more.

"All of our experiences have meaning and many are meant to teach us something."

"And what exactly am I supposed to learn from this?"

"We're not meant to live in unhappiness, nor are we meant to hold on to anger. It doesn't serve us to live this way and it is really important that we learn how to let go. Buddha said that to be happy, we need to want what we have."

"You mean, we're supposed to spend more time being grateful for what we've got and less time worrying about what we don't have?"

"Yes!"

"So I guess I should be happy that I can still talk to my brother, even if he's not like he used to be."

"That would be a great start."

"I don't know if I can do that right now."

"Give yourself time. Sometimes it takes a while to turn a ship."

"You like metaphors don't you?"

"Yes, I guess I do. They can be helpful in explaining things."

"I guess that's why Jesus spoke in parables and metaphors."

"Do you often get angry when you don't get the things you want?" Teach asked carefully.

"Ya, I guess I do. My mother says that anger is my default emotion. My mother's always focusing on people's faults."

"What do you suppose is at the root of your anger?"

"I don't really know."

"If you had to take a guess, what do you think it might be?"

She sat quietly for a moment, then her expression slowly changed and he thought she was going to cry. "My old man," she said, her lip quivering. "He never loved me. He never told me he loved me. Never hugged me. Never kissed me on the cheek. Never spent time with me. He only spanked me and yelled at me. I just wanted him to love me."

"That's what we all want, but unfortunately, far too many of us don't get it."

"But why does it have to be this way. If parents are going to bring us into the world, shouldn't they love us?"

"Many parents are too caught up in their own emotional pain and lack of self-love to properly love their children."

"Then they shouldn't have kids."

"Growing up with dysfunctional parents who are unable to express love seems to be part of the process."

"What process?"

"The process of learning the lessons we need in order to grow spiritually and understand who we really are."

"And what am I supposed to learn from this?"

"There are a number of lessons that can be taken from this experience and there's a little girl inside you who needs to express her anger," he said softly. "Perhaps the reason you're holding on to so much anger about your brother's situation is because you've learned to hold on to it, because anger feels far better than rejection and the loss of your father's love."

Caitlyn turned and looked at John. "That actually makes sense," she said, astonished that she was seeing eye-to-eye with him. "Man, I never thought I would agree with anything you had to say. You just never know do you?"

"Yes, there are many uncertainties in life. That's part of the reason I love it so much," he offered looking at his watch. "I'm afraid it's time for me to get ready for class. I hope this has been helpful."

"It has been very helpful." She turned to head up the stairs, then suddenly stopped and looked back at him. "You know, what you said about Anthony's brother and about death and loss helped me understand my relationship with my father a little better. And while I don't totally understand why it happened, I'm way more at peace with it. I know how to find more happiness in my life."

"That's good Caitlyn," he said quietly, slowly nodding his head.

"I'm really sorry that I've been such a bitch to you."

"Thank you."

"I'm also really sorry that I wasn't nicer when Ms. Connors left the school and I'm *really* happy that you went to see my brother, Teach," she smiled.

"I understand," he acknowledged, surprised and pleased that she called him Teach, "and I'm happy too, because I just figured out today's topic of discussion."

"Let me guess," she smiled.

"You got it," her teacher replied, as he turned and bounced happily down the hall.

"Happiness is an important aspect of living a long, healthy life," John began, standing before the class. "And yet, true happiness seems to evade most people. Many of us live with enormous anger, resentment and hatred, inflicting physical and emotional pain on one another and ourselves. Clearly this doesn't serve mankind."

"My parents and their friends like to sit around and complain about everything," observed Tracy. "It makes me not want to be around them."

"It seems that people spend a lot of time bitching and moaning about government, millionaire athletes, the price of gas, you name it," added Jordan.

"And is anybody ever happy about the weather," asked Scott. "It's too hot in the summer and too cold in the winter. Blah, blah blah!"

"What can we do to change this?" asked Tracy.

"Let's put that to everyone," the head of the class suggested. "What brings happiness into our lives?"

"Money," replied Stuart.

"That's for sure," agreed Blair.

"Friends," added Tracy.

"A good job," remarked Ryan.

"Love!" said Jessica. "Being in love really makes people happy."

"A hot girlfriend," commented Eric.

"A nice home," said Jordan.

"Good video games," remarked Adam.

Several students looked at Adam with puzzled expressions. "Well, they make me happy!" he added, causing a few snickers amongst his classmates. "Why are you laughing at me?"

"We're not laughing at you, buddy," replied Josh. "What you said was funny. We're laughing with you."

"Oh, I get it," Adam smiled.

"Good health," added Tom, continuing the discussion.

"Nice weather," suggested Mike.

"Those are all certainly things that are nice to have," John agreed. "But what if you didn't have them? Would you still be happy?"

"I don't see how you could be happy without money," Josh replied.

"Or without your health," added Eric.

"I would be pretty sad without friends," said Jessica.

"Then you must be the saddest person in the world," joked Blair. "I'm sorry, I'm sorry," he added before anyone could jump in. "I just couldn't resist."

"That's okay," Jessica sympathized. "We know you can't help yourself."

"Hey! Good one, Jessica!" Mike said dryly, bringing a few more snickers from the class.

"I guess I deserved that," acknowledged Blair. "Maybe someday I'll learn."

"Sometimes it takes a while to turn a ship, Blair," Caitlyn said, eyeing John with a cheerful smile.

"Yes it does," he agreed, returning the smile.

Several of the students exchanged puzzled glances, not quite sure what to make of what just occurred between Teach and Caitlyn.

"I guess the question you're asking," concluded Tom, "is, if we we're destitute, alone, living in a shelter and experiencing health issues, could we still be happy?"

"I don't see how anyone could be happy under those circumstances," observed Mike.

"I guess it depends on how you look at it."

"What do you mean by that?" asked Terry. It had been several days since his return to class after his brother's very emotional funeral. John and most of the students had attended and Terry and his mother were grateful for their support.

"Let's begin with childhood. It is said that much of our beliefs and views of the world are shaped during our early formative years. What are the things that make for a happy upbringing?"

"The love of your parents," replied Tracy.

"That is absolutely the single most important thing."

"Is that why there are so many unhappy people in the world?" asked Adam. "Because people grow up without that love?"

"Without a doubt. If every child grew up feeling loved, we would be living in an entirely different world."

"What about the other things you've been teaching us?" inquired Josh. "Like feeling wanted, accepted and appreciated. I don't think your childhood would be very happy if you grew up without these things."

"That is also true. As children, we absolutely must feel wanted, accepted and appreciated, because if we don't, it affects us in a profound way. It makes us feel unlovable, insecure, angry, resentful, and full of hatred. It leads to jealousy and other self-sabotaging behaviours."

"Children also need a stable family environment," remarked Tracy. "Marriage breakups can have a very damaging affect on children. It certainly affects their sense of well-being and security."

"Particularly if the marriage breakup is acrimonious," commented Tom.

"Say what?" asked Mike.

"If there is a lot of resentment and hostility."

"Oh, ya. Now I understand."

"It's hard on children when they have to stay at two homes, adjust to their parents dating other people and possibly move from the family home," remarked Ryan. "The disruption in their lives can be really traumatic."

"People also need to be really careful who they get into relationships with after they separate," remarked Scott.

"Ya, it's amazing how many divorced people get involved with someone who doesn't get along with their children," observed Josh.

"I don't know how people can do that," said Jessica. "You'd think they'd be more concerned about their children than their love life."

"Some parents are blind to what's going on. Or perhaps they're so happy to be in a new, loving relationship, they think everything will work out. If people only realized that if things are bad before they move in together, they're only going to get worse afterwards."

"That's for sure," agreed Jordan. "I've read about some horrific things that stepfathers and stepmothers have done."

"But it's also not good for parents to stay together when they're unhappy with each other," said Terry. "It teaches kids that it's okay to settle for something less than what you want and that it's okay to be miserable."

"That's quite true. Unhappiness in a marriage creates a very toxic environment in the home and as much as parents might want to believe that it's better for the children for them to stay together, children are deeply affected by this negative energy."

"It's also important for children to have friends," added Eric.

"Having friends validates our lovability and makes for a happier childhood. Whereas being rejected by other children can have a devastating effect on our sense of self."

"It's pretty hard to be a happy kid when you don't have any friends," added Travis. "You feel so alone."

John looked at Travis for a moment, realizing that he had just revealed some deep sadness about his life.

"What are we supposed do if we grow up without being loved, wanted, accepted and appreciated? What if we have a really unhappy childhood?" asked Tracy.

"Until there is a societal change, until we start living in a more loving, compassionate, accepting way, whether we've grown up in a happy, loving household or not, we will be constantly challenged to live joyfully. There is a great deal of unhappiness in the world and we will constantly be confronted with miserable people."

"So what can we do?" asked Ryan.

"There are several things we can do to bring joy into our lives. First, it helps immensely to understand who we really are and why we're really here on the planet. When we understand that we are divine spiritual beings participating in the flow of life, at one with God and each other, it helps us make sense of what is going on in our lives and on the planet. It gives us faith that we can end the individual and collective suffering we are experiencing. It encourages more loving behaviour and acts of kindness."

"I guess that would create more happiness, wouldn't it?" remarked Stuart.

"Well, duh!" kidded Josh.

"Perhaps your last remark wasn't the kindest thing you could have said, Josh," chided Tom.

"I was just kidding!"

"Did Josh's remark make you feel good, Stuart?" asked Tom.

"Well, not really," Stuart replied.

"I'm sorry, Stu," said Josh, offering his classmate a fist pump.

"Any joke made at someone else's expense is never funny," said Caitlyn.

"Thank you, Caitlyn. That's a very important point. The second thing we can do to bring happiness into our lives is to learn to trust. When we trust that everything is happening as it is meant to and that no matter what happens, we can handle it, we let go of fear. And this gives us peace of mind."

"Is peace of mind the same as happiness?" asked Matt.

"Happiness and peace of mind go hand in hand. It's hard to have one without the other."

"You mean, happiness comes from peace of mind and peace of mind comes from happiness?" asked Travis.

"Yes, just like that! They're pretty much one and the same. Third on the list of things we can do is to heal and release our emotional pain and change our faulty beliefs. It is almost impossible to experience real joy when we are holding on to unresolved emotional pain."

"That doesn't sound easy," remarked Eric.

"It isn't. It is perhaps the most difficult challenge we face. Awareness that we even have emotional pain is something that eludes most people. They don't understand why they get so angry or why they cry all the time. They don't realize how it affects their behaviour, health, relationships, career and finances."

"Emotional pain affects your finances?" questioned Mike.

"It certainly does. It's difficult, if not impossible, to attract wealth into your life when you're holding on to shame and guilt."

"I guess that makes sense."

"And if you do attract it into your life, you likely won't hold onto it for very long," remarked Tom.

"That's quite true. We typically find ways to sabotage ourselves."

"What else can we do?" asked Jessica. "I bet there's more stuff, isn't there?"

"Yes, there certainly is. Next, we need as Buddha said, to want what we have, which means we need to spend more time appreciating and being grateful for what we have and less time bemoaning what we don't have."

"Basically, does that mean it's not good to want things?" asked Adam.

"Not at all. It's natural to want things. Wants lead to ideas and ideas lead to creation. Our wants motivate us. What I'm saying is that it doesn't serve us to be unhappy when we don't get or don't have the things we want."

"That makes sense," said Jessica. "Cause my mom always tells me to stop asking for stuff. She says things don't make you happy."

"Your mom is making a very good point."

"I think she's just being cheap." Jessica's last point prompted more snickers from the class.

"Next, and we've talked about this before, we need to live in the present moment. Most of us spend far too much time fretting about the past and worrying about the future, neither of which brings us happiness."

"Nor does it accomplish anything," agreed Tom.

"When you live in the now, you feel nothing but euphoria, because there's nothing else to feel."

"But how do you do that?" asked Mike. "What if you've got an exam coming up and it's in a subject you're not very good at. You can't help but worry."

"What would you be worried about?"

"Failing!"

"And what if you failed?"

"I would be embarrassed, my parents would be angry and I'd have to repeat the course."

"Yes, I suppose those are all possibilities, but let's examine this more closely. First, have you done everything you can to prepare for the exam? Have you made sure your notes are complete and understandable? Have you sought help for topics you don't quite comprehend? Have you put in sufficient study time? Are you focused on doing your best, rather than passing or failing?"

"Well, not really."

"If you did all of these things, would it make you feel more confident?"

"Definitely."

"Great. And even if you did all of these things and still failed, can you say with absolute certainty that each of those things you just mentioned are going to happen…that you're going to be embarrassed, that your parents are going to be angry and that you will have to repeat the course?"

"Well, I'm pretty sure they're gonna happen."

"But not one hundred percent certain?"

"No, not one hundred percent."

"That means you're projecting…you're assuming something will happen when it's not absolutely certain that it will."

"I guess."

"And even if all of these things did happen, could you handle it… would you be okay?"

"Yes! I guess eventually I'd be okay. I'd stop being embarrassed at some point and my parents would get over it."

"And you could always take a summer course," offered Tracy.

"Maybe. But I wouldn't want to."

"But you could."

"Yep."

"So if we're prepared and if we imagine a positive outcome rather than a negative outcome and if we have faith that no matter what happens in our lives, we can handle it, then we stop worrying. Right?" asked Tom.

"Yes! And more importantly, at this moment, you're not writing the exam, you haven't failed it, you're not embarrassed, your parents aren't angry and you do not have to repeat the course. So is there any reason to worry *at this moment?*"

"No, I guess not. I guess it would make more sense for me think about what I need to do to ensure that I am fully prepared for the exam…and do it."

"Exactly. Focus on the solution, not the problem."

"Okay, I gotta go!" Stuart joked, bringing a burst of laughter from the class, as he jumped out of his seat in a mock show of panic.

John chuckled along with the students and after everyone had settled down, he continued. "Another important aspect of bringing happiness into your life is doing what you love. Be it your work, your hobby, playing a sport, spending time with friends, spending time in nature. Whatever! Doing what you love is sure to make you feel joyful."

"It also helps keep you in the moment," observed Ryan.

"It certainly does. When you're doing what you love, you usually aren't spending much time worrying about the future or fretting about the past.

"The final thing we can do to create happiness is be forgiving, especially towards ourselves. Forgiveness is freedom from suffering because it helps us let go of anger, resentment and hatred. And one of the best things we can do to forgive is to know that everyone is doing the best they can with what they've learned."

"It's not easy to forgive," observed Tom.

"That's for sure," agreed Travis. "I'm not sure that I can ever forgive my father."

"Maybe one day you will, Travis, especially when you know in your heart that it doesn't serve you not to forgive."

"Why is it so hard to forgive?" asked Jessica.

"It's because we're not taught how to do it. It's also from holding on to victimhood and emotional pain."

"A lot of stuff comes back to holding on to emotional pain, doesn't it?" asked Mike.

"Ya, it sure causes us a lot of grief…pardon the pun," agreed Josh.

"Yes! As I said before, it's one of our biggest challenges." As he was speaking the words, John thought about the difficulties he had in his own life forgiving people. It didn't come easy to him. He was never taught how to forgive. Instead, he learned how to hang on to anger, bitterness and self-loathing like a baby baboon learns to cling to its mother.

"Letting go is an important part of being happy, isn't it?" asked Tracy.

"It's very important. Letting go of emotional pain, bitterness, attachment, judgment, projections and expectations is like letting go of a huge albatross. It eliminates a great deal of unnecessary stress from your life."

"What do you mean by letting go of attachment?" asked Scott.

"I'm referring to letting go of things or ideas."

"You mean like a kid not wanting to share his toys?" asked Mike.

"Yes, that's a good example."

"Or not wanting to let go of a relationship," Eric added.

"My brother wouldn't get rid of his old clothes," observed Terry. "They meant a lot to him." It was the first time Terry had mentioned anything about his brother and the class fell silent. It was a very poignant moment.

"Anthony was a really sentimental guy," said Jordan, breaking the tension.

"Yes, he was," Terry smiled.

"I guess we hold on to them because of what they represent to us," Matt suggested.

"Yes! There's an emotional attachment."

"You mean like a relationship represents love?" Jordan inquired.

"And a house represents success," added Travis.

"I guess money represents safety to a lot of people," added Ryan.

"I think my brother's clothes represented good times," said Terry.

"Those are all terrific examples. But if we understood our emotional connection and if we understood impermanence, we'd be more likely to let go of our attachments and we'd be much happier, because we're not taking them with us when we leave this planet."

"What do you mean by impermanence?" asked Eric.

"When we look around us, we get the sense that things are real… they have form… and thus, our perception is that they are permanent. But they aren't!"

"Ask someone whose house has burned down if things are permanent," offered Caitlyn.

"Right! Now I get it," smiled Eric.

"And I guess relationships aren't permanent, are they?" asked Josh.

"You'll figure that out pretty quickly when you've had your heart broken by the death of a spouse," Caitlyn added

"Or any loved one for that matter," added Tracy.

"Think of a majestic oak tree being chopped down and cut into lumber to be used to build a house. Everything you see around you, is, has, or will, change form. It may happen in an instant or it may take thousands of years, but it will change."

"But we should still treat our things with respect, right?" asked Jessica.

"Definitely," Teach heartily agreed. "I don't think we want to be cavalier about it. How we treat things is a reflection of how we feel about ourselves."

"You also said we need to let go of projections. I don't really understand that," said Mike, looking somewhat embarrassed.

"No worries," replied his teacher empathetically. "Here's an example. You meet a girl, fall in love and your heart is set on marriage. But then she breaks up with you and in the process, breaks your heart. You're devastated and you fall into a state of depression."

"So projecting is where we imagine something happening," said Mike.

"More like you're convinced something is going to happen," added Jordan.

"And you're emotionally attached to it," added Tom

"Exactly! It's when we believe something is going to happen in the future, rather than living in the moment and enjoying what is."

"Another example would be when we go to a baseball game, thinking our team is going to win," added Matt. "And when they don't, we get angry."

"What's more, we likely don't enjoy the game very much because we're so worried about them losing," added Terry.

"Now I see," said Mike. "Thanks."

John found himself grinning again at how all the students, not just Tom and Ryan, were grasping these ideas. He thought about all the people who wondered why he liked teaching so much and his smile grew even bigger.

"What about expectations?" inquired Travis. "Isn't it sort of like projecting where we think something is going to be a certain way?"

"Yes it is, but here's the difference. Let's say you're planning to go on a vacation and you expect the weather to be warm and you see yourself doing a lot of swimming. But then you get there and the weather is too cold so you can't swim. You expected it to be warm and you projected yourself swimming. Your reaction to this situation depends on your emotional attachment."

"When my old man gets home, he expects dinner to be ready and he gets pissed if it isn't," remarked Blair.

"He imagines himself sitting down to a nice dinner as soon as sets foot in the door and so he expects dinner to be ready," John clarified.

"Yep."

"I see how our expectations can get us into trouble," added Travis. "If we go on vacation and don't care about the water temperature, we won't get angry when we find out it's too cold for swimming."

Just then the bell rang. "Thank you for a very valuable discussion," Teach praised the class.

"Now I've got a better idea of how I can make my life happier," said Caitlyn after everyone else had left. "I've spent so much of it being bitter, but I don't want to be that way anymore."

"That's wonderful," John replied, suddenly feeling very choked up.

"Thank you for helping me see that there is a better way to live," she added, before turning and heading out the door.

Her ecstatic teacher smiled and wiped away a tear.

Fred Phillips

As John made his way through the early evening traffic, he was reflecting on the discussion about what we can do to bring happiness into our lives and he was reminded of a recent conversation with Sandra. How often, she had asked, do we let the past interfere with the present? Something that happened two days, two weeks, two years ago, continues to play over and over in our minds. It haunts us and we suffer. He considered how this is particularly true in relationships. Something our partner did, no matter how long ago, continues to bother us. It upsets us and we can't seem to let it go... even things they did before we met them.

It is important to understand why it upsets us. Is what they did something that goes against our values and therefore serves as a red flag? Or is it something that is triggering a deep emotional wound? Either way, we need to deal with it before it poisons our relationship, as it surely will. And perhaps most importantly, we need remind ourselves to stay in the present moment and let the past go.

CHAPTER 18:
HEALING

The white walls of your dressing room
are stained in scarlet red
You bled upon the cold stone
like a young man

— Elton John, *High Flying Bird*

"Mr. Stevens," Jessica began. "You keep talking about healing our emotional pain and I just don't understand it. What is emotional pain and why is it so important for us to heal it? I'd really like to know."

"Emotional pain is one of the least understood aspects of our experience," her teacher replied. "And it's certainly one of the least understood aspects as it relates to modern medicine and our health. Its affect is significant and in spite of that, doctors tell us nothing about it. It's at the root of all health conditions and pretty much every other form of human suffering, whether it's our finances, relationships, career or whatever."

"That's a very bold statement," remarked Tom. "Can you back it up?"

"Yes I can, Tom. Let's take a few steps back. The state of health of our bodies is managed by one thing. Does anybody remember what that is?"

"Bacteria," answered Eric.

"Bacteria play a role in our health, but they don't manage it."

"What about viruses?" asked Mike.

"Like bacteria, viruses play a role in the state of our health, but they don't control it."

"The food we eat," suggested Jessica. "My mom keeps telling me I'm gonna get sick if I keep eating so much junk food."

"Again, our diet is important, but it doesn't regulate our health, although your mom is right in encouraging you to eat healthy foods."

"Basically, it's gotta be stress," exclaimed Adam.

"Ah, now you're getting closer. What happens to our bodies when we get stressed?"

"We become susceptible to illness," replied Ryan.

"And why is that?"

"Because it weakens our immune system," said Matt.

"Precisely! It weakens our immune system. The state of our health is maintained by one thing and that is our immune system.

"The human body was created with perfection. Look at it. Millions of tiny cells that form a complex network of internal structures and systems that operate in harmony, allowing us to see, hear, taste, digest food, walk, throw a baseball and figure out a mathematical equation. It is an incredible machine."

"Mine certainly is," Blair grinned, flexing his biceps.

"Man, you're so weak even your insecurity feels powerless," quipped Josh.

"I guess I set myself up for that, didn't I," Blair admitted, laughing along with the rest of the class.

"As we discussed previously, our bodies were also designed with an immune system and its sole purpose is to keep the body healthy," John continued after everyone had settled down. "The only way the body can become unhealthy is when the immune system reaches overload...when it is no longer able to function normally. This is when bacteria, viruses and other intruders are able to cause sickness."

"That makes a great deal of sense," agreed Tom.

"And I guess stress is one of the things that causes the immune system to break down," added Travis.

"It's the only thing, Travis."

"But if our bodies were built with such perfection, why weren't they designed to handle stress?" asked Caitlyn.

"They were! When humans were first evolving, we were both predator and prey. We hunted and gathered food, but we were also hunted by lions, tigers and other carnivores. Our bodies were designed to cope with this."

"You must be talking about the fight, flight or freeze response," said Jordan.

"Exactly. When we detected danger, we took action. We hid, we ran or we defended ourselves. And during this period of stress, our normal body functions, like digestion and immune defense, shut down temporarily in order for our energy to be directed to saving ourselves. But these were short term periods of stress and they likely happened infrequently. In today's society, we are constantly being bombarded with stress."

"That's for sure," agreed Terry. "Just watching the news is bad enough."

"Yep, think about it," remarked Adam. "Bills arriving in the mail, driving in traffic, stock market fluctuations, mortgage payments, business meetings or getting fired from your job. That's a lot of stress."

"What about us?" added Josh. "We've gotta get good marks in school, find a job, earn money to pay for our college education. That's a ton of stress, man."

"And what about peer pressure?" asked Tracy. "You're always worrying about what other people think of you. It's really bad."

"Bullying is really bad too," added Scott. "It's awful coming to school when you're afraid of getting beaten up."

"That's why you've gotta be tough," chided Blair.

"You don't really learn very quickly do you?" snarled Caitlyn. "If you don't have anything intelligent to say, you should shut up."

"You just told me to shut up," said Blair, looking very dejected.

"Yes, well, I'm sorry. It wasn't a very appropriate thing to say, but quite frankly I'm tired of your behaviour."

"Ya, I guess I can be a jerk sometimes."

"Sometimes?" said Josh, raising his eyebrows.

"Blair, if you're going to continue to disrupt the class with unacceptable behaviour, you can expect a backlash," added Tom.

"I hear you," Blair said, smiling for a change. "Sorry guys."

"I'm sorry too," added Caitlyn, surprising everyone.

"I think we can all agree," Teach continued, beaming with pride over the way the students handled this incident, "that things have changed and human beings, and by association, our immune systems, are under constant stress. And this pressure eventually takes its toll. The immune system breaks down and we get sick."

"I get that," said Ryan. "But why do things stress us out? What is it that makes us worry about this stuff?"

"Ya!" added Eric. "Why is it that some people freak out about things and other people don't?"

"It's largely because we're preconditioned by our unresolved emotional pain in addition to our upbringing and cultural and societal beliefs."

"I don't get that," said a rather puzzled Mike, furrowing his brow.

"Let's begin by examining emotional pain. If we're holding on to shame, grief, resentment, rage and humiliation from woundings earlier in our life… from being harshly punished by our parents, sexually abused by a family member, embarrassed by a teacher or bullied by an older child… our reaction to current experiences is going to be considerably different from someone who hasn't had the same experiences. The better we feel about ourselves, which also means the less emotional pain we are carrying with us, the less likely we are to be stressed by events in our life."

"You mean like traffic jams or money problems?" remarked Scott.

"Precisely. And, if we've been conditioned to believe a certain societal ideal, for example, that money equals power, we're bound to feel powerless, embarrassed and even shamed, when we're without money, which of course is going to cause us to worry and be stressed."

"I get that," said a smiling Mike. "Thanks."

"What about mental illness?" inquired Terry. "I don't get where the immune system fits into things like bipolar disorder and schizophrenia."

"All of our internal systems are integrated. Our immune system operates in harmony with our central nervous system, endocrine system, lymphatic system, digestive system and so on. These systems constantly interact with each other through chemicals called hormones and neurotransmitters. What is more, the same hormones and neurotransmitters, or at least complimentary versions of them, are produced in different systems. So, when the immune system is stressed, every other system in our body is stressed, and vice versa, resulting in chemical imbalances in every part of every system including the brain, which is part of the central nervous system. This leads to conditions like bipolar."

"Amazing!" exclaimed Travis.

"Yep, go figure," agreed Adam. "Crazy stuff!"

"Pardon the pun, right?" Tom stated dryly.

"Oops!"

"How does our diet affect our immune system?" Tracy asked.

"A poor diet, you might recall, also puts our immune system under stress because 80% of it is situated in the gastro-intestinal tract, so everything we ingest has a direct impact on it. If we're taking in a lot of sugar, particularly refined sugar or high fructose corn syrup, we're promoting the growth of yeast and unhealthy bacteria in our intestines, which compromises the immune system."

"So, kids get sick and parents give them pop and ice cream thinking that it's making them feel better. But it actually works against them getting healthy, doesn't it?" asked Ryan.

"It certainly does."

"What a mess!" stated Tracy.

"It seems to me that if we want to stop getting stressed," summarized Tom. "We need to heal our emotional pain, help everyone feel good about themselves and eat healthy."

"Absolutely! And I would add three other things that we have already talked about to that list."

"Would you remind us what they are?" asked Eric.

"Exercise, live in the present moment and learn about who we really are and why we're really here on the planet. In other words, become spiritually conscious."

"I can see where that would ease somebody's stress level," Tom agreed.

"That's really great," added Jessica. "But I have one more question that I'd really like an answer to."

"What's that?" John inquired.

"How do we heal our emotional pain? I just don't understand that part and that's what I really want to know."

"Yes! This gets us back to your initial question. There are a lot of ways to heal and release emotional pain. I have a simple prayer mantra that I intuited many years ago that I continue to use. I have modified it over the years and it goes like this:

> *Thank you Spirit [God I Am]for severing and dissolving the synapses and neural pathways, neutralizing the energetic frequency, healing and releasing from my body and being, all unresolved emotional energy, all fear and all faulty beliefs that need to be healed and released in connection with…whatever it is I wish to heal… and I thank you for this healing.*

"What does it do?" asked Jessica.

"It's like praying to God and asking God to heal something. Prayer has enormous healing power that has been proven since the beginning of time. I believe it also connects me with healers in the spirit realm and using the principles of quantum physics, I use thoughts…which are just energy…to create change or healing. It's all about intention."

"Wow, that's really cool!" said Jessica, grinning from ear to ear. "I wish I could do that."

"There is no reason why you can't. Just use the prayer."

"I will. I really will. I can do it, you know."

John looked at Jessica and couldn't help but smile. Her innocence and thirst for knowledge was very refreshing. He had great admiration for the entire class. Their backgrounds and home lives were extremely troubled. They had challenges at school. They felt marginalized and yet he had found a way to connect with them. He didn't judge them or consider them unreachable. He respected them, admired their intelligence and talked to them as equals. He spoke to them about things that were meaningful to them. Perhaps it was because he understood them. He could empathize with the group because he had felt marginalized much of his life. He too had felt different. John Stevens felt enormous satisfaction and gratitude at that moment.

"Is there anything else we can do to let go of emotional pain?" asked Travis.

"Yes, actually, there is. Practice forgiveness and gratitude. When we forgive, including ourselves, we let go of anger, bitterness, hatred, guilt, shame and so on. When we practice gratitude, we let go of jealousy and envy."

"Thank you, Teach!"

"Mr. Stevens," said Tom, looking very pleased.

"Yes Tom?"

"I can say with unequivocal certainty that you backed up what you said. Thank you."

"Terrific!."

As the students quietly exited the classroom their teacher couldn't help but feel befuddled and frustrated that so little was known about the importance of healing emotional pain. It is such an important part of the five essentials of health and happiness and yet we don't teach it in schools. It seemed that there was little awareness about any of the five essentials. Doctors seem to know little or nothing about it. Maybe this lack of awareness is a necessary part of our spiritual awakening. He needed to talk to the students about it.

"Do you have a minute?" asked Matt after the rest of the students had departed.

"Certainly," John replied, sitting on the edge of his desk.

"I spoke to my father about my mother's death. At first he didn't want to tell me what happened, but then he opened up." Teach sat quietly as his student continued. "He didn't want to tell me what happened because he blamed himself for her death. He admitted that he was a workaholic and had ignored my mother's depression. He said that he worked long hours so he wouldn't have to be at home. The day she took her life, she called him at work, but he refused to leave the office. He said he was too busy. When he came home that night and found her he went ballistic and he's never gotten over it."

"I can't imagine the guilt he must be feeling. What a tragic experience."

"It's been a nightmare for my dad, but I don't know how to help him."

"You've already started to. He needs to express how he's feeling, so getting him to talk about it is really important."

"He's so angry, he doesn't want to talk."

"That's understandable. The anger that he is feeling because of his unresolved grief from losing his wife, the guilt from not preventing it and the shame from running away from it all these years is probably too overwhelming for him to face."

"So, what can I do?"

"Keep talking to him. Let him express. Let him rant and yell and most importantly, let him cry."

"He's too proud to cry."

"I suspect that he wants desperately to cry. He just needs to find a way to do it. Maybe talking to you will help him find the way."

"I hope so, cause he won't talk to anyone else."

"He needs to be reminded that he was doing the best he could with what he had learned. This will help him forgive himself. And if need be, he needs to stick his face in a pillow and scream and cry until all the anger, grief, guilt and shame are gone."

"Thank you," said Matt, reaching out to shake hands. "Do you remember the first time we spoke?"

"I certainly do," replied John smiling, recalling how menacing it felt to have the big teen standing in front of his desk.

"Well, you're not a bull-shitter."

"Thank you! That might be the best compliment I have ever received," Teach beamed.

"Awesome!" Matt laughed, echoing his teacher's favourite word.

As Matt rounded the corner and headed up the street towards his aunt's place, his cellphone rang. He quickly retrieved it from his pocket and held it up to his ear. "Ya?" he said abruptly.

"Matt Hills?" asked the voice on the other end.

"Ya. Who's this?" he asked, looking at the call display, which read, *Unknown*.

"That's not important."

"It is to me, man."

"I want you to listen and listen carefully," commanded the voice. "I have a job for you to do."

"I'm doing diddly-squat until you tell who you are," the burly teen bellowed.

"If you don't want to go back to jail, I would advise you to shut-the-fuck-up and listen."

"Jail? Fuck you! Is this Blair?"

"Look, shit for brains, take this seriously, very seriously, if you know what's good for you."

It didn't sound like Blair or anyone else he knew, and suddenly he started to feel anxious. "Okay, what?" he asked after a short pause.

The caller quickly explained what he wanted done, as he listened in disbelief. "You want me to do what?" he exclaimed.

"By the end of the week!" And with those final words, the caller hung up.

Matt stood on the sidewalk, his mind racing, his head spinning and his knees ready to buckle. "This can't be real," he said out loud.

CHAPTER 19:
THE UNAPPRECIATED

There's a fossil that's trapped in a high cliff wall
There's a dead salmon frozen in a waterfall
There's a blue whale beached by a springtime's ebb
There's a butterfly trapped in a spider's web

— The Police, *King of Pain*

John was late arriving at school. He walked into the classroom to begin the day and found the students huddled around Stuart's desk. When he asked them to take their seats, they ignored him. "Would you take your seats," he repeated a little louder. Slowly the huddle broke up. As they cleared away he was shocked by the bruises and scrapes on his student's face.

"What happened?" he asked looking worriedly at the distraught teen.

"The cops beat him up," snarled Blair.

"What do you mean, the cops beat him up? Is that true?"

Stuart slowly nodded his head. It was evident that he wasn't feeling right.

"Stu was in the wrong place at the wrong time," said Mike. "And some cops beat the shit out of him."

"What they did was ridiculous," said Tracy in disgust.

"Basically he should file a lawsuit, yep" remarked Adam.

"Hold on a minute," said a bemused Teach, holding up his hand. "It would be helpful if someone told me what happened."

"Do you want me to tell him?" Blair asked, looking at his friend.

"No, it's okay man. I'll tell him."

Stuart sat silently for a few moments, looking down at the floor. He was clearly feeling very emotional. "I was walking by the bar at the plaza last night on my way home from my girlfriend's, when a bunch of cops pulled up. I guess there had been a fight. I've been in trouble with them before and they recognized me. One of them asked me what I was doing and I told him I was going home. Then he said, 'Get the fuck over here.' I hesitated cause I didn't do anything, so he screamed at me again. So I shrugged my shoulders and walked over to the police car. The cop grabbed a hold of me and threw me up against his cruiser. I turned my head and said, 'I didn't do anything,' and he punched me in the kidney. I started to struggle a little bit, so he whacked me on the side of the head with something. Then another cop grabbed me and slammed me on the pavement face first. The next thing I knew I was in the back seat of the cop car."

"My goodness!" exclaimed John, trying not to overreact.

"Then I saw the cops talking to the bar owner. He came over and looked at me and told the cops I had nothing to do with it. So one of them pulled me out of the backseat, uncuffed me and told me to get the fuck out of there."

"They didn't apologize?" asked his incredulous teacher.

Some of the students laughed. "You're kidding, right?" asked Caitlyn. "You think the cops are going to apologize?"

"I don't think it's in their code of ethics," agreed Tom. "Cops never apologize."

"They think they can do anything," added Josh. "They're the kings of pain."

"Did you say anything to them?"

"No way! I just got out of there as fast as I could."

"I'm shocked, Stuart."

"This shit happens all the time, Teach," said Eric.

"It does?"

"Of course it does," agreed Terry. "Cops are power trippers and bullies."

"Just like a lot of teachers," added Mike.

John looked at his student with a raised eyebrow.

"It's true," said Scott. "Teachers and cops are all alike. All they want to do is tell you what to do. They don't want to talk and they sure as hell don't want to listen."

"Not wanting to talk or listen is one thing, but beating up an innocent person is something totally different. It's unacceptable."

"I agree. Did you tell your parents, Stuart?"

"Naw! They were in bed when I got home and gone before I got up this morning."

"And I assume you haven't seen a doctor."

"Nope."

"It's quite possible that you have had a concussion."

"How could you tell the difference?" Josh quipped.

"I'm not sure that this is the best time for that type of humour, Josh."

"Sorry," he replied sheepishly.

"How would I know if I had a concussion?" Stuart asked.

"Were you knocked out when you hit the pavement?"

"I think so, cause I don't remember the cops putting me in the cop car."

"And did you have a headache?"

"Ya, my head was pounding when I got home. And when I got up this morning, at first I couldn't remember everything that happened yesterday."

"I'm pretty sure you've had a concussion and you need to go to the hospital to get checked out."

"Why? Isn't it too late now?"

"No, it isn't. We need to make sure there's no swelling in your skull. Blair, would you take Stuart down to the office and ask Ms. Brooks to call his parents, so he can be taken to the hospital?"

"I don't want to go to the hospital," pleaded Stuart.

"It is in your best interests. Would you please go with Blair?"

The battered teen nodded his head, trusting his teacher. Given the students' experience and mistrust with authority figures, this was an important step for Stuart... for the entire class!

After the pair had left the room, Scott raised his hand. "What can we do about this?"

"I have an idea."

Driving home from school, John Stevens was mulling over the incident with Stuart. He felt very torn. He had a great respect for police officers. They had a difficult and dangerous job. They had to regularly deal with unpleasant and dangerous people and situations… domestic disputes, disrespectful teens, hardened criminals and gangs. What is worse, quite often they receive little support or praise from the governments or communities they serve. John remembered a police officer friend of his telling him that nobody ever expressed any gratitude for the work he did. He seemed to feel enormously unappreciated.

He also remembered another officer friend telling him that the most dangerous situation for police officers is a domestic dispute. They could be confronted by angry husbands with knives and guns, and more often than not, the women who they were trying to help, would turn on them. He said that more officers were harmed during domestic disputes than any other situation. Even standing on the side of the road after pulling someone over for a traffic violation can be extremely risky. Officers are regularly exposed to horrific scenes of violence, automobile collisions and other situations that most people would find unimaginable.

But he was also troubled by the growth in *American-style* policing. This *shoot first and ask questions later* attitude that prevailed among many police officers was very alarming. He knew from talking with young people that police brutality was out of control, and for the most part, unreported. It was far more widespread than people realized. He thought about the way many officers were bulking up and weightlifting in order to look bigger and more menacing. He wondered when it all changed… when the focus of policing switched from a culture of serving and protecting to an attitude of *law enforcement*.

He recalled an incident that happened several years earlier. Walking home one night, he happened upon several boys skateboarding in a public park. They appeared to be around thirteen or fourteen years of age and they were laughing and having a lot of fun. At that moment, a police car pulled up and two burly officers jumped out and started screaming at the kids to get out of there and go home. One of the officers said, "You little shits know you're not supposed to be skateboarding here, so get home now." He swore several times. John was appalled at the officers' behaviour and he couldn't help but think that all they had accomplished was to make these boys hate the police. This experience with Stuart happened for a reason and he needed to take action.

Karen Brooks knocked on the door and opened it briskly. "Officer Baker is here," she announced. The smartly dressed officer strode confidently into the classroom and Karen closed the door quietly behind him. He was in full uniform with his tunic tucked smartly underneath his right arm. He walked over to the teacher's desk and shook John's hands.

"Thank you for coming this morning."

"It's my pleasure to be here, sir," replied the officer.

Constable Baker was the community services liaison in the area and he spent much of his time at schools speaking about police work. He had been on the force for over twenty years, but was relatively new to his current role.

John turned to address the class. "I asked Officer Baker to come here this morning to speak to you about the incident with Stuart. I briefed him beforehand on what Stuart told us and he is prepared to discuss the matter with you. Officer Baker, they're all yours."

"Before we talk about the events of the other evening, let me begin by giving you some background on me and our policing strategy. I've been a police officer for over twenty years. I began as a beat cop, worked in the detective squad and in the major crime division for several years before being assigned to community services. Our strategy is to provide community focused policing. We want to have a very visible presence in order to prevent crime, rather than having to deal with it after the fact."

"Does that involve beating up innocent people?" Blair interrupted.

"It certainly doesn't," the officer replied.

"Then why did Stuart get beat up?"

"I'm going to discuss that incident momentarily, if you will allow me to finish telling you about our policing strategy."

Blair was about to say something, but John jumped in before he could begin. "Please allow Officer Baker to finish his introduction."

Blair nodded his head.

"As I was saying," the officer continued, "we have created a strong police presence and we believe this visibility has been instrumental in reducing crime in our town. Depending on the day of the week and time of the day, we have a predetermined minimum number of officers in patrol cars, walking the beat and riding bicycles."

"What's the minimum number and how were these numbers determined?" inquired Ryan.

"That information is confidential," the officer replied.

"Why is it confidential?"

"Because criminals could use it to decide the best time to commit a crime."

"That makes sense," Ryan agreed, satisfied with the officer's response.

"And what is the purpose of this strategy?" asked Tom.

"It is simply to let people know that we are here to protect them and to let criminals know we are here to prevent them from committing crimes or catch them if they do."

"And is this strategy intended to get to know the kids?" Tom continued.

"Well, that is one of the things we hope to accomplish."

As the students peppered the officer with questions, John was reminded of a valuable lesson he learned as a young boy. There were two elderly neighbours on his street. One was a crotchety old curmudgeon who constantly yelled at the children, frequently threatening to run them off his property if they even stepped on his lawn. The other was a gentle, considerate man who always spoke kindly to them, told them stories and fixed their bikes when they needed fixing. The kids went out of their way to help the second man and did everything they could to make the first one's life even more miserable. They played nicky-nicky nine door, ran through his garden and soaped his windows at Halloween.

The lesson John learned is that people generally treat their friends well and so it was best to be friendly. He had also learned over time that you had to know your values and you had to have boundaries or people would invariably take advantage of you, but he never forgot the lesson about how people treat their friends. He realized that this approach could help both teachers and police to be more effective at their jobs.

"So why are the cops... er, police officers... always yelling at kids?" asked Mike.

"And beating them up!" added Blair.

"I don't think police officers are always yelling at kids... and beating them up," replied the officer, looking irately at his antagonist.

"Tell that to Stuart," said Josh.

"Ya!" echoed Blair. "The cops sure beat him up."

"I spoke to two of the officers who were there that night and while they are very sorry about what happened, they assured me that they did not hurt Stuart intentionally."

"That's bullshit," Stuart yelled, igniting an uproar.

John held up his hands and asked the students to let the officer continue, although he didn't think his statement that Stuart wasn't hurt intentionally was the appropriate thing to say.

After a few moments the students quieted down, allowing the officer to go on.

"The officers said that Stuart was being belligerent and that he took a swing at one of them."

Again, everyone started shouting at once. "I'll take a friggin lie detector test," Stuart yelled.

"You cops are all liars," added Blair.

Again, their frustrated teacher held up both arms and asked for order. "Regardless of who's right and who's wrong, or who is telling the truth, we're not going to accomplish anything by yelling at Officer Baker."

"But Mr. Stevens," pleaded Tom, frowning, "surely you don't believe what he is saying."

"I am not in a position at the moment to determine who is telling the truth. I... we... don't have all the facts and we haven't heard directly from the officers involved in this incident. The reason I invited Officer Baker to come and speak to us today, is so that we can begin to heal the rift between the police and the young people of this town."

"But surely that has to begin with the truth," replied Tom.

"Absolutely! But this is not a trial."

"Police officers have a very difficult job," the officer interjected. "We never know when our lives might be in danger. In certain situations we may react in a specific way if we are uncertain of the danger or if we feel our lives might be threatened."

"Look at Stuart," interrupted Josh. "Does he look like a threat?"

"I'm not referring to your classmate or this specific incident."

"It sure doesn't look like we're gonna to get a straight answer," added Travis.

"That's for sure," added Jessica. "My father always said cops are just a bunch of bullies."

"That's the first intelligent thing you've said all year!" chimed in Blair.

"Shut up!" Jessica snapped.

"Perhaps this would be a good time to move on," said John, shaking his head at this inappropriate exchange. "Does anyone have any questions for Officer Baker?"

"How long were you in the major crime division?" Ryan inquired.

"Seven years!"

"You must have seen a lot of bad stuff during that time."

"Yes, I did."

"And you must have had to deal with a lot of bad asses."

"Yes, I did," the officer replied looking somewhat puzzled.

"It couldn't have been easy doing that every day."

"No, it wasn't."

"It always intrigues me when I watch cop shows on television and I see these guys pretending to be bad asses, acting all tough, and then after a little interrogation they wimp out and tell the police everything."

"That's not uncommon. The police have years of experience in interrogating suspects and gaining confessions that are invaluable in securing convictions in court."

"Did you have to do a lot of interrogating?" asked Matt, joining in on the exchange.

"Yes, I did," replied the officer.

"And how did you feel after you got finished torturing these people?" he continued calmly.

"I didn't say we tortured anybody!" responded the officer.

"I know," replied Matt. "I said it."

"I don't think I need to answer that question," Officer Baker stammered.

"Why not?" asked Tracy.

"It's not related to the purpose of my visit."

"Yes it is," countered Ryan.

"The police culture had a lot to do with what happened to Stuart," added Tom.

"Let's face it," said Caitlyn, she too jumping into the conversation, "It seems that any cop with a short dick and lack of self-esteem has license to treat people any way they please."

"That's not the way it works," said the officer, now on the defensive.

"Really?" Caitlyn asked.

John sensed that the officer felt trapped, that the students had cleverly backed him into a corner and he had no choice but to answer their questions.

The rattled officer paused for a moment before continuing. "You have to understand, police work is very difficult. We have to deal with some terrible situations and we see unspeakable things happen to good people every day. We have to deal with some of the worst people you can imagine, people who don't care about anything, who don't care about you or me or who they hurt. We get lied to, and sometimes we have to use aggressive tactics in order to secure information, gain confessions and ensure convictions."

"And so, how do you feel after you torture someone?" Matt repeated.

"I've never tortured anyone," responded the officer.

"Well you must have beaten the shit out of a few suspects," scoffed Travis. "How did it make you feel?"

"I felt like I was doing what I had to do, in order to protect our community." Several students gasped at the officer's unexpected admission.

"Let's back the film up for a second," said Tom. "The *suspects*," he said, "as you describe them, came into this world as innocent little babies, and then they were exposed to a lot of suffering, a lot of heartache. Perhaps they didn't have a father or perhaps their parents beat their innocence out of them."

John watched as the officer's expression softened. He felt his energy crash. He saw anguish in his eyes.

"Maybe," Tom continued, "they were teased or bullied mercilessly at school and responded in a way they thought was necessary to survive. They became hardened and tough. Perhaps they lived in a culture where they believed they had no choice but to turn to crime in order to live. Maybe they were poor and felt like outcasts living on the edge of society, disenfranchised. Perhaps they tried hard and wanted to be a good person, but everything was stacked up against them. Now how do you feel about what you did?"

"I thought I was doing what was right."

"The only way you could have done what you did and thought it was okay, was by completely shutting down your sense of compassion," said Scott. "There is no way anybody can hurt another human being and feel good about it. No matter the circumstances. It's impossible!"

John smiled at his student's insightful statement about how we can't feel good about ourselves when we hurt another being. Clearly he had taken to heart the things they had been discussing in class.

Officer Baker slowly hung his head towards the floor. The students had touched a nerve and he was immersed in guilt. He brought his right hand up to his face and wiped away tears.

Jessica got out of her seat and approached him cautiously. She held out a tissue and the officer took it from her. Slowly, he wiped his eyes. Jessica gave him a hug.

Then Ryan walked up and put a hand on his shoulder. "It's okay, man," he comforted.

John Stevens couldn't believe what he was witnessing.

The students were dumbfounded. Here was this hardened police veteran standing before them… a group that quite frankly felt like misfits on society's fringe… and they had driven him to tears.

"Thank you," he whispered.

They both returned to their seats as the officer took a few moments to compose himself. "This isn't easy. We never start out meaning to do any harm. We begin with honourable intentions. But then things happen. We see vicious criminals getting off with light sentences or perhaps no sentence at all. This happens all the time because a lot of judges dislike the police."

"That sounds like bullshit," scoffed Eric.

"You think so. Many judges used to be defense attorneys. They've gone up against the police their entire careers. They've tried to discredit us, humiliate us and make us out to be liars. It's not easy to turn that switch off when they become judges."

"I never thought of it like that before," Eric admitted. "I can see how you would become cynical and perhaps take the law into your own hands. And I guess I can't really blame you."

"We also get caught up in all kinds of bureaucratic nonsense. We feel unappreciated by the politicians and public we serve. We walk in constant awareness of the possibility of what could happen the next time we approach a car, bust down a door or answer a call to a domestic dispute. And so we create this protective barrier for ourselves."

"I suppose the black uniforms and bullet proof vests you wear and the cars you drive in are representative of that," noted Caitlyn, who was still not empathizing with the officer.

Maybe that's when it all changed John thought. Perhaps this American-style policing attitude started when officers donned black uniforms and vests. It created this symbolic barrier between police and the public.

"I suppose that is true," the officer acknowledged. "We don't always feel good about what we do."

"It can't feel good to feel unappreciated," noted Tracy.

"It certainly doesn't." Officer Baker looked completely dejected.

It suddenly occurred to John that perhaps part of the reason for this attitude that seemed to be causing the police to distance themselves from the people they serve is a form of protection. Unlike firefighters and paramedics who are greatly admired and appreciated, police officers are largely feared and even hated. They feel unappreciated and unwanted and these feelings mirror the feelings many of them experieenced growing up due to dysfunctional relationships with their parents. This in turn triggers the resentment, anger and hatred they are holding in their hearts. Because these feelings are so painful… the feeling of being rejected by a parent is unbearable… we don't want to feel them, so we shut down… we stop feeling them. And when we stop feeling, we are able to do things like yell at children and brutalize teenagers.

This was an important epiphany, but before he could say anything, Eric jumped in with another question. "So what's your story?" he asked, abruptly.

"Pardon?" Officer Baker replied, still reeling.

"How did you end up working in community relations?"

The officer stood silently for several moments. His hands were visibly shaking. "I've never spoken to anyone outside of policing about this before," he began, his voice trembling. "That's part of the problem with the police culture. We rarely talk about our experiences, particularly the traumatic ones."

"Macho bullshit," Caitlyn remarked.

The officer looked at her for a few seconds, then nodded his head in agreement. "I was involved in a hostage taking incident during the last year I worked in major crime. I was the hostage negotiator for our unit and it was the first time I had to do it. A distraught father had kidnapped his five year old daughter after losing a custody battle with his ex-wife. When two police officers went to his house as part of the search for the child, he met them at the door holding a knife to his daughter's throat."

A couple of the student's gasped. "That's horrible," exclaimed Tracy.

"It was a really bad scene. My unit was called in as part of the rescue operation and I did the negotiating. I was on the phone with him for many hours and he assured me numerous times that he hadn't harmed the girl and that he had no guns in the house. I believed him and when the Superintendent who was in charge of the scene asked me if I thought it was safe for the tactical unit to rescue the child, I said yes. I also told him I didn't believe he would harm his daughter, because I had assured him that if he surrendered peacefully, at the very least he would have visitation rights to see her and he seemed to believe me. Then the police brass got impatient, so they ordered the tactical unit to storm the house."

"Yep. Basically, the idiots in charge always mess things up," said Adam.

"And they couldn't have been more wrong in this case. When the tactical unit broke down the front door and charged into the house, the father started shooting at them, and while trying to back out of the house they instinctively returned fire."

"Oh my God," exclaimed Jessica.

"What happened?" asked Tracy, tears streaming down her face.

"Two police officers were wounded and so was the father."

"What happened to the little girl?" Tracy screamed.

The officer began crying. "She was killed! And it was my fault!"

Tracy too, burst into tears.

"I remember that!" exclaimed Josh.

"Me too!" said Ryan, shaking his head sadly in disbelief. "I saw it on the news."

As the officer stood before them, head hung, weeping, Caitlyn stunned the entire class by walking up to him and holding him in a compassionate embrace, her head resting gently on his chest. "It's okay. You're safe here," she whispered.

John was blown away, completely taken by surprise at her immensely caring gesture. He would never have imagined she was capable of it and he was deeply moved.

The entire class sat in silence as the officer wept openly.

Finally, after several minutes, Officer Baker lifted his head and Caitlyn stepped back, still holding both of his hands.

"I'm sorry," he said to the class.

"You don't have to be sorry," replied Travis.

"How did the little girl die," Caitlyn asked softly, looking directly into his eyes.

"It was determined that she was killed by the father. Unfortunately, he had a history of mental illness."

"That's so sad," she said, stepping away from the officer and quietly returning to her seat.

Teach was having a hard time grasping what had just taken place. When he invited the police to come and speak with the students he certainly hadn't imagined anything like this and as he looked around the room, he could see that the entire class was shaken. He felt that this was going to result in enormous healing for everyone; far more than he had envisioned.

"Why do you think it was your fault?" asked Josh quietly.

"I thought I could trust him. I was certain he didn't have a gun and I was even more certain he wouldn't harm his daughter."

"How could you possibly have known that he had a gun?"
"As a street cop, I relied on my instincts and I trusted them."
"I don't know," countered Terry. "That seems like a lot to ask of yourself."
"I guess it is."
"Did you know he was mentally ill?" asked Jordan.
"Yes! We did! And we certainly took this into consideration. But I still thought I could trust him."
"Sometimes," John said, "we will have experiences that are meant to test us in a certain way, like test our beliefs and our trust. And not just our trust in life, more so our trust in ourselves."
"If that's true," asked Mike, "why couldn't it have been something less horrific than killing a little kid?"
"Sometimes, the experiences must happen in the extreme… to really test us. If it was something easy, we might not get the lesson."
"I guess that makes sense."
"And do you still trust yourself?" asked Caitlyn, being very direct.
"No, I don't," admitted the officer. "That's why I'm in community services."
"There's something here I don't understand," said Tom. "Wasn't it the police brass who made the decision to storm the house?"
"Yes, it was. But that decision was in part based on my belief that he didn't have a gun and wouldn't hurt his child."
"But the police brass had the same information you did, correct?"
"Yes they did."
"It seems to me that they're letting you take the fall for this."
"Ya! Tom's right!" agreed Mike.
"I agree," added Ryan.
"I think we all agree," observed Terry.
Officer Baker stood silently for a few moments before speaking. "My wife said the same thing and I told her she was wrong and that I never wanted to discuss it again. Perhaps now I can talk to her about it."
"That's awesome," beamed Jessica. "Talking is the best thing!"
"You also need to acknowledge that you are experiencing PTSD," suggested Jordan.

"Yes! Post-traumatic-stress-disorder is becoming more recognized as a condition that needs to be addressed among emergency and police service workers."

"You know," said Caitlyn, "Teach has been telling us something that might help you get over this experience."

"What is that?" the officer asked.

"No matter what it might look like, we're all doing the best we can in each moment of our lives with what we've learned. And that applies to you, your superiors and even the little girl's father. Knowing this helps us to forgive, and in this case, a lot of forgiveness is needed."

"And something else Mr. Stevens has taught us," added Tracy, "is that when we truly understand what life is all about, we understand that there are no victims and that no one is to blame for anything, because we are all co-creators of our experiences."

"We are all part of the flow of life," observed Jordan.

"That understanding would help a lot of people," agreed Baker. "And I guess it also applies to how police interact with teenagers and people we perceive to be criminals. It doesn't serve anybody if we continue to have an attitude of distrust."

"It goes for us too," added Terry. "Both sides tend to look at each other as the enemy. There's no empathy and no attempt to understand the other. We each think we're right and the other is wrong. As long as we maintain these attitudes, nothing will change."

This was an incredibly transformational moment for the class and John couldn't have been prouder. As he listened to the exchange between the students and the beleaguered officer, he realized that they had reached a pivotal turning point in their understanding of life. It seemed that they were ready to step out of their victim roles and let go of their anger, and in that instant, he knew they were going to be okay.

"The bell is going to ring any second and this seems like an appropriate time to wrap up the discussion. I would like to thank Officer Baker for coming in to speak with us today and I would like to thank all of you for being part of such an amazing session."

"This was awesome, Teach," said Ryan.

"It certainly was," agreed Scott.

"There is one other thing I would like to do before I go," said the officer, as he walked over to Stuart's desk. "Stuart, if you can find it in your heart to forgive us, I would like to offer my apologies to you for the treatment you received the other night and I give you my word that I will be speaking to my colleagues about it."

Officer Baker held out his hand. Stuart stood up, shook his hand and simply said thank you.

At that moment, the bell rang and on the way out of class each of the students offered their thanks and best wishes.

After they had left, the officer turned to John. "I don't know what to say."

"You don't have to say anything."

"I feel so much better, like an enormous weight has been lifted from me."

"Then that truly is awesome."

"How would you like to come to our detachment and speak to our officers about the same things you are teaching your students? We would really benefit from it."

"I would love to."

"Terrific. I will call you to schedule a date."

Matt removed his knapsack with a slight shrug of his shoulders and tossed it lightly on his bed. He liked living at his aunt's place. It was peaceful and orderly, something he had missed after his mom died. His aunt was cheerful and quick-witted and she kept him on his toes. She was also a no-nonsense type of person. She had clearly defined values ... like integrity ... and she didn't stray from them. He admired her.

As he prepared to head downstairs to watch television, his phone rang. Before hitting the green *Call* button, he checked the call display. *Unknown Caller* again.

"Ya?" he said.

"Why haven't you done as you were instructed?" asked the caller.

"*Fuck you!*" he replied, recognizing the voice.

"Pardon?"

"You heard me."

Fred Phillips

"I would advise you to do as you were told."
"Up yours!"
The line went dead.

CHAPTER 20:
ESCALATION

A couple of the sounds that I really like
Are the sound of a switchblade and a motorbike
I'm a juvenile product of the working class
Whose best friend floats in the bottom of a glass

— Elton John, *Saturday Night's All Right for Fighting*

John was home alone, enjoying a quiet Saturday evening. He felt like he was finally coming to terms with Sandra's departure and was ready to move on with his life. It hadn't been an easy time. He was very fond of her and certainly hadn't been expecting anything like this.

He was quietly scanning the menu on the TV screen when the phone rang. Reaching over and picking it up, he was greeted by a barrage of indistinguishable noise. It sounded as though someone was calling from a party. "*Hello!*" he said, thinking perhaps he was about to be invited out for the evening.

The panic in the voice that responded on the other end took him by surprise. It was female. At first he couldn't make out what she was saying, and then he heard, "hurt really badly." Next he heard, "blood all over the place." Then the line went dead.

He stood up and began pacing. He had no idea who was calling. It wasn't long distance so he reasoned that it wasn't Sandra or his kids, but he didn't recognize the voice or the number on the call display. He was about to call back when the phone rang again.

"Sorry Mr. Stevens, it's Tracy." She was crying and very upset.

"What's the matter?"

"Matt's been hurt. A couple of guys jumped him and one of them smashed a bottle across his face. We're at the hospital now."

"My goodness! Is he okay?"

"We don't know. He's in the ER and they won't let us in. Mr. Stevens, can you come down here quickly? Some of the guys are really angry and they want to get payback."

"I'll be right there."

When John Stevens walked into the hospital, he was immediately surrounded by a throng of angry students. They were all talking at once and he couldn't understand a word they were saying.

"Hold on a second," he pleaded. "Can someone first tell me how Matt is doing?"

"We still don't know," replied Tracy.

"They won't tell us what the *f* is going on," added Mike.

"Tell that kid to watch his mouth," snarled a security guard standing nearby.

"Mike, you can't talk like that in here!"

"I don't give a shi…" Tracy covered his mouth before he could finish the word.

"Don't touch me," Mike scowled, looking her directly in the eye.

"I'm telling you sir, that boy's gonna get himself locked up if he keeps it up," snapped the guard.

"Do you need me to call more security, Tim?" asked the admitting nurse.

"Please don't," John interrupted before the guard could respond. "Give me some time to talk to them. You don't know what these kids have been through."

"I don't care what they've been through, this is a hospital and they need to behave."

John quickly took charge of the situation. "I need everyone to come with me," he commanded. "Immediately!"

It was a calculated risk. These kids had experienced issues with authority all their lives. They didn't like being told what to do. They stood for several moments looking at him, not budging.

"If you want to do what's best for Matt, please come outside with me." Without giving them a chance to respond, he turned and walked out the front door of the ER. He was relieved when the students, led by Tracy, reluctantly followed.

"Why do we have to come out here?" demanded Blair.

"Because we're gonna get locked up if we cause trouble in there," replied Tom, pointing towards the hospital.

"I don't give a shit," said Eric.

"Well you need to."

"You think I care if I get locked up," snapped Blair.

"How will that help Matt?" asked Ryan.

"Screw them all."

"A lot of us are really angry," said Tom. "Matt gets whacked across the face and they're treating him like a criminal."

"Us too," added Ryan.

"What?" asked their incredulous teacher.

"Ya," said Mike. "It's like they think he deserved it."

"Have they been mistreating him?"

"They certainly weren't very gentle with him," replied Tom.

"Has his father been notified?" John said evenly, hoping to calm the students.

"No, Matt didn't want him to know."

"Well, I guess that's understandable. Is anybody with him?"

"No, he's by himself," replied Stuart. "They wouldn't let anybody go with him."

"Would everyone be okay out here if I went in to find out about his condition?"

"I don't know," Tracy replied, looking genuinely concerned. "The guys are really angry."

"Look everyone," he commanded. "What Matt needs most right now, is our support. He has worked hard to turn his life around and as you've seen in class, he has a very promising future ahead of him. He would be very upset if he found out that you went out and did exactly what he was trying to stop. I think he would want you to show some restraint and focus on trying to find a peaceful solution to this matter. I know you don't want to get the police involved because you've had some bad experiences with them, but I was hoping we could change that after our session with Officer Baker. I need to go inside the hospital and check on him, but I need to know you're going to be okay until I get back."

The students were all standing quietly at this point, and surprisingly, Blair was the first to speak. "We'll be okay. You go do what you need to do. We won't let Matt down."

"Thank you," John answered, feeling somewhat relieved.

Tom put his arm around Blair's shoulder. "You're coming around, Blair," he said.

"Matt's a good guy."

As he turned to head into the hospital, a nurse who had been watching the exchange motioned him to the door. "I am guessing you are Mr. Stevens," she said as he approached her.

"Yes," he replied.

"The young man who your students are so concerned about would like to speak with you," she continued, leading him into the hospital.

"Is he okay?"

"He's got a nasty gash on his forehead, which took several stitches to close, but otherwise he seems fine. There's no sign of a concussion."

"That's good."

As they walked by the admitting desk, the security guard who had snapped at the students earlier, scowled at him.

"I'm Marnie Rowe," she added. "You're very good with these kids. I'm glad you came. We were getting quite worried."

"I'm pleased to meet you Miss Rowe and glad to be able to help" he said, looking away from the guard and returning his attention to the matter at hand.

"Please, call me Marnie."

"Is that guard always so angry… Marnie?"

"He's not the friendliest one we've had."

"Too bad. I guess it's not an easy job."

"Situations like this can make it challenging, but an easygoing manner can be helpful in calming people down. This guy doesn't seem to understand that concept."

As they walked down a hallway lined on each side with admitting rooms it was noticeably quiet in the ER.

"The rooms are empty," he remarked.

"We've been blessed with a quiet night," she agreed guiding him through the fourth door on the right. "And we never complain about that."

Matt was lying on his back facing the door. His forehead was swathed in bandages and he smiled faintly when they entered the room.

"How are you doing?" his teacher asked softly.

"I've had better nights."

"I bet you have."

"How are the guys doing?"

"They're doing okay at the moment, but they're quite angry and very concerned about you."

"You can tell them I'm okay."

"You'll be able to tell them yourself!" said Marnie. "The doctor says you're free to go."

"He is? That was quick."

"The benefits of a quiet Friday night."

"The doc was in a few minutes ago," said Matt. "He said the x-rays were good and I don't have a concussion. I'm feeling okay right now."

"You might feel some pain when the freezing wears off," remarked the nurse, "so make sure you've got painkillers handy."

"I will."

"I'll grab a wheelchair for you," she said.

"I don't need a wheelchair," assured the wounded warrior.

"Hospital policy. You don't have a choice young man."

"Fine."

"What happened?" John inquired, as she left to retrieve a wheelchair.

"Two kids were arguing, looking like they were about to get into a fight and I tried to break it up. Two of the kid's buddies jumped me and one of them smashed a beer bottle across my face." Matt figured it must have something to do with phone calls, but he wasn't absolutely certain, and either way, he didn't want to say anything to his teacher.

John felt sick to his stomach at the thought.

"After the kid bottled me, the other one kicked me and then they took off."

"Were the police called?"

"Nope. Everyone beat it."

"I can't tell you what to do, but I think it would be best to notify them."

"Why? I know how this works. The cops will take one look at me and say that I got what I deserved. They won't give a shit." Matt didn't want the police nosing around asking questions until he knew what was going on.

"We have to give them a chance. Were there witnesses?"

"None of my friends were there when it happened. They were in another room. It'll be my word against theirs."

"That may be true, but they assaulted you with a weapon. I would ask you to at least consider calling the police."

"Maybe."

"Otherwise, the other students are going to want to take matters into their own hands."

"This is not their business."

"I think they plan to make it their business."

"We'll see."

"The other kids were also concerned about the way they were treating you in here."

"Ya, at first they were kind of rough, but when I explained what happened, they lightened up. Nurse Marnie was really good."

Just then, she returned with a wheelchair. The big teen sat up and swung his legs over the side of the bed, then she and Teach each grabbed an arm and helped him to his feet. "Really," he said, "I'm fine."

"Just making certain," she assured him.

As he plunked himself in the chair, Nurse Marnie grabbed the rear handles and gently guided him out into the hallway. As they made their way to the front door, John noticed for the first time that she was quite attractive. She appeared to be in her mid to late forties and had a nice figure.

"Your friends are going to be happy to see you!" she said.

He was struck by her friendliness. "Are you always this happy?"

"No point in being unhappy, it's not good for your health," she smiled.

"You can say that again," he heartily agreed, returning the smile.

Making their way through the front door, they were quickly surrounded by the other students.

"You alright Matt?" asked Mike.

"Ya, I'm good."

"Why are you in a wheelchair then," asked Jessica. "You must be hurt badly if you're in a wheelchair."

"Hospital policy," he said, looking up at his nurse.

"Oh. Well that's a relief. We thought you couldn't walk," she said, breaking the tension with a much needed round of laughter.

"What?" she asked innocently.

"Look," Matt said, addressing the guys after everyone had quieted down. "I don't want anybody going after the guys that did this to me. I need some time to think about what I want to do."

"I really wish you'd call the police," pleaded Tracy.

"Ya, Matt," added Blair. "They shouldn't get away with this."

"Maybe this is my punishment for some of the things I've done," he said, trying to put everyone off for now.

John thought that perhaps his reluctance to call the police was borne of guilt for things he had done in his life. "Let's honour Matt's wishes and give him time to think about this. It's been a challenging night, so why don't we all head for home and let things cool down."

"Okay," agreed Blair, suddenly acting as spokesman for the group. "We'll let it go for now."

"Thank you," Matt said, clasping hands and bumping shoulders with his classmate.

Tom looked at Blair with a puzzled expression. "Now I really believe you've turned a corner."

Their teacher was equally dumbfounded, but smiled nevertheless. "Does anyone need a ride?"

Driving home, after dropping Matt off at his aunt's, John couldn't help but wonder about his misfortune. It was the first time he had been out with his classmates and this happens. On the surface, it seemed very unfair, given everything he's been through. But he also knew that sometimes, this is how karmic debt gets repaid. Unfortunate things happen to the people who least deserve it, and quite often, when they're doing something good.

He felt very strongly that his gifted student had karmic debt to clear, perhaps from things he had done in this lifetime and likely from experiences in other lifetimes. If only we would stop creating karmic debt for ourselves. Each time we mistreat someone or something, each time we do something with ill intent, we just create more of it. Awareness is the first step in putting an end to it. People just don't realize that their actions create a *karmic* energy and we have a choice between creating positive or negative energy for ourselves.

Pulling into his parking spot behind Sammy Wong's, he vowed to do what he could to bring awareness to this notion. It is too important to ignore.

CHAPTER 21:
KARMIC DEBT

What in the world you thinking of
Laughing in the face of love
What on earth you tryin' to do
It's up to you, yeah you.

— John Lennon, *Instant Karma*

On Monday morning, the class was still abuzz over the assault on Matt. They were talking about it with immense concern as they entered the classroom.

John waited until they took their seats. "How is everybody feeling this morning?"

"We're still pretty pissed," said Ryan.

"You got that right," added Blair, with renewed anger.

"At the risk of asking the obvious, what are you pissed about?"

"We should have beat the shit out of those guys," exclaimed Stuart.

"And what would that have accomplished?" asked Caitlyn.

"They shouldn't get away with what they did," said Scott. "Matt's a good guy."

"Of course they shouldn't get away with it, but beating people up isn't the solution."

"Then what would you do?" asked Eric.

"Caitlyn's right," interjected Terry. "You don't end violence with more violence."

"What are you talking about?" asked Stuart. "Even Nelson Mandela realized that they couldn't end apartheid in South Africa using peaceful tactics."

"That was different. What Mandela was trying to do, was end oppression. What you're talking about is revenge. And Mandela didn't want to hurt people. In fact, after he got out of jail he encouraged reconciliation."

"This is stupid," said Blair, not really talking to anyone in particular.

"Basically, it's crazy," said Adam. "My dad said that when he was our age, guys used to fight one on one."

"That's true," John acknowledged. "It was very unusual to see two on one, three on one, or six on one fights. There was no swarming. Weapons were pretty much unheard of and nobody ever got bottled."

"You gotta keep your head up when you're out," said Jordan. "There's always somebody looking to cause trouble."

"So many kids want to fight," remarked Jessica. "Even girls, man. People think they're so tough. They should just stop it."

"Why do you think this is happening?" asked Josh. "Why are things getting so bad?"

"There are a couple of factors. First, kids… boys especially… are not allowed to express themselves, particularly when it comes to sadness and anger. They have many wounded children inside themselves; an accumulation of all the emotional woundings they've experienced. Then they grow up to become teenagers and they're holding on to all this unexpressed emotion. The next thing you know, they're out at a bar or a party, they've had a few drinks, somebody says something and it triggers all that emotional energy, so the fists start flying."

"I guess a lot of people don't feel good about themselves," remarked Ryan. "They feel unlovable and powerless."

"That's a big part of it too. In addition to all this unexpressed emotion, we have a society that individually and collectively doesn't feel good about itself. Unfortunately, we enact these feelings of self loathing on others."

"It discourages kids from wanting to go to parties," observed Tom. "There is far too much fighting."

Just then, the door swung open and Matt walked in. His forehead was still bandaged and his right eye was a ghastly black and blue. He actually looked worse than he did Friday night and a few of the students gasped at the sight of him.

Their embattled classmate quietly took his seat.

"How are you doing?" John inquired.

"Not too bad. It looks way worse than it feels."

"That's for sure," said Jessica. "It looks really bad. Are you sure you're okay?"

"Ya... I'm fine."

This was one of the few times none of the students corrected Jessica for her bluntness. She was saying what the others were clearly thinking.

"That's good," added Josh, "cause I gotta tell you, Matt, you look like you've been to war."

"That's sometimes what it feels like going out to parties," remarked Ryan. "It feels like we're at war. Most of us just want to have fun, but a lot of guys want to cause trouble."

"Actually, it feels like the entire planet is at war right now," observed Tom. "It's like good versus evil. Government vs. the people. Police vs. teenagers. Religion vs. atheism. Communism vs. democracy. Terrorism vs. Westernism. Wealth vs. poverty."

"Ya, it's like my side is right and yours is wrong, so pow!" echoed Jordan.

"Many people believe this conflict is the result of the immense fear that is pervading the planet as we transition into the next stage of our evolution."

"What do you mean by that?" inquired Travis.

"There is a belief that holds a lot of merit, that we're entering a stage of spiritual awakening where we will live with love, compassion and acceptance and a better understanding of who we really are, because if we don't change the way we live, we will soon get to the point where the planet will no longer sustain life."

"Can you visualize this planet with no life on it?" asked Tom.

"That sounds pretty scary," admitted Eric.

"It is scary and it has a lot to do with why there has been such an escalation in violence. It's like this is what we need in order to get everyone's attention."

"You mean things have to get worse before people will want to change?" asked Mike.

"That seems to be the way it is in our society. People as a rule are complacent. They won't act unless they're directly affected by something. A little bit of minor violence affects only a few, so people do nothing. A lot of serious violence affects the whole and so people take action."

"That makes sense," agreed Travis.

"If we're evolving into a better way of living, why is there so much fear?" asked Jordan. "You would think we would welcome this."

"Any change creates fear. Change leads us into the unknown and humans seem to have an inherent fear of what they don't know. If we trusted, we wouldn't have this fear."

"Yep, if we knew who we really are and why we're really here on the planet, we would trust wouldn't we?" asked Adam.

"I believe we would indeed. We would have no reason to fear."

"It seems silly to be afraid of a better life," observed Eric.

"Yes, it seems silly, but there is no rationale to fear."

"Maybe it's because we can sense that change is coming, but we don't know it is change for the better," observed Tracy.

"That's a very good point! And there is one other thing we need to do before each of us can achieve this state of bliss. We need to clear our karmic debt."

"You said that a few days ago?" said Mike, looking very puzzled. "What does it mean?"

"I saw Shirley MacLaine being interviewed a few weeks ago," said Tracy. "She said, 'when are we going to stop going to war, cause we're not really killing each other, we're just creating more negative karma for ourselves.'"

"Who's Shirley MacLaine?" asked Mike.

"She's an actress and she's written a lot of books, including one about reincarnation. What did she mean when she said we're not really killing each other, just creating more karma?"

"I believe what she meant is that we are spiritual beings that exist in perpetuity, coming into human form whenever we are ready for more spiritual growth and when we achieve what we need to achieve, we return to spiritual form."

"So, we never really stop existing… we just change form," Ryan commented.

"Yes, I believe that's how it works."

"And when we do bad… I mean, inappropriate things, like killing… do we create karmic debt?" asked Terry.

"I believe we do."

"So if we went after the guys who attacked Matt, would we be creating karmic debt for ourselves?

"Absolutely! Anytime you mistreat another being, you create it."

"Even when you're seeking retribution?" asked Tom.

"Beating up Matt's attackers would be more a case of revenge than justice, I'm afraid."

"There won't be any retribution on our part!" interjected Matt, looking around at his classmates. "The cops came to my place on the weekend to interview me cause somebody called them to report the incident. Then one of the cops called me last night to tell me that they're pretty sure these kids are from out of town."

"So what are they doing about it?" asked Jordan.

"There's not much they can do. Nobody knew them and nobody got a license plate."

"That sucks!" remarked Stuart.

"That's for sure!" agreed Blair.

"Shit happens!" Matt replied.

"So, if we don't resolve our karmic debt in this lifetime, we come back in another lifetime to clear it?" asked Josh, getting back to the discussion.

"Again, I believe that is how it works."

"I don't get it," said Mike. "Why does it work like this?"

"And why aren't we taught this in school?" asked Tracy. "It seems like it would be important for people to know about it."

"It's because people don't know, or don't want to reveal, the truth," remarked Matt.

"But why?" asked Jordan. "Why wouldn't people want to know this?"

"To answer your question," John offered, "let's go back to the fear aspect of this forthcoming change in the human experience. What specifically do you think people might be afraid of?"

"This change will likely alter the power structure," observed Caitlyn.

"Basically, what do you mean?" asked Adam.

"In order for us to achieve a better way of living a lot of things have to happen and these things are going to reduce or eliminate the dominance and wealth of a lot of very powerful people, corporations and governments."

"You hit the nail squarely on the head," her teacher praised. "A better way of living means better for everyone and this isn't possible when there is such a wide and growing gap between the very powerful haves and the increasingly powerless have nots. There has to be balance and harmony. People must have money which means they need jobs…everyone! The haves must give something up in order to create this balance and right now, they're afraid to do that."

"What about these rich and powerful corporations?" asked Terry. "They have to change as well."

"Especially drug and biotech companies," added Travis.

"That's right. In order to have joyful living, we need to have good health, but this isn't possible when people are poisoning themselves with toxic medications produced by incredibly powerful drug companies, and stuffing themselves with genetically modified, processed foods that are sprayed with chemicals that are produced by very powerful factory farms and food processing and chemical manufacturing companies. These companies are going to fight like hell to maintain the status quo."

"We also need to eliminate all the conflict on the planet," remarked Travis.

"We certainly do. We must have peace, but this isn't possible when we have huge war machines, run by very powerful people in very powerful governments."

"I went to the demilitarized zone between North and South Korea a few years ago," remarked Tracy. "I couldn't believe the amount of money and resources that are being spent by both countries in order to protect themselves from one another. It was very sad."

"I recently read about a family that was separated during the Korean conflict," added Ryan. "Part of the family was kept in the north while the rest escaped to the south. They've never been able to reunite."

"That's ridiculous," exclaimed Mike. "How can that happen?"

"When you're motivated by fear, anything can happen," observed Caitlyn.

"We want freedom, but it's not possible when we have dictatorships such as those in Syria, Iran, North Korea and China, and oppressive laws, even within democratic countries."

"Oppressive laws is right," agreed Tom. "Some of the laws that exist in this country are appalling. They seem to totally lack common sense."

"Ya, it's dumb," agreed Stuart. "We have all these laws that people have to abide by, but then we allow corporations to pollute."

"Yes! In order to have a better life, we must have clean air to breath and water to drink and this isn't possible when we have a very rich and powerful petroleum industry and very powerful corporations producing enormous amounts of pollution."

"How do we change all this?" asked Ryan. "It seems like an impossible task."

"You're right, it does seem rather daunting, but remember, anything is possible."

"I'm with Ryan," agreed Jordan. "I really don't see how we're going to radically change the way we live."

Just then the bell rang.

"We'll have to get to this tomorrow," replied John, as the students closed their books and bolted for the door. "In the meantime, have an awesome day."

Terry stopped in front of his teacher's desk. His expression conveyed enormous concern. "I can't imagine the negative karma we're going to create for ourselves if we destroy this planet," he said sadly. "We'll carry that burden around with us for lifetimes." Without waiting for a response, he wheeled and strolled out of the classroom.

John Stevens sat there for a moment considering this disturbing proclamation. It was incredibly profound. *We simply can't let that happen!*

Matt's phone rang for the fifth time and after mulling it over it for a few moments he decided to pick it up. "What the fuck do you want?" he bellowed.

"Apparently, you haven't learned your lesson," said a calm voice on the other end.

"Do you think you can cause me more pain than I've already experienced in my life?"

"I don't think you understand the meaning of pain, young man. You have until the end of the week to do as I instructed."

Before he could reply, the line went dead. In frustration, he slammed his phone down on the bed. "You chicken bastard!"

CHAPTER 22:
NO TRESPASSING

And the sign said anybody caught trespassin'
Would be shot on sight
So I jumped on the fence and I yelled at the house,
"Hey! What gives you the right?"

— Five Man Electrical Band, *Signs*

Before John could begin, Josh eagerly raised his hand to ask a question. "Yes Josh?"

"Yesterday, you said that part of the reason the level of violence is escalating in our society, particular with teenagers, is because we've got wounded children inside us. Would you remind us what this means?"

"When a child has an experience, such as being rejected, scolded, spanked or bullied, he or she experiences one or more negative emotions, like sadness, shame, grief, anger and fear. There is an emotional wounding. If that wounding isn't resolved, if the child doesn't express those emotions in a constructive way, including forgiving, he or she holds onto the emotions, and as a result, ends up with a *wounded child* inside themselves."

"Each of us must have lots of wounded children."

"I believe we do… a wounded child for every unresolved experience."

"I guess that would really be a problem with a really bad experience like being sexually abused or losing a friend."

"Absolutely! Sometimes the experience is so traumatic a child is not able to move past it. A large part of that child stays stuck at that age level. It's why so many people behave immaturely. They are literally acting like a child."

"So how do you get over it?"

"Therapy is one way. The person has to find a way to let go of the emotional pain through some form of expression and they need to forgive whoever caused the pain."

"I guess that's why it's so important for parents to talk to their children and let them express themselves in a constructive way. So they don't hold onto their emotional pain."

"Definitely. Parents play a crucial role."

"Don't parents cause most of it?" inquired Eric.

"Unfortunately, they do."

"Then they're not likely gonna let a kid express themselves are they?" asked Travis.

"Not likely," replied Ryan.

"It creates a serious dilemma, doesn't it?"

"It starts with helping people to feel good about themselves," remarked Tom, joining the conversation in his typically insightful way.

"Yes, it does. Which leads us into today's discussion, unless you have any more questions about wounded children."

"Nope, I'm good," smiled Josh.

"Since the beginning of the school year, we've been talking about the importance of feeling good about ourselves and how our inability to feel this way affects us on a daily basis. It affects our health, our behaviour, the way we treat other people and so on. We've witnessed and discussed a few real life examples that illustrate this important aspect of life on planet Earth. We've talked about many of the archetypal experiences that reflect a society that doesn't feel good about itself; things like betrayal, infidelity, incarceration, persecution, abuse, murder, war, racism, discrimination, terrorism, greed, exploitation and so on. Today, I would like to talk about the things that we see and experience on a daily basis that are indicators of this phenomenon. For instance, consider *no trespassing* signs. If we felt good about ourselves, would there be a need for such signs?"

"No, there wouldn't be," replied Jordan. "If we felt good about ourselves, we would respect other people's property and we wouldn't walk on it."

"And if we had to fence off an area for safety reasons, like around electrical stations," observed Eric, "we would put up friendlier caution or warning signs using language that says we are concerned about your safety."

"How do you feel when you see a no trespassing sign?"

"Angry," said Mike. "It's like I want to say, 'screw you,' and tromp all over their property."

"I actually feel sad," added Tracy, "because the energy is so unfriendly. It makes me think the person who put the sign up must live in a lot of fear."

"I saw a sign recently that read, 'no trespassing, violators will be prosecuted,'" remarked Scott. "I wanted to rip it down."

"You set foot on our property boy and we're gonna throw yer ass in jail. Now git!" mocked Josh.

"Fences in general," said Caitlyn. "They reek of fear and hostility."

"*No more than two students at a time*," said Terry. "You see those signs in stores everywhere. It makes students want to terrorize the place."

"It pretty much encourages them to shoplift," agreed Tom.

"So, it seems a lot of the signage we post reflects a society that doesn't feel good about itself. What are some other indicators?"

"Barbed wire," added Terry.

"Traffic fines," said Stuart.

"All types of negative incentive," remarked Tom.

"Absolutely," agreed Ryan. "We're always using the threat of punishment to get people to do things in a certain way. If you speed you get a ticket. If you spit on the sidewalk, you get a ticket."

"If punishment was an effective way of encouraging good behaviour," observed Jordan, "kids wouldn't misbehave. You'd think we would have figured it out by now."

"What about parking enforcement?" asked Matt. "It's gotta be one of the most negative forms of *energy* work on the planet. Can you imagine going around all day handing out parking tickets, bringing unhappiness into people's lives. You really have to hate yourself or be very desperate to do that kind of work."

"Ya," agreed Stuart. "Just because some white collar bureaucrat sitting in an office at city hall came up with a brilliant idea to generate more money for the city."

"Road rage is another one," said Stuart. "When people get behind the wheel of a car, they do things and say things they wouldn't do anywhere else."

"They get a false sense of bravery... of empowerment," suggested Caitlyn.

"Price gouging," added Tom.

"Jails," said Travis, shaking his head.

"The entire judicial system," remarked a clearly incensed Ryan.

"Zoos," added Jessica.

"Hey, zoos are good things," argued Adam. "Yep, they save a lot of animals."

"They might rescue some, but many animals that end up in zoos are poached, especially dolphins. I read about it recently. And besides, if we were really concerned about animals, we would preserve their natural habitat, rehabilitate them and return them to the wild. We wouldn't put them in cages and charge people money to come and look at them. Have you ever looked at gorillas at the zoo? They look so sad."

Several of the students exchanged glances, surprised that Jessica was able to articulate her point so well. "That was well said, Jessica," praised Tom, as she grinned from ear to ear.

"The wanton destruction of our natural environment," added Caitlyn. "There is an orangutan sanctuary in Indonesia whose slogan is, *when the orangutans are gone from the planet, humans won't be far behind*. We should be paying attention. We build subdivisions on perfectly good agricultural land. It's insane."

"I couldn't agree more," said John, pleased with the discussion.

"Factory farms," remarked Tracy. "Animals are housed in horrid conditions and the meat is really toxic. We really shouldn't be eating it."

"Horse racing," added Travis. "Horses are bought and sold without any thought as to how it might affect them. They're whipped to get them to behave and run faster, and if they don't perform, they're sent off to glue factories. Horse racing is all about money and prestige."

"Charity," said Matt.

"Why do you say charity?" asked Travis.

"Charities disempower people. They keep people trapped in poverty. If we were truly a compassionate society, we would make sure there was lots of work and money for everyone, so that nobody needed charity."

"That's socialism," observed Jordan.

"In a caring civilization, socialism could work because we would evolve into it naturally. It wouldn't be forced on people. It's like communities that come together to build barns and look after people during times of disaster."

"The risk is, that it could lead to communism," noted Terry.

"Communism, which is basically socialism that benefits the elite, wouldn't exist. Not in a society that felt good about itself. In this type of society, everyone would contribute and benefit equally."

"That makes a lot of sense, Matt," agreed Blair.

"Gambling is another symptom of how messed up we are," said Adam.

"All forms of lotteries are," added Caitlyn. "They feed greed. They cause way more harm than good... if they provide any good at all."

"What about fast-food joints?" asked Travis. "If we really felt good about ourselves, we wouldn't put that crap in our bodies."

"It sounds like we need to look at all the things we do and ask ourselves if this is the way we want to live," observed Josh. "The way we live and treat each other isn't exactly the hallmark of an enlightened society?"

"That's a good way to look at it," agreed Ryan. "But in doing so, we are focusing on the effect of not feeling good about ourselves. I think we also need to look at the cause and put our efforts towards changing it."

"You both raise good points," John smiled. "At the moment, we are living a certain way without understanding the meaning of it or how it got this way. We need to examine our lifestyle and ask ourselves if it is working for us. Is it bringing us peace of mind? Is it bringing us joy? Then, in order to make change, we need to look at the cause and start changing that."

"You know," observed Travis, "it might have been a shorter conversation if we had listed the things that actually reflect a society the feels good about itself."

"Sadly, that's very true."

"What can we do to change things, to create a more compassionate, accepting and loving world, where people treat each other with respect and where everyone lives in abundance?" asked Tom.

Just then, the bell rang signaling the end of class.

"That's an excellent question and we'll address it on Monday," Teach replied. "Enjoy the rest of your day and have an awesome weekend."

"You too, Mr. Stevens."

As Matt walked uneasily up the hallway, he spotted Ryan, Jordan and Tom engaged in an impromptu conversation outside the cafeteria. They were discussing their own experiences with karma. Not wanting to talk to anyone just yet, he considered turning around and heading in the opposite direction. But before he could, the group caught sight of him.

"Hey Matt," said Ryan, "feeling any better?"

He paused for a moment considering his options, but before he could make a decision, Tom spoke. "We understand if you don't want to talk about it."

At that moment, Matt made a very meaningful decision. He chose to ask for help. "Can I trust you guys?" he asked, cautiously approaching the group.

The three exchanged puzzled glances. "Certainly," said Jordan. "What's up?"

"I know why I got beat up."

"You do?" exclaimed Ryan. "What do you mean?"

The muscular giant explained the phone calls. He told the shocked threesome that the caller ordered him to create a confrontation with their teacher, Mr. Stevens. He wanted the student to make it look like the teacher started it. He wanted Stevens to lose control. "He told me to 'make him hit you,'" Matt explained. He said that if I didn't do it, he would arrange it so I would go back to jail."

Ryan, Tom and Jordan stood in stunned silence. It almost sounded too absurd to be true. "How were you going to do that?" Ryan asked.

"I have no idea. I didn't get that far. Anyway, I told him to get stuffed."

"I can understand that," offered Tom.

"And the weird thing is that he wanted me to do it in the classroom."

"He did?" asked an incredulous Jordan.

"Ya, he told me to make sure I did it in class. Fucked, eh?"

"Maybe not," said Tom, a look of 'you won't believe what I just figured out' spreading over his face!

"What do you mean, Tommer?" inquired Ryan.

"Perhaps whoever is behind this caper put hidden cameras in our classroom."

"Holy fuck!" exclaimed Jordan. "That's heavy, man!"

"Ya, but it makes sense," agreed Matt. "Why else would he tell me to do it there?"

"Wow!" echoed Ryan. "If somebody planted cameras, this is big shit, man!"

"It sure is," agreed Matt.

"So, what do we do?" asked Jordan.

"We gotta find the cameras," said Ryan, with a sly smile.

"That should be easy," said Tom, matter of fact. "They'll be in the ceiling."

"Let's meet after school and figure out a plan," suggested Jordan.

"I'm in," said Ryan.

"Me too," said Matt.

They all looked at Tom. "I'm not missing out on this!" he smiled, eyes lighting up.

The four new amigos pumped fists before departing in different directions for their next class. As he walked away, Matt felt very relieved. Since the incident with his father after his mother's death, he had done everything on his own, not letting anyone else into his world. For the first time since then, he didn't feel so lonely. *I have friends*, he thought. And it felt good!

John decided to take the evening off. It was Friday night and he had been working hard all week, including moderating several intense discussions with the students about the ills of our society. He thought about driving out to Henderson Lake, but quickly dismissed the idea. Memories of times spent there with Sandra were still very fresh and he wasn't quite ready to risk reopening those wounds.

He reasoned that it might be better to enjoy a glass of wine and settle in for the evening. There were a couple of movies he had been planning to watch and this seemed as good a time as any to enjoy them. As he was reaching for the TV remote to search the on demand station the phone rang.

"*Hello!*" he said.

"*Mr. Stevens?*"

"Yes!" he answered, thinking it was a call centre.

"Hi, it's Marnie Rowe."

"Who?"

"Marnie Rowe. I spoke with you at the hospital last week."

"Oh, I'm sorry. Nurse Marnie," John responded, pleasantly surprised.

"I'm glad you remember me."

How could I forget he thought? She was a knockout... and very friendly to boot. "Of course I remember you. You were incredibly helpful that night."

"Thank you. You handled those kids very well. We all thought there was going to be a riot in the ER."

"I was concerned about that as well. The students were quite upset."

"We were all very grateful for what you did. You were wonderful with them."

"Thank you," John Stevens said, feeling a little embarrassed.

"I was calling to see how Matt was doing."

"Oh, are you at work?"

"No, I'm at home. Got the weekend off."

"Lucky you," he said flirting a little. "He's recovering well. Came back to school on Monday."

"I'm so glad to hear that. He suffered a nasty cut."

"Fortunately, most of the damage was above the hairline, so he won't have much of a scar."

"That's good. He seemed like a nice young man."

"He's had a troubled life up until now, but he's really getting it together."

"That's wonderful."

"Tell me, do you always call to follow up on your patients?" he asked playfully, realizing of course that he wasn't the patient.

"Only the special ones."

"I'll take that as a compliment."

"That's certainly how I meant it."

He thought about it for a second and then decided to go for it. "Are you free tomorrow night?"

"Unfortunately not… but I'm free tonight," she replied taking him by surprise.

"Well, um… would you like to get together?" he stammered.

"I would love to."

Taking their seats a short while later, John noticed that she was sporting a tattoo. It was a dolphin, subtly placed on her right hip, just above her jeans.

"I like your tattoo."

"Thank you," she said, looking slightly self-conscious. "I just had it done. My first one."

"It's very nice."

"Do you have any?"

"No. Haven't been brave enough to experience the pain."

"I know what you mean. It was much worse than I thought. My girlfriends put me up to it. They each got one."

"Nice friends."

"I considered ditching them, it hurt so much," she said with a playful laugh.

"Why a dolphin?"

"They're amazing animals. Very sacred."

"Yes, they're quite special."

Despite her friendly manner, Marnie seemed quite reserved, almost shy, although he didn't like to use that term because it infers powerlessness… that we can't do anything about it. He preferred *reserved* or *private*, because these words infer that it is our choice. He was surprised that she was reserved because nurses had a reputation for being outgoing.

He was about to ask her how long she had been a nurse, when their waiter appeared.

"What would you like to drink folks?" he asked.

The pair placed their order and the young server wheeled and scooted off towards the bar.

"I like this place," John said, continuing the conversation. After deciding to meet for a drink, Marnie had suggested the Wolf Hound, an Irish pub. It was a little out of the way; a charming little spot where they could enjoy a friendly drink.

"I come here occasionally with my friends. I like the atmosphere."

"I can see why. It's pretty lively."

She smiled at his approval.

"How long have you been a nurse?"

"Over twenty years."

"You must like it then."

"I love it. I've worked all over the hospital. In ICU, palliative care and maternity. But I like ER the best. It can be overwhelming at times, but as a whole, I like the pace."

"I guess you've seen some interesting stuff over the years."

"I have. One moment you might be dealing with a senior, the next moment, a child. I've never had to deal with a gunshot wound, thankfully."

"GSW," added the teacher, using the medical acronym. He was feeling more comfortable. "I used to watch *ER*."

"A pretty realistic show," she agreed. "And what about you, how long have you been teaching?"

"Only a few years. I was drawn to it after many years in the corporate world and a failed business venture."

"I'm sorry to hear that, but I can relate. My ex-husband's business went bankrupt. It's part of the reason we broke up. He couldn't handle the humiliation and blamed everyone else for what happened."

"Well I'm sorry to hear that," he sympathized.

"It wasn't the only reason, but it had a lot to do with it."

Just then, the waiter arrived with their drinks. He carefully placed a glass in front of Marnie, before setting another in front of John. They both watched as he filled her glass, careful not to overflow it with too much foam.

John picked up his drink and gently clinked it with hers. "Cheers," he smiled, "I'm so glad you called."

"Me too!" she replied.

They looked at each other for a moment and before it got awkward, she continued the conversation. "How is it that you have such a wonderful rapport with your students?"

"Hmmm. Where do I begin? I treat them with kindness."

"They certainly seemed to have a lot of respect for you."

"Thank you. I have learned that whatever you give to people is what they give back to you. If you want people to behave a certain way, you need to treat them accordingly."

"You know," she agreed, "it's the same with our patients. I see certain staff treat them poorly while others treat them respectfully and it makes a huge difference in how the patient cooperates and responds."

"It's like the way we treat children. When we're kind to them they behave the same way. What's sad is that adults are more likely to be kind with other adults, but not children… even their own."

"That's so true."

"I'm also teaching the students about the importance of self-image. Feeling good about yourself is the most important thing for our health and happiness."

"I never thought about that before, but it makes a lot of sense. What do you teach them?"

"That feeling good about yourself means that you feel lovable, worthy, adequate and empowered, and when we don't feel these things, it leads to all manner of suffering. We mistreat others and others mistreat us. We also attract negative experiences into our lives."

"That's like the law of attraction."

"Yes, it is!"

"How is it that we end up with a poor self-image? Is it because of how our parents raised us?"

"That has a lot to do with it. Certainly for most people, growing up feeling unloved, unwanted, unaccepted and unappreciated is at the root of a poor self-image. But it's not the only thing. Bullying at school and sexual abuse play a role for many people."

"Do you think it can change?"

"I sure hope so. If we want to save humankind, we have to."

"What do we need to do to change the way we live?"

John was thrilled that Marnie was taking an interest in something that was very important to him. She listened intently as he spoke and he was excited to tell her more. "People need to be inspired. They need a compelling reason to change. Scare tactics clearly don't work. If they did, people would have stopped smoking years ago."

"I couldn't agree more."

"At the risk of going on a rant, I think three things need to happen. First, it would be great if parents would raise their children differently; second, it would be ideal if the education system would make this a part of the curriculum; and third, it would be awesome if each of us would live our lives differently. We need to put an end to the psychological inferiority that exists on the planet."

"How can we live differently?"

"To begin, we can be kind… every moment of every day. Everything we do, every interaction we have with another person, needs to come from a place of kindness. I really don't think you can feel good about yourself when you mistreat another being, and similarly, you can't help but feel good about yourself when you are kind."

"That makes so much sense and it seems a very simple thing to do."

"It is, but people don't realize the significance of kindness."

"My grandmother taught me how to be nice to people, but I never thought of it before from the perspective of how it affects how you feel about yourself."

John nodded his head in agreement.

"Wow, this is a heavy conversation for our first one."

"I haven't overdone it, I hope."

"Not at all. I share your concerns and I love your ideas and your enthusiasm. They seem so practical, and quite frankly, so easy."

"They are. All we need is awareness and willingness. And willingness comes from having a compelling reason."

"Saving ourselves and treating the planet better would seem to be compelling enough."

"Yes, but people have to see it and it seems that many people aren't ready for it yet. They're not aware of the urgency of our situation."

"That's true."

"People need to see a picture of what is possible. For example, imagine what it would be like if you could walk down any street in any city anywhere in the world, any time of day or night, and not have to fear being beaten up, robbed, raped or murdered."

"That's a very enticing picture."

"It is indeed! It's something people can relate to. Similarly, imagine if you never had to lock your front door. Wouldn't that be awesome?"

"It certainly would. And wouldn't it be nice if parents could send their children out to play and never have to worry about them being abducted by a stranger."

"That too would be awesome. These are concrete things people think about every single day."

"It seems like a good way to get people's attention… get them thinking about it."

John again looked admiringly at his attractive companion. She looked up at him and returned his smile. He felt very at ease with her.

They spent the rest of the evening getting to know one another, talking about their childhood, families and careers. He learned that she had been married for twelve years and that she had no children because she was unable to conceive. He told her about his own marriage, his three children and his years in the corporate world. He was pleased that she seemed unconcerned about his art store experience. She was easy to converse with and before they knew it, the waiter announced last call. The evening had slipped away rather quickly.

"I'm fine," Marnie smiled.

"As am I," John echoed.

As they waited for their bill, she glanced at him, still smiling. "I've had a wonderful time."

"I have too," he readily agreed, returning her smile. "Would you mind if I called you sometime next week?"

"I would love it!" she replied.

When the waiter returned with their bill, he offered to pick up the tab, but she insisted they split it. It could have been an awkward moment, but she playfully said there was no way she was going to allow him to pay for their drinks after she had called him.

The teacher relented, not wanting to make it uncomfortable and the two of them made their way out to the parking lot.

He walked her to her car and was about to say something, when she surprised him by reaching up and kissing him on the cheek. He reflexively embraced her and they kissed passionately on the lips. The kiss lasted several seconds.

"Wow," she exclaimed. "You're a great kisser."

"Thank you. And so are you," he grinned.

"I'm looking forward to your call," she beamed, climbing into her black Toyota Camry.

"You won't have to wait long," he smiled, waving goodbye as she pulled out of the parking lot. He felt a strong attraction towards her and he was excited about the prospect of seeing her again.

CHAPTER 23:
MELTDOWNS

And it seems to me you lived your life
Like a candle in the wind
Never knowing who to cling to
When the rain set in

— Elton John, *Candle In The Wind*

"I trust you have provided sufficient inspiration for our client to complete the job," said the very powerful man on the other end of the line.

"He is being somewhat stubborn," replied the middleman.

"Perhaps he needs another visit."

"He needs some time to consider his 'situation,' so I have given him until the end of the week."

"Are you confident the job will get done?

"Yes, I believe that he will come to his senses."

"I want to remind you that the people I represent are anxious to see this come to a successful conclusion."

"I understand."

"I hope our friend is not falling victim to the teacher's propaganda."

"A leopard never changes its spots."

"I hope you are right."

The middleman hung up the phone. "I hope I am too!" he said out loud, nervously wringing his hands together.

"As a follow up to our last discussion about the things we see on a daily basis that are indictors of a society that doesn't feel good about itself, we were going to talk about what we can do to change things," John Stevens began, looking at the class. "Before we get into this discussion, I would like to talk about another phenomenon that reflects a society that doesn't feel good about itself and more importantly, reflects how we've lost touch with who we really are.

"I was watching TV last night and I happened to see a special on the rise and fall of movie actor Mel Gibson and it made me think of all the celebrities who have succumbed to fame; who've exhibited bizarre behaviour, had major meltdowns and who have fallen from grace or lost their lives due to inappropriate behaviour, excess, drug use, addiction and unhappiness.

"Besides Mel Gibson, in recent years there have been Charlie Sheen, Robert Downey Jr., Michael Jackson, Heath Ledger, Brittany Spears, Whitney Houston, Lindsay Lohan, Christina Aguilera and Chris Farley, to name a few."

"And what about Tiger Woods?" asked Adam. "Basically that was a major fall from grace."

"That's for sure," agreed Stuart. "Talk about a guy that is the poster boy for someone who feels inadequate."

"He plays golf with so much anger," observed Tom. "And then, despite being married to an extremely beautiful woman, he's out having sex with all these other women... as if he didn't have enough."

"There haven't been too many golfers who've had meltdowns" remarked Terry.

"What about John Daly?" asked Eric. "He's had a bit of a rough go of it."

"That's true," agreed Terry. "Especially with his ex-wife."

"And a few have had troubles with alcohol," added Mike. "I saw a special recently on the golf channel about a couple of pro golfers who've had to deal with alcoholism. Otherwise, golfers seem to be a pretty level headed bunch."

"Hollywood has sure had a lot of tragedy over the years," remarked Travis. "In the past, there was River Phoenix, John Belushi and Freddie Prinze."

"One of the saddest was Judy Garland," observed Tracy. "I still have a hard time watching The Wizard of Oz without wondering how she could have ended up the way she did."

"And, of course, Marilyn Monroe," added Teach. "Possibly the most famous tragic celebrity."

"And then you've got all the childhood actors who couldn't handle life after their careers ended, or at least after their fame ended," added Terry. "Todd Bridges and Dana Plato from the TV show Different Strokes. Danny Bonaduce from the show The Partridge Family and Anissa Jones from the TV series, Family Affair.

"Look at the music business," observed Ryan. "Kurt Cobain from Nirvana and Michael Hutchence from INXS, both committed suicide, although there's some question as to whether Hutchence's hanging was actually suicide."

"Either way, it kind of reflects the lifestyle," observed Tom.

"Think about the sixties and seventies," lamented Josh. "We lost Jimi Hendrix, Janice Joplin, Jim Morrison, John Bonham, Keith Moon and Elvis Presley… some of the best musicians of our time."

"And there was Dennis Wilson from the Beach Boys," added Stuart.

"And Pete Ham and Tom Cole from Badfinger," said Ryan. "Two guys from the same band who both took their own lives. How crazy is that?"

"And Sid Vicious from the Sex Pistols and Bon Scott from ACDC," remarked Travis. "They both died tragically."

"Nothing was more heartbreaking than Karen Carpenter," said Caitlyn. "What a beautiful voice."

"How did she die?" asked Adam.

"Complications from years of anorexia."

"That's too bad."

"You should listen to *Superstar*, a song by the Carpenters. It's so beautiful."

"What about Phil Spector?" asked Jordan. "That's about as bizarre as it gets."

"Who's he?" asked Adam.

"One of the most successful music producers of all time," Jordan replied laconically. "He created the *wall of sound* production technique, which was basically a big sound using lots of musicians and instruments and over dubbing to create a huge orchestral effect."

"Didn't he also produce the Beatles last album, *Let It Be*?" asked Mike.

"Yes, he did," answered Jordan.

"What happened to him?" asked Jessica.

"He murdered his girlfriend a few years ago."

"Wow, that's crazy!" Jessica's unintended pun prompted a few snickers from the class. "Oh, I get it," she added.

"How is it that people who have everything, throw it all away? Why do they have meltdowns?" asked Terry.

"Why do you think so many celebrities have had such difficulties?" Teach asked directing the question to the entire class.

"There's a lot of pressure when you're in the public eye all the time," suggested Ryan.

"There is enormous pressure," agreed Jordan. "Especially, once you've achieved some success."

"Record companies, movie studios and even publishing companies pay big bucks when they think they have a star on their hands," John remarked. "And they expect big returns on their investments. Musicians and actors give up a lot of their independence. At least until they get big enough to control their own destiny."

"And they give up their privacy too," added Josh.

"It's not a normal lifestyle," remarked Tom.

"Those are all good observations, but Tom raises an important point. What did you mean when you suggested it's not normal?"

"When you become a celebrity, you lose the ability to do normal everyday things like go for a walk, go to the store or go to a movie. Everywhere you go, people want your autograph, they want to talk with you and get their picture taken. You are constantly harassed by the paparazzi. You get treated like you're something special, like you're better than everyone else."

"I couldn't handle that," observed Jessica. "I always want to be able to go shopping and other stuff. I wouldn't want to be treated like I'm better than other people. That would drive me crazy."

"Everyone wants a piece of you," said Ryan. "They want you to endorse this product or appear at that event. It seems like you have little time to yourself."

"And people are always telling you how great you are," added Josh. "If you aren't well grounded, it can create an unrealistic, over inflated self-image."

"That's an excellent observation. That type of flattery can be very damaging to someone who doesn't know how to handle it effectively, especially someone who has grown up with a poor self-image."

"Groupies want to sleep with you," remarked Tracy. "You can have sex with pretty much anyone you want."

"What's wrong with that?" joked Stuart.

"For starters, it might create unrealistic expectations."

"I guess so. But it's too bad," he added with a wry smile.

"It seems that many of these people came from very modest backgrounds and couldn't handle the lifestyle change," said Travis. "It was too much for them."

"And I guess there was a part of them that didn't feel good about themselves, right?" asked Scott.

"And this would have led to self sabotaging behaviour, wouldn't it?" asked Ryan.

"I suspect so," their enthused teacher replied. "When you don't believe you are deserving… when you have no self-worth… you will undoubtedly experience self-sabotage."

"This must happen on an unconscious level," observed Matt.

"Yes, it does," John agreed.

"What is the higher purpose of this celebrity meltdown phenomenon and what is the lesson to be learned from their burnouts?" asked Tom.

"Would anybody like to take a shot at answering Tom's question?" Teach asked the class.

"If we are all aspects of God," offered Matt, "and if we live in Oneness with all that is, then being treated as if you are better than everyone else is unnatural. It's not the way we're meant to live. It creates enormous *hidden* stress."

"On a certain level," added Ryan, "we know this to be true. We know that we are the same as everyone else and it unsettles us. It causes us to suffer in a certain way."

"Celebrities feel trapped," observed Caitlyn. "They don't know how to escape what they inherently know to be a false way of living."

"You know," Tom observed, "if we didn't have celebrity worship, we likely wouldn't have celebrity burnout."

"I never understood why people go so crazy over celebrities," remarked Caitlyn. "It seems absurd."

"I agree," said Eric. "They're just people who happen to be good at something."

"Ya, but we've put an illogically high value on what they do," observed Ryan.

"We've got our priorities messed up for sure," agreed Scott.

"It all stems from our collective negative self-image. We don't feel good about ourselves, so we think others are better, particular people who are in the public eye. And that leads to all sorts of trouble."

"Ya, it's like you've told us," Travis added. "When you don't feel good about yourself, nothing else matters. It seems that this celebrity worship and burnout thing is meant to guide us back to the truth."

"So it has a purpose?" asked Josh.

"It has to have a purpose," replied Tom. "Knowing things have a purpose gives us hope."

John Stevens was both surprised and elated at how well the students were articulating their thoughts on this issue. Clearly they grasped the concepts he had been teaching them and were able to apply them to current life situations. He felt confident that with this awareness they were well on their way to overcoming their individual dilemmas. "Your points are all very well made. It seems that this celebrity meltdown phenomenon, just like bullying and the rapid increase in the rate of autism, Asperger's and ADHD, is meant to help guide humanity back to a more spiritual, loving, caring way of living. It's meant to guide us to the truth of our existence."

"It appears that a lot of what seems like suffering and inhumane living is actually meant to eventually bring us towards peace and the compassionate treatment of others, once we figure it out," said Caitlyn.

"Ya, that's true," added Josh. "But we're so caught up in our misery, we don't see it."

"Again, you're points are well made," John praised.

"So, what is the point?" Tom said matter of fact. "What can we do?"

"Create awareness," Caitlyn replied.

"We need to talk about it," added Travis. "The more we talk about it, the more awareness we create."

"That's certainly true, Travis," Teach acknowledged. "And that brings us to another perspective we need to consider. Before they became famous, most celebrities grew up in homes just like you and me. They led non-celebrity lives. Some grew up in dysfunctional homes with dysfunctional parents and consequently, they too became dysfunctional. Some experienced trauma. Some were physically and sexually abused. But they also had talent and they became rich and famous. And then, because of their dysfunctionality and unresolved emotional pain, they had meltdowns and people wanted to know why. And when the truth came out many celebrities became spokespersons for all those who had similar experiences. They brought awareness to these experiences."

"So, perhaps they are serving a higher spiritual purpose," suggested Tom.

"Because if somebody rich and famous can be sexually abused, then I don't feel so bad, right?" added Ryan.

"Which creates the potential for mass healing," remarked Jordan.

"It certainly does."

"You know," said Tom. "It's okay to acknowledge and admire someone for their ability and for what they do, whether it's an actor, musician, athlete, teacher, police officer, maintenance worker or whatever. What we need to stop doing is treating them as if they are better than everyone else."

"Because we all have our own purpose," said Caitlyn. "Regardless of whether it's on a grand scale or not, we are all meant to serve."

"Which means we just plain need to treat everyone with the same level of kindness, compassion, integrity and respect," stated Blair.

The class suddenly went quiet as all eyes turned to look at their apparently converted troublemaker, not quite believing what he had just said.

Teach couldn't contain his smile.

As they exited of the movie theatre, Marnie quietly took John's hand. It was a warm evening and the night sky was alive with the glow of a million stars. "Would you like to go for a walk?" she asked.

They had been on several dates already and he was beginning to feel comfortable with her. He was stirred by her upbeat energy. "I would love to."

The theatre was in the downtown district, not far from his apartment, and they headed northward towards the town's central park.

"Thank you again for taking me to the movies," she began. "I really enjoyed the film."

"I've wanted to see it for a while now. I'm glad you were able to go and thrilled that you wanted to see it too."

She squeezed his hand a little tighter. "I love this time of the year. It's getting warmer and the flowers are starting to bloom. It's so beautiful."

"New beginnings. It's very invigorating."

"John," she said walking quietly for a few minutes. "There is something I would like to ask you and I'll understand if you don't want to talk about it."

"Um, sure," he replied. "Go ahead."

"I think... you've had your heart broken... recently."

He was a little surprised she had noticed. He was being guarded with her, but thought he was doing a good job of hiding it. "Why do you say that?"

"I get the feeling you like me, but I sense that you're holding back."

"I guess I have been kind of cautious. I wanted to make sure this wasn't a rebound thing. I wanted to be sure my feelings were genuine."

"You must have cared for her a great deal?"

"I did. We dated for a couple of years. She taught at the school, but she left several months ago to take a teaching position at an arts college. It was something she had wanted for a long time. She was...er, is...very spiritual in her outlook on life and we shared many common beliefs."

"I'm so sorry that you were hurt."

"I'd be lying if I said I wasn't. It was very difficult, but I understand why she left, I understand why she came into my life when she did and I accept that I had to let her go. In my heart, I know what happened was meant to be and I'm ready to move on."

"I'm glad I met you, no matter what happens."

He stopped and looked at her. "And I'm thrilled that I met you." He kissed her on the lips and held her for several moments. "I couldn't be happier that you came into my life."

"Ditto on that. When you're single you often wonder if you're ever going to meet *the right person*... someone you're compatible with, who shares your interests, beliefs and values. Even though I've been single for a while and I've had these thoughts in my heart, I've always believed that when the time was right I would meet someone."

"You just never know how things might turn out," John agreed, squeezing her hand a little tighter.

Four determined students walked boldly through the front door of the school. They were on a mission. A basketball game underway in the gym would provide ample coverage for their operation. The plan was simple. Tom would stand guard at the corner of the hallway, Matt would guard the door, while Ryan and Jordan would search for the cameras. If anyone asked, they were looking for Jordan's ring.

With Tom and Matt on the watch, Ryan and Jordan entered the classroom and quickly went to work. It didn't take them long to find what they were looking for.

"Found one," proclaimed Jordan in a low voice, one foot perched on a chair, the other on a book shelf, in the front corner of the room. "They operate by sensors, so we've likely triggered them." He waved into the camera, but didn't touch it.

"Got another one," announced Ryan from the back of the room. "These little buggers aren't easy to see unless you get up really close. They blend in perfectly." Then he too waved to the camera and said, "Gotcha dickheads!"

The pair scoured the room high and low for several minutes but there were no additional cameras.

"Let's get out of here," implored Matt.

"Somebody has a real hard on for Teach," observed Ryan after the foursome had safely exited the school. "What do you think it is?"

"Got me," replied Jordan shrugging his shoulders.

"What's next fellas?" asked Tom.

They all looked at each other. "I say we tell Teach," suggested Matt.

"I'm good with that," agreed Ryan.

"Me too," said Jordan.

"I'll make it unanimous," added Tom.

"Oh fuck! We've been busted!" exclaimed the blonde haired man, watching the smiling face on the screen giving him the finger.

"What?" asked the second man.

"Look," said the first, pointing at the computer.

"Fuck is right! Shut it down."

"What?"

"Shut it down! You know the drill. Anything goes down, we shut it down and get the fuck out."

"Right. I wonder how they found it?"

"Doesn't matter. Let's go!"

"What about the cameras?"

"They're not traceable."

CHAPTER 24:
ANYTHING IS POSSIBLE

Some will win, some will lose
Some were born to sing the blues
Oh, the movie never ends
It goes on and on and on and on

— Journey, *Don't Stop Believing*

As John was leaving the school, he noticed Blair sitting alone under a tree reading a book. The amiable teacher thought this very peculiar.

"I'm surprised to see you still at school," he said, approaching casually.

The troubled student continued to look into the book, pretending that he didn't hear.

"Aren't you normally hanging out with your friends at this hour?"

"Huh," Blair grunted, turning to look at Teach.

"Why are you still at the school? I thought you didn't like this place."

"I don't, I hate it."

"Then why are you here?"

"I'm afraid to go home."

John was quite surprised by his student's truthful admission, given how disruptive and belligerent he had been. "Why is that?"

"Cause I broke my bed this morning," he said, looking down at the ground. "My dad's gonna kill me."

"Why'd you do that?"

"I was mad."

"What were you mad about?"

"I couldn't close my dresser drawer properly."

"I see," Teach consoled. "Do you get angry a lot?"

"Ya, I guess."

"Why do you get so angry?"

"I dunno," he replied, shrugging his shoulders. "Things just make me mad."

"Things used to make me angry too. Still do sometimes. Would you like to talk about it?"

"Ya, I guess," he said, looking suspiciously at his teacher.

"I don't think things make us angry. They just trigger the anger that's already there."

"You mean I get angry at things because I'm already angry with something else?"

"Yes. And my experience is, when kids get angry, quite often it's because of something that is going on at home."

"I hate being at home."

"Why is that?"

"Cause my dad's a prick. Every time I turn around, he gives me shit about something. He loves to yell at me and criticize what I do."

Blair's emotional pain was evident in the expression on his face. He wore it like a warrior wears a cruel battle scar. John had not seen this in him before and in that moment, he felt great empathy. "Father and son relationships can be extremely difficult. How does it make you feel?"

"I hate him, especially because he never says anything to my sister. It doesn't matter what she does, she never gets in trouble."

It was apparent that the teen was in victim mode and so the empathetic teacher needed to choose his words carefully. "I had a really difficult relationship with my own father, so I know how you feel."

"Oh ya, what did he do?"

"Spanked me a lot when I was a kid. Scolded at me. He expected his children to behave in a certain way and if we didn't, we got it."

"My dad said the next time I stepped out of line, he was gonna kick me out of the house."

"How does that make you feel?"

Blair sat quietly for a moment, appearing to be on the edge of tears. "It rips my heart out. I can't believe a parent would want to kick their kid out of the house," he mumbled, his voice trembling.

"It's not something any parent really wants to do. They just don't know any other way to deal with it."

"Then they're stupid," he snapped, showing a little more defiance.

"You may see it differently when you have your own kids."

"I'm never gonna have kids."

"Perhaps there is a different way of looking at this that might help you feel better about your relationship with your father."

"I don't know if I want to feel better about it. He's such a prick, I don't think I want to like him."

"I didn't say you had to like him. Maybe just feel differently about it. So you're not so sad and angry."

"Ya, I guess."

"It helps to understand a few things. First, most, if not all, parents don't feel good about themselves. Because of the way they've been raised, they don't feel lovable, worthy, good enough or empowered. Just like you, they've been yelled at, hit, criticized, ignored and in too many cases, abused or abandoned."

"You'd think they'd want to raise their kids differently."

"A lot of parents do, but they don't know how. They only know what they've learned. They're so deep in their emotional pain and they don't even realize it. And of course, some parents have no awareness at all. They just raise their kids the same way they were raised. The reality is, if you don't feel good about yourself, you're not likely going to raise your children to feel good about themselves."

"So, are you saying my old man doesn't like himself?"

"You cannot possibly mistreat another being, particularly your children, if you feel good about yourself. Your dad has all these wounded little boys inside of himself, quite possibly from the punishment he received as a child, and they want to lash out at someone in order to ease their suffering."

"My old man doesn't know anything about wounded children. He keeps telling me that I'm the problem… that I'm the one who's bad and who keeps doing stupid things. He makes me feel like I'm a burden and that I don't deserve to be part of the family."

"Well, that brings us to the second point. Children misbehave… that is, they act out… because they don't feel good about themselves, mainly due to a dysfunctional or non-existent relationship with one or both of their parents."

Blair turned and looked at his teacher with a very puzzled expression. "How stupid is that. Parents mess up their kids and then spank them when they act up"

"Seems rather ironic, doesn't it. What is more, children are incredibly impressionable and they treat everything their parents say as gospel. If Mom or Dad says something, it must be true. Certain things parents do or say may not seem all that big a deal, but they can have a huge affect on a child. A parent cannot call a child stupid or bad and a parent cannot physically punish a child by spanking them or slapping their hands or any other form of physical punishment, without it having a tremendously damaging affect on the child's self-image."

"My father used to spank me all the time. Now he just yells at me."

"If a parent's only physical expression of emotion towards their children was that of love and encouragement… hugging, cuddling, patting on the back… it would make such a difference. The moment they lay a hand on a child in an inappropriate way is like the most heart breaking form of betrayal for a child. It destroys their self-esteem."

"Ya, I can see that, but don't parents need to discipline kids?"

"A lot of parents think the proper way to raise a child is to teach them to do things out of fear or reward. If you do this, you're gonna get spanked. If you do that, I'll buy you an ice cream cone. They don't teach their children to behave in a certain way simply because it is the proper thing to do.

"Children certainly need to be taught boundaries and they need to understand what acceptable behaviour is and what it is not. They also need to know that there will be consequences when they step outside the boundaries, but it all begins with raising a child to feel good about him or herself. A child who has a positive self-image is more likely to honour those boundaries."

"Ya, I get that" Blair said, looking a little more confident, but one thing I don't understand is why my dad only yells at me. Why didn't he spank my sister or yell at her? It makes me feel like there's something wrong with me…like I'm a bad person. I remember one time when we were kids, my sister and I were playing in the backyard. She got mad about something and threw a toy at me. It hit me and it hurt, so I threw it back at her and hit her in the face. She started screaming and my dad heard what was going on, so he grabbed me and dragged me around until he found a big stick and then he whacked me with it. But he didn't spank my sister. He didn't even say a word to her."

"I'm very sorry to hear that. It must have been very upsetting for you."

"It was, and that's when I really started hating him."

"That's really unfortunate and I can understand why. But there's an explanation for it and it gets us to the third point, which is this, quite often, children reflect back to their parents things about themselves that they were denied or that they don't like about themselves and so the parent turns on the child."

Again, Blair looked at Teach with a puzzled expression. "I don't get that."

"If a parent, for instance, was a very sensitive child and had that sensitivity beaten out of them, quite often they will do the same with their own children. Or if a parent has grown up in fear of expressing themselves and has a child who is outgoing, energetic and expressive they may be harsher with that child."

"So, maybe my dad is so mean to me because I'm a lot like him. People say I'm like him, anyway."

"That's very possible."

"You know, Mr. Stevens … Teach … I do feel a little better about my dad, but what can I do to make things better?"

"How would you feel about talking to him?"

"Scared!"

"I can imagine, but you've got something you need to talk to him about, right?"

"Ya, my bed," the student said smiling sheepishly, remembering why he was hanging out at school. "What can I do though? When I tell him, he's just going to yell at me."

"He's likely gonna yell for sure if he finds out on his own, but he might not if you tell him first."

"But what if I tell him and he starts yelling anyway?"

"If he starts yelling at you, very calmly say, 'Dad, when you yell at me, I feel scared and I feel that you don't love me.'"

"Knowing my dad, he'll just tell me to man up."

"If he does, simply say, 'Dad, I've felt like this all my life.'"

The appreciative teen looked at his teacher and although he was smiling, he had a tear in his eye.

"It's been my experience that it's always best to tell people the bad news before they find out for themselves. Do you think you can go home right now and tell your father what happened?"

"Ya, I can do that. And maybe he won't yell at me," he added excitedly, reaching out to shake his teacher's hand.

"Anything is possible!"

The young man smiled.

"And I would encourage you to do one other thing. Stay in the moment. It's okay to plan what you want to say, even write it down, but if you find yourself worrying about how he might react, bring yourself back into presence. Focus on your breath. Look around and observe. It will help diffuse any nervousness."

"I will."

Teach watched as his student left the schoolyard. He was extremely pleased that he had finally connected with him. He always felt that anyone could be reached with the right approach. Blair was simply another wounded soul acting out in the only way he knew how. To everyone else it was misbehaviour. To the wounded teen, it was an unconscious cry for help. John hoped it would go well with his father.

He also thought about the cycle of emotional pain parents continue to inflict on their children. Like an unattended scratched record that just keeps going round and round, skipping at the point of the nick. People who don't feel good about themselves become parents and unwittingly raise their children to feel the same way. In most cases, they want what's best for their children, but their parenting behaviour has the exact opposite effect. The concerned teacher wondered if this cycle of insanity could ever be changed.

"J. K. Rowling went from living in poverty to becoming the first billionaire author, with seven books on the all time top one hundred list of best selling books. The initial idea for her first book came to her while riding a train from Manchester to London, England."

As John walked around the room, Blair looked at him, gave him the thumbs up and smiled, indicating that things had gone well with his dad. "Arnel Pineda," he continued, returning the smile, "went from living on the streets in the Philippines to being the lead singer for the rock band Journey after a video his friend posted on Youtube was discovered by Neil Schon, Journey's lead guitarist.

"Nelson Mandela rose from prison inmate to become the president of South Africa, while Wilma Rudolph went from being crippled as a child due to polio and scarlet fever to winning three gold medals in track and field at the 1960 Olympics! Anything is possible!

"Jesus, the renowned spiritual teacher and healer whose teachings led to the creation of Christianity, began as a carpenter. The Buddha turned his back on his royal family, lived in the forest and meditated for years, almost starving to death, before reaching a state of enlightenment. His teachings led to the creation of Buddhism. Muhammad, an orphan, was a merchant and shepherd, before receiving revelations from Allah which later became the text for the Qur'an, the book that is the foundation of Islam."

Throughout his talk. Ryan and Jordan were continually whispering to one another, which was out of character for them and it piqued the teacher's curiosity. "Everything okay, gentlemen?"

"Fine," replied Ryan apologetically.

"Sorry," added Jordan.

"These examples," Teach continued, satisfied that nothing was out of order, "demonstrate that anything is possible and that goes for each one of you. As you walk through the next door or around the next corner, do so knowing that anything is possible."

"Do you really believe that?" asked Caitlyn, sincerely.

"Yes, I do. It doesn't mean anything *will* happen, but it's certainly possible."

"You're mostly talking about individuals," observed Tom. "What about society? The fact is, it's a mess. Can we really change society? Is it really possible?"

"When you look around and see what is happening in the world, it is easy to feel a sense of despair and doubt that anything can realistically change. But we are creators and we can create anything we want. If we want a life that is characterized by love, joyful living and peace of mind, we can create it. If we want to live in a society where everyone feels good about themselves, we can create it."

"What about destiny?" inquired Terry. "What if it is our destiny to continue living this way?"

"Ya," agreed Eric. "What if it is our destiny to destroy the planet?"

"And ourselves," added Matt.

"Again, anything is possible. The question is, what do we want?"

"That should be rather obvious, shouldn't it?" asked Tom.

"It may be obvious to us," remarked Caitlyn, "But I don't think it's quite so obvious to the people who run corporations that poison and pollute, or the people who run banks and oil companies that rake in billions of dollars in profits on the backs of people who are barely getting by, or the people who run governments that are totally corrupt."

"I know that, but these are smart people. They must know that this can't possibly go on forever. They must know that the population can't continue to grow unabated."

"Yes!" added Ryan, "And they must realize that at some point, if the gap continues to widen between the haves and have nots, and if the middle class continues to disappear in developed countries, there is going to be a revolution on a far more massive scale than the one in Egypt in 2011."

"They're so caught up in the here and now, that they don't believe it," Caitlyn observed.

"Karl Marx said that industrialization would put more and more workers out of work," observed Matt. "He said that eventually workers would rise up and overthrow the capitalists, which would lead to a class-free, conflict-free society. Marx's theory didn't prove correct in his lifetime, but his ideas were adopted by people like Lenin in Russia, Mao Zedong in China and Fidel Castro in Cuba. It led to the creation of Communism which resulted in the oppression of millions and millions of people. Aren't we risking the same thing with this growing gap between the haves and have nots?"

"Yes we are," John replied. "But what Marx's theory failed to consider was the role of self-image. As long as there are people who feel inadequate and powerless, there will be oppression. If everyone was spiritually conscious and felt good about themselves, there would be no *revolution*. A class-free, conflict-free society would just happen."

"I guess that's why bringing awareness to the concept of *feeling good about yourself* is so important," remarked Jordan.

Just then, the bell rang.

"That was a terrific discussion!" John praised. "And I would like to continue it next class. Have an awesome day in the meantime."

As the students made their way out of the classroom, he was overcome with an enormous sense of pride. These kids were so wise and so well informed. If anyone can start a revolution, they can, he mused with a smile.

While he was in the midst of his revelry, Jordan, Ryan, Tom and Matt gathered in front of his desk. "What's up gentlemen?" he asked.

Ryan was the first to speak. "You're not gonna believe this, Teach!"

"Believe what?" the puzzled teacher inquired innocently.

"You're being spied on," said Jordan.

"Pardon?" John replied, thinking this was some kind of joke.

"There are hidden cameras in the ceiling," explained Tom, pointing to the front corner and back of the classroom. "Somebody planted them there to spy on you."

"Show me," he said, not quite sure what to make of this.

Jordan pulled a desk up to the front corner of the room, climbed on top of it and pointed up to the ceiling. "It's right there."

The camera was barely visible and John had difficulty seeing it at first. When he finally spotted it, he almost fell over.

"The other one is back there," said Ryan, pointing to the back of the room.

"My goodness," he exclaimed. "Do you know who put them there?"

"I might know," replied Matt.

"Please explain," John suggested, unable to take his eyes off the camera.

Matt told the whole story, including the phone calls, his suspicions about the assault and their impromptu operation to find the cameras.

John Stevens was flabbergasted. This appeared to be some sort of clandestine undertaking, right out of the movies. "I don't know what to say!"

"That's how we feel," said Tom.

"Did you touch the cameras?"

"No way," Jordan replied, hopping down from the desk.

"Good."

"What do we do next?" asked Ryan.

"We'd better call the police."

After the police had left, John, Ryan, Jordan, Tom, Matt and Principal Clark stood in a circle, still bewildered at what had just taken place. The police were taking this very seriously. They had removed the cameras and dusted for finger prints. They took Matt's phone and each of the boys had given a statement. The police said the cameras were custom made and would be difficult to trace.

"How are you boys feeling?" asked Principal Clark.

"Numb," replied Tom.

"This is crazy," added Ryan.

"It certainly is," agreed John.

"You young men did the right thing," said Clark proudly. "Let's just keep this to ourselves for the time being, at least until we hear back from the police."

"Yes, sir," the boys replied in unison.

"We'd better get going," Matt said, looking at his new friends.

After the students had left, John looked at his boss. "If someone had told me when I left home this morning that this was going to happen, I would have thought them daft!"

"We'd better take this seriously. Someone is clearly out to discredit you."

"I'd surely like to know who!"

"Hopefully, the police will find out!"

John was just finishing up the breakfast dishes, still thinking about the bizarre set of events that had taken place, when the phone rang. "Hello," he answered cordially thinking it might be the police.

"Hi John," said Marnie. I was just thinking about you, so I thought I'd call."

"Hi," he said grinning from ear to ear. "I'm glad you did."

"How would you like to go for a drive?"

"I would love to."

It was the weekend and he had no plans, so Marnie's suggestion that they go for a day trip pleased him enormously. When she pulled up in front of Wong's he opened the door and slid easily into the passenger seat.

She leaned over and kissed him on the lips. Her kiss was warm and he felt unexpectedly aroused. "Where are you taking me?" he asked playfully.

"To a farmers market and conservation area about an hour north of here."

"Sounds awesome!" he said. John had decided not to tell his new girlfriend about the cameras. He reasoned that there was no threat, and therefore, no need to alarm her at the moment.

As they drove northward, the observant teacher noticed a marked change in the terrain and vegetation. It was much hillier and the forest was dominated by coniferous trees, mostly spruce and pine, that enclosed the highway in a warm blanket of green. It was a beautiful trip.

Their conversation was easy and before long, they were pulling into the parking lot at the market. It was much larger than he had envisioned and it was bustling with a crowded throng of cheery weekend shoppers ready to part with their cash in exchange for the verdant organic fruits and vegetables that adorned the tightly packed merchant stands.

They made their way from stall to stall, checking the rich offerings, bantering with energetic merchants and enjoying each other's company. She was clearly in her element and he was quite taken with her joyful manner. She was very respectful of the merchants and despite her reserved personality, interacted with them easily.

Afterwards they went to a nearby café, well-known for its gluten free menu and natural dishes. The food blew Teach away and he vowed to go back on a regular basis.

"That was one of the best meals of my life," he beamed, taking Marnie's hand as they exited the café and walked casually towards a nearby canal.

The sun was almost directly overhead and the cloudless sky was alive with a charming variety of colourful birds, whose aerial maneuvers seemed skillfully choreographed to entertain the appreciative crowd below.

There were several boats moored alongside the canal and the walkway was alive with free spirited folks enjoying the sunshine and warm air. A young couple was tossing a Frisbee back and forth while their ever determined dog tried valiantly to snatch it in mid-flight. It was an idyllic setting.

"I would like to know more about the healing work you've been doing," she said as they made their way slowly among the crowd. "Until I met you, I didn't know anything about healing emotional pain."

John was surprised, but pleased with her desire to know more about his healing journey and he was delighted to share his story with her. "I would love to," he replied.

She listened intently as he recounted in considerable detail his initial introduction into emotional healing, the physical manifestations that came one after another as he got deeper into his journey... headaches, joint pain, digestive problems, sudden intense pain that sent him scurrying for pain remedies that he loathed having to take... as well as financial issues, being mistreated by coworkers and managers, and memories from childhood, adolescence and adulthood that regularly popped up. He told her everything.

"I guess every experience we have that results in unresolved emotional pain has to be healed, doesn't it?" she asked inquisitively.

"I believe it does. When we don't resolve them at the time they happen, they get stored in our cell memory and limbic brain. With each successive wounding, more and more negative emotional energy... guilt, shame, grief, bitterness and so on... gets layered on. We continue to accumulate it and eventually it manifests in physical illness."

"I understand what you are saying and it makes sense to me. Listening to your story, it sounds like it's been a rollercoaster ride for you. You're very brave."

"It's been at times, both difficult and fascinating. I've had days when I wanted to rip my hair out… when I shouted at the universe to leave me alone… when I yelled myself hoarse. But each time I got through it and I felt better."

"What made you stick with it?"

"I don't know. I guess an inherent belief that this is what I need to do and this is the way to do it. Somewhere along the line, I came to the conclusion that healing emotional pain is an integral part of the human experience. It's one of the main reasons we're here on the planet. But I also think it's one of our most difficult challenges, because it's not easy and it's certainly not fun."

"Is it just experiences from this lifetime that you've healed?"

"No, actually, I've done a lot of healing around experiences that happened in other lifetimes."

"That's fascinating. I'd love to know more sometime."

"It's really what turned me on to the whole idea of emotional healing. When I went back into previous lives, saw images, felt the intensity of the emotions and then experienced positive changes in my life as I healed them, I was hooked."

"What has been your most difficult challenge?"

John thought quietly for a moment. At first he was unsure if he should tell her, as she looked on patiently, waiting for his response. He was concerned that it might scare her away, but he knew if he was to have a meaningful relationship with her, he had to be truthful.

"Anger," he admitted.

For a moment there was silence between them.

"I can believe it," she said, taking him by surprise. "I see it every day at the hospital; men of all ages who end up there because of their anger. Injuries from fights and road rage incidents. Automobile accidents from aggressive driving. Addictions, heart disease and cancer.

"And I've also seen the victims of this anger... spouses, girlfriends and children who have been abused by angry men. Rape victims. The carnage left on the streets and roadways and in homes is heartbreaking."

"Yes, I guess you see a lot of the end results."

"We talk about it a lot. We all think hospitals would be empty if it weren't for all the anger in the world."

"I guess that's true."

"Has it been difficult for you?"

"It was initially. Actually, it took a long time for me to recognize that I was holding on to all this rage. I used to get angry all the time, but I thought it was things that happened that made me angry. I didn't realize that external events were triggering anger I already had. For the longest time, I fought it. I didn't want to feel it. It upset me."

"That's probably because we're taught that it's bad to get angry. In fact, a lot of parents scold or punish their children when they get angry."

"That's quite true. But then one day I had an anger release and I felt really good afterwards. I had been feeling pain and stiffness in my body for several days and after the release it all went away. I felt energetic. Since then I have accepted that if I want to have peace of mind, I have to release all the negative emotional energy in my body, so now I say, 'bring it on!'"

Normally John would have felt quite awkward telling somebody about his healing process, but he felt surprisingly comfortable talking to Marnie about it.

"How do you release the anger?" she asked

"Transforming anger is a process. The first step is recognizing that we're holding on to it, which isn't all that difficult. If you get angry a lot, you can be assured that you're holding on to anger. Once you have this awareness, you can start to transform it."

"That makes sense."

"The second step is to understand that anger sits on top of deeper unexpressed emotional woundings, like fear, grief, shame and guilt."

"How does that work?"

"Let's say you're a child and you just hurt your younger brother. Then you get scolded and spanked by one of your parents. Now you're likely feeling guilty for what you did and you're also likely feeling a lot of anger towards your brother for getting you in trouble, your parent for spanking you and yourself for doing something inappropriate and disappointing your parent."

"That makes sense too," she nodded.

"Another example might involve loss. Let's say that your best friend has moved away and you're feeling grief over your loss. You're also likely feeling very angry that your best friend has been taken away from you. You might be upset at your friend's parents or you may simply be angry with life."

"I can see that."

"The third step is to talk about it. Admit your anger. Forgive the person who has mistreated you and apologize to those you have mistreated. Forgiveness helps you to release anger and bitterness, and apologizing helps you to let go of guilt and shame."

"People find it hard to apologize and forgive, don't they?

"Yes, we do, because our ego gets in the way. We don't want to admit that we're wrong."

"But this just hurts us."

"Yes it does and that's why expression is so critical. Actually, expression is the way to prevent ourselves from holding on to emotional pain in the first place, but unfortunately, we're not taught how to do it. In fact, most often, we're taught how not to express."

"That's very true. I just had an image of a parent cuddling their child, encouraging him to cry in order to express his grief or yell and scream to express his anger."

"We'd be living in a different world if all parents did that. Experiencing sadness, anger, frustration and other forms of emotional pain is part of the human experience. It's part of why we're here on the planet. What gets us into trouble is in how we deal with it."

"You mean, how we suppress it?"

"Yes. Or worse still, when we get punished for expressing it."

"What about punching pillows or yelling and screaming? Does that work too?"

"It certainly does. As strange as this may sound, when I used to feel anger well up inside me, I would either go for a drive and scream my lungs out, or stick my face in a pillow and do it. Either way, it worked!"

"It's really that simple?"

"Yes, it is, although it took a while to get comfortable with it. I was always concerned someone would hear me."

"I can understand that. Heavens, they might call the police!"

"Wouldn't that be awkward," he laughed.

"It certainly would."

"Now I use a different technique. When I feel anger welling up, I quickly say to myself matter of fact, 'This is interesting. I am having an emotional reaction. This isn't me, the conscious observer. It's simply unresolved emotional energy I'm holding on to. It's ego. Then I just observe, objectively, until it passes. I don't personalize it."

"Fascinating! It must take practice."

"It does. But if you trust and stick with it, it's an effective way of diffusing anger."

"And does this type of release allow you to get at the underlying emotional pain like grief and guilt?"

"It seems to, because I always feel better when I'm done. And that is key, to keep talking and observing until you actually feel better. You can actually feel the release in your body."

"That sounds amazing."

"It is. And there is one other thing we can do."

"What's that?"

"Live in the present moment. When we live in the now, we can't be frightened by the future or haunted by the past. The more we focus our attention on what we are doing or simply observe things around us, the less time we spend in thought, which quite often, is self destructive."

"You need to come to the hospital to work with some of our patients. They could really use your help."

"What an awesome idea. I would start with the cancer ward."

She was smiling and he could see that it was genuine. "So dating a guy with anger issues doesn't scare you?"

"Try to find a man who doesn't have anger issues. I don't think it's possible. I'm very pleased that you have the awareness and courage to take it upon yourself to heal it," she said, slipping her arm into his.

At that moment, a smile came over his face because he knew, as his family liked to say, that Marnie was a keeper!

CHAPTER 25:
THE REVOLUTION

You say you'll change the constitution
Well, you know
We all want to change your head
You tell me it's the institution
Well, you know
You better free your mind instead

— The Beatles, *Revolution*

"We've been discovered," said he voice on the other end of the line.

"Have you closed down the operation?" asked the very powerful man.

"We shut it down immediately."

"Good. Meet me for lunch tomorrow. You can explain what went wrong."

"The usual place."

"Yes," he said hitting the *End* button on his cell phone. Although disappointed that the operation had failed, he was not discouraged. Undertakings such as this had their inherent risks. Besides, his determination was exceeded only by his patience. They would find a different way, just as they had done in the past.

"Last week," John Stevens began, standing before the class, "we listed some of the things that need to change in order for us to achieve a more peaceful, harmonious way of living. Some of you said you didn't see how this was possible."

"I have to admit," said Josh, "I still don't."

"On Friday we talked about how anything is possible," Teach continued, nodding at Josh, "and we cited several examples of individuals who went on to accomplish great things despite their humble beginnings. Today I would like to continue the discussion, but I would like to look at it from more of a collective basis."

"Awesome!" remarked Tom.

"Hey, you're starting to sound like Teach," kidded Mike.

"I'll take that as a compliment," Tom replied, fist pumping with his friend.

"It's great to see that you are feeling so joyful this morning. I hope what I'm about to say doesn't dampen your enthusiasm because unfortunately, we, and by we, I mean the human race, seem to be very rapidly heading in a direction that will lead to our extinction."

"You didn't just dampen it," said Josh, "You drowned it."

"Sorry, but it's important to be open and honest. The population continues to grow at an alarming rate. There are already places on the planet where there is a shortage of water to drink, where the air is unfit to breathe and where the fish are too toxic to eat. As the population continues to grow, as we continue to gobble up arable land, strip more forests and consume more water, it's just going to get worse. This is inevitable."

"Are you trying to scare the shit out of us?" asked Matt.

"You're really scaring me," added Jessica looking very frightened.

"We need to be aware, because we can no longer be complacent about what is happening on the planet. There are too many people who are oblivious to our situation. There are many more who are so caught up in their own greed or suffering that the condition of mankind is of little consequence to them. There are still more who are aware, but are not compelled to take action."

"A lot of people are just trying to cope," remarked Ryan. "Their biggest concern is having enough money to pay their bills."

"No doubt about it, Ryan."

"And then you've got all those people who don't give a damn," added Tom. "They're more concerned about how many Mercedes are parked in their driveway. Try to convince them we need to change."

"You may believe that it is impossible for us to change... that it is too monumental a task. There was a time when people didn't believe the Berlin Wall would ever come down or that apartheid would ever end in South Africa or that democracy would ever come to Egypt. But all of these things happened.

"It takes a revolution to bring about radical change and revolution begins with a desire for something different... something better...and a conviction that change can be achieved. It is not necessarily a call to rise up and take arms against those who would control us. Rather it is a call to rise up and change our way of being, to understand what is truly important and to stop blindly supporting and adhering to systems and institutions that no longer serve us. It is to no longer accept systems and practices born of greed or a lust for power. It is to rise above apathy, doubt and despair. It is to say that there are more important things in life, like love, peace of mind, joyful living, wisdom, equal opportunity and abundance for everyone, not just the privileged few."

"This all sounds well and good in theory," said Tom, "but changing our entire society is a lot different than bringing down the Berlin Wall."

"Ya," added Josh. "I watched *Slum Dog Millionaire* and after watching them burn kids' eyes out with acid because blind beggars can make more money, I thought, man, there's no hope for some people."

"True, we have some daunting challenges, but perhaps if we looked at things a little differently, we might see that they've already begun to change."

"What are you getting at?" asked Ryan, as the class looked on with very puzzled expressions.

"There are a number of interesting phenomena happening on the planet that when you look at individually seem quite alarming, but when looked at collectively, tell a compelling story. They tell us that perhaps the revolution has already begun."

"Like what?" inquired Travis.

"Let's examine them and see what you think," Teach replied. "What are some of the significant developments that are taking place on the planet right now?"

"You mean, like the wave of bullying in schools?" asked Jordan.

"That's one of them."

"Yep, but bullying has always existed," protested Adam.

"Yes it has, but lately it has become an epidemic, particularly with cyber bullying," observed Tom.

"Everywhere you go people are talking about bullying and anti-bullying," added Terry.

"It seems like every school has an anti-bullying campaign," said Scott. "It's crazy."

"And yet there is more and more bullying," remarked Mike, shaking his head.

"I read recently about indigo and crystal children," said Tracy, jumping into the conversation, "and I'm puzzled that there has been such a rise in bullying at a time when all these wise, gentle souls are coming to the planet."

"What are indigo and crystal children?" asked Eric.

"They're children who are extremely sensitive, empathetic and intelligent and seem to possess special gifts," said Ryan, grinning at his teacher.

"Yes, it's believed that indigo children first started coming to the planet in the late-seventies and crystal children started coming in the mid-nineties," added John, returning Ryan's smile.

"I heard about them too," added Travis. "They're supposed to have special gifts like mental telepathy and psychic abilities."

"Everybody is supposed to have those abilities," countered Scott.

"Yes, but they're supposedly more evident with crystal children."

"My aunt is an elementary school teacher," added Jordan, "and she's always talking about how much smarter kids are today and how they don't just believe everything they're told like kids used to. She says they blow her away with their wisdom."

"What do you think, Mr. Stevens?" asked Tom.

"The critics say there is no scientific proof to support the idea of indigo and crystal children, but all you have to do is look around. There are so many extremely sensitive, super intelligent and super-gifted kids that it's hard not to acknowledge its significance. They even look older."

"Maybe like the book said, they're old souls," added Tracy.

"That could very well be."

"My aunt also says kids cry way more than they used too," Jordan added. "Especially boys."

"That's what the article said," agreed Tracy. "Because they're so sensitive, they cry easily."

"The first time I cried at school a bunch of kids teased me," stated Blair, sadly.

The students turned in disbelief to look at him, surprised at his admission. "Kids can be really cruel," empathized Matt.

"What about all the kids with ADHD?" remarked Jordan.

"And autism and Asperger's," added Travis.

"Ya, what is with that anyway?" asked Josh. "My dad said the first time he ever heard of autism was when he saw the movie *Rain Man*. Now it seems that the schools are full of kids with autism and Asperger's."

"Isn't it just because we're doing a better job of diagnosing these diseases?" asked Stuart.

"First," said Caitlyn, looking quite agitated, "we've talked about this before. If it were simply a case of doing a better job of diagnosing, then where are all the adults with autism?"

"Ya, I remember that," Stuart admitted sheepishly.

"And second, please don't refer to these conditions as diseases. They're not diseases and people with these conditions are not diseased or disabled. Every kid I've ever known with autism is very intelligent. It's just that their brains seem to be wired differently, so they're differently-abled than other people."

"Sorry," Stuart apologized.

"You don't have to be sorry, Stuart. It's not your fault we've been led to believe autism is a disease."

"I heard that autism was caused by vaccinations," said Travis.

"There seems to be a lot anecdotal evidence to support that assertion, but the medical community won't admit to anything," remarked John.

"Of course," scoffed Matt. "Nobody wants to be held liable for it."

"Plus drug companies are making huge profits vaccinating kids," added Ryan.

"Somebody told me one time that a lot of kids who have been called ADHD just have food allergies and if they ate properly, they'd be okay," said Scott.

"Yes, there seems to be a great deal of evidence to support that theory," Teach agreed.

"That's another thing," remarked Eric, "man there are a lot of kids with food allergies."

"There is no doubt about it! When I was young, there were hardly any kids with food or environmental sensitivities. Now it seems like every other child has an allergy."

"Lots of adults too," added Tom.

"The book I read said indigo and crystal children are more prone to allergies," offered Tracy.

"It seems then, that we have a growing bullying phenomenon and a rapid increase in the rate of autism and allergies in the last few years and these conditions may or may not be connected to the arrival of indigo and crystal children," their teacher summarized. "What else is happening?"

"What about cancer?" Eric inquired. "We spend all this money on research and treating cancer and yet more and more people are dying every year from breast cancer, ovarian cancer, prostate cancer, colon cancer, lung cancer and other forms of cancer. It seems to me that this too is an epidemic."

"People are being taken down the garden path," added Tom.

"That's for sure," agreed Blair. "I heard recently that cancer societies spend more money on fundraising than they do on research. That's nuts!"

Several of the students looked at each other with puzzled expressions, still not quite believing the change in Blair.

"And it's not just cancer," remarked Jordan. "It seems that there is way more arthritis, asthma, MS, ALS, Parkinson's and other diseases than there used to be."

"Ya!" agreed Jessica. "I know lots of people who have arthritis. Even my dad has it and he's not very old."

"It sounds like soaring cancer and disease rates is the fourth phenomenon. What else is going on in our society?" John asked.

"What about the divorce rate?" asked Tracy. "There was a time when hardly anybody divorced. Now it's over fifty percent."

"The traditional family doesn't seem to exist anymore," Tom lamented. "We've got a whole generation of kids growing up in broken homes."

"Maybe that's why prisons are filling up with people who are mentally ill," suggested Mike.

"What do you mean by that?" Caitlyn asked.

"I saw something on television not too long ago about how prisons are filling up with people who aren't really criminals. They are mentally ill people who are committing criminal acts."

"Yes, that's true," observed John. There has been a marked increase in the rate of depression, schizophrenia, bipolar disorder and other forms of mental illness, although I don't know of any connection to the increasing divorce rate."

"Maybe so," added Caitlyn, "but it certainly seems that these conditions are more prevalent."

"I agree with Caitlyn," said Ryan. "Schizophrenia and bipolar are on the rise. Maybe it's because people are overwhelmed by everything nowadays. Life isn't as simple as it used to be."

"There is one other alarming trend that seems to be happening right across the globe," noted Tom, "and that is the growing gap between haves and have nots."

"If anything is gonna start a revolution, that's it," agreed Terry.

"That's what caused the revolution in Egypt," added Jordan.

"Yes, it certainly did. The collapse of the middle class is very alarming."

"Poverty can really motivate people to change," added Tracy.

"So we've got a bullying epidemic, an autism epidemic, an allergy epidemic, a cancer epidemic, a divorce epidemic, a mental illness epidemic and a poverty epidemic," Tom summarized. "Seems like we've got a lot of chaos happening."

"We have an epidemic of epidemics" kidded Josh, causing a few snickers among his classmates.

"And if we consider these various phenomena how does it make you feel?"

"Depressed," replied Stuart, "and I'm not kidding."

"I believe you, Stu," sympathized Ryan. "Thinking about these things could certainly lead to a lot of despair."

"Without a doubt," the teacher agreed. "But what if we looked at them from a different perspective. If we first consider that everything happens for a reason, then it would be reasonable for us to conclude that these aren't simply independent random phenomena. Rather that they are coordinated and they have a purpose."

"Looking at it from that perspective has the potential to eliminate a lot of fear," Tom remarked.

"Ya," agreed Mike. "It makes us feel less powerless."

"That was an interesting way of expressing your point," Josh said smiling. "Sort of like the poodle that thought being with a great dane made him feel a little smaller."

John smiled himself. "If we next consider that it typically takes some sort of crisis…some significant suffering…to knock us out of our complacency and inspire us to take action, then it also makes sense that extreme conditions would need to be created to get our attention."

"That does make a lot of sense," agreed Travis. "If you're some rich dude, who is only concerned about money, you might change your priorities when your kid starts getting the shit beat out of him at school."

"Or if someone in your family develops a psychiatric disorder," Caitlyn added, quietly.

"Yes! And if we next consider the five essentials for creating happiness and heaven on earth," continued Teach, looking at Caitlyn empathetically, "then it is quite possible, if not probable, that these phenomena are meant to guide us in the direction of those essentials. They are meant to guide us to the truth."

"To finding peace, love and joy," added Jessica.

"I guess we can't continue to live the way we've been living and expect life on the planet to go on forever," observed Josh.

"I don't think we were ever meant to live this way," added Matt.

"It's interesting," noted Ryan, looking very deep in thought, even Hollywood seems to be getting into the act."

"What do you mean?" inquired Scott.

"Well, look at all the movies that have come out recently that are about things like our obsession with money and the suffering we'll inflict on each other to get it."

"You must be talking about *Slum Dog Millionaire* and *No Country for Old Men*?" remarked Terry.

"Exactly!"

"And what about *The Informant* and *Margin Code*?" asked Scott. "That's the epitome of corporate greed."

"At the expense of people's health," added Eric.

"I thought corporations were run by people," remarked Ryan.

"It doesn't seem that way. It seems more like they're run by some sort of alien entity that cares little about people's welfare."

"That's a good analogy," praised Tom.

"Is it any wonder people are living with so much fear?" asked Travis.

"That's just it. We don't have to live in fear. We have a choice. We can take charge. We have an opportunity to examine these phenomena collectively to understand their significance."

"How do we do that?" asked Terry.

"Let's begin with bullying," John suggested. "Tracy raised a good point a few minutes ago. Why would there be such a rise in bullying at a time when all of these gentle crystal children are coming to the planet?"

"Maybe it's because our priorities are messed up," replied Josh.

"Yes! Maybe it's meant to teach us that there are more important things in life than what we're presently focused on," added Tom.

"Like what?" Teach inquired.

"When you think of what is at the root of bullying, perhaps it's meant to remind us that the most important thing on a day to day basis is how we feel about ourselves."

"Ya! And it needs to become an epidemic to get people's attention," added Scott.

"Otherwise, people won't take action," added Terry.

"And maybe these *crystal children* cry easily cause they're trying to show us something as well," observed Mike.

"That it's okay to cry," Tracy remarked, raising her eyebrows at the guys.

"Crying when we're upset about something is important, isn't it?" Adam asked, looking at his teacher.

"It certainly is. It allows us to let go of our emotional pain."

"Do you think all of these crystal children are also developing autism because we need to change the education system?" asked Adam.

"I certainly do. We're already seeing it happen."

"So much of what we learn in school is meaningless, when you consider that we don't learn about kindness, compassion, acceptance, gratitude and forgiveness," observed Tracy.

"And if it's true that autism is triggered by vaccinations..." suggested Caitlyn.

"And milk allergies are due to pasteurization, homogenization and the crap we feed cows..." added Mike.

"Then it's easy to see why so many kids are developing these conditions," Caitlyn continued.

"Because we need to stop these unhealthy practices," concluded Mike.

"Yes, we do."

"I'm beginning to see what you mean," remarked Tom. "Looking at the big picture, these phenomena have a higher spiritual purpose."

"Like cancer," agreed Josh. "It seems like we're not meant to find a cure for cancer. Otherwise, we wouldn't change the way we live."

"Ya! We wouldn't stop eating crappy foods and putting so many toxins into our bodies," added Scott.

"Or understand the importance of healing our emotional pain," observed Jordan.

"Or become spiritually conscious," remarked Ryan.

"I guess that's why there are also so many people with food sensitivities. So we'll learn to eat better and stop poisoning our food," agreed Jessica.

"So the revolution has begun, we just don't realize it," enthused Matt.

"It would seem so," agreed John.

"It's unfortunate that there needs to be extraordinary suffering in order to motivate us to change," lamented Travis.

"It's the nature of the beast," observed Tom.

"But it's like you said, right?" asked Ryan, looking at the head of the class. "We have a choice."

"Yes, but the first step is awareness. The second step is making the choice."

"How could you not choose to change?" asked Josh.

"Some people are stuck in inertia," replied Tom. "They don't think they have the power to change."

"Other people don't want to change," added Matt. "They don't want things to be different. They're in positions of power and wealth and they want to maintain the status quo."

"Most people just don't have a clue or they just don't want to know," said Jordan.

"What about the religious fundamentalists?" asked Scott.

"And political zealots," added Ryan.

"Is there any chance of getting them to change?" Scott continued.

"Is that why the gap between the haves and the have nots in widening…why society's middleclass is shrinking in so many countries?" asked Matt, "because the more people who are suffering…who are forced to do without…the more likelihood that we will take action."

"I believe it is," John replied. "Once a certain number of people are suffering… when we have reached a watershed point… the gates will open and change will come."

"The gates of heaven?" asked Eric.

"The gates of love, compassion and acceptance, which I suppose could be considered heaven," Teach smiled.

"Yes! And we can overwhelm the fanatics and zealots," observed Caitlyn with reverence.

"It's possible for everyone to change. Some are going to take longer than others, but I believe that once it starts, just like the fall of communism in Eastern Europe, there's no stopping it."

"I hope so," said Jessica, "cause it sure would be nice to live in a happier world, where people treat each other better."

"You got that right, Jess. Let the revolution begin," Blair said triumphantly, again, causing the class to look on in wonder.

"Teach, you mentioned the five essentials," said Mike. "What are they?"

At that moment, the bell rang. "We'll have to talk about that another time," John bellowed above the racket, as the students clamoured for the door. "Have an awesome day!"

Matt was last to leave. He stopped and stood quietly in front of his teacher's desk. "At the start of the class, you said that revolution begins with a desire for something better," he said, looking John in the eyes.

"Yes, I did."

"Because we want to end our suffering."

"Yes, we do."

"And suffering occurs in the mind, doesn't it? We have an experience that, because of how we interpret it, leads to a negative thought, which in turn leads to emotional pain, and it all occurs in the mind."

"Yes, it does."

"And one person's suffering is not necessarily that of another's because our interpretation or situation might be different."

"That's true. We've all had different experiences that have shaped our perceptions."

"But because we are all connected, the more minds that are suffering, the greater the possibility that there will be a call to action. The higher probability that we will look for something different. Like getting out of our minds and getting into our hearts. And reconnecting with our true spiritual essence."

Teach nodded his head in agreement.

"So that's why all of these phenomena are occurring simultaneously. Not only are more people being affected, but more people are being affected by more things. And their children are being affected."

"People will die for their children."

"I would," the big teen concluded, before turning and walking confidently out of the classroom.

Moments later, John noticed Adam pacing back and forth outside in the hallway. "Adam, would you like to speak with me?"

"Yep!"

"Well, c'mon in."

He nervously entered the room, eyes glued to the floor. "I have Asperger's," he declared.

"Yes! That is the name commonly used to describe what you are experiencing."

"Yep! Basically you said people with Asperger's are here to change the world."

"That's right! I believe that to be true!"

"So I'm not a weirdo or retarded, cause that's what people say about me."

"Absolutely not! Those are words used by people who are uninformed. You are participating in the flow of life in your own unique way, just like everyone else."

"Yep! Sort of like Stephen Hawking!"

"Yes indeed! His is definitely a unique experience!"

"He has a lot of courage."

"He certainly does!"

"Awesome!" With that, Adam smiled and marched confidently out of the room.

After he had left, John Stevens sat quietly reflecting on the moment. It had been a spirited discussion with the class followed by insightful and encouraging chats with Matt and Adam. It seemed that the concepts he had presented made sense to them and he had a feeling that they were ready for change.

Looking up at the calendar he realized it was getting close to the end of the school year and he really hoped that he had made a difference in the lives of these students. Throughout the term, they eagerly grasped the ideas he introduced. He hoped he had given them something to think about. He hoped he had given them hope, or better still, faith!

"We pulled the plug on the operation," said the middleman without a hint of emotion.

"What happened?" asked Jonathan Fox.

"That's not important," the caller scolded.

"What's next?"

"We will let you know when your services are required again."

"I understand."

CHAPTER 26:
GRADUATION

No more pencils
No more books
No more teachers
Dirty looks

— Alice Cooper, *School's Out*

The square was abuzz with a packed crowd of extremely agitated citizens. Though they were orderly, their mood was of enormous determination, like a herd of water buffalo intent on protecting one of their own from a pride of ravenous lions. They had come not only to witness the poisoning, but also to lend their support, for they believed the death sentence rendered by the court was not just. Elpidios did not deserve to die and they were incensed, fully prepared to take action.

Many great thinkers had met similar fates, victims of a fearful administration who sought to still the voice of the populace, much in the way a leopard seeks to silence a noisy baboon.

Elpidios knew the risks, but he believed that it was far less harmful to the soul to endure suffering than it was to cause it. And he believed that it was far more damaging to one's self-image to remain silent than it was to speak the truth... and so, despite the counsel of his closest advisors, he spoke.

He challenged people to think beyond that which was evident; to search deeper into the mysteries of life. He asked them to confront their fears… to step out of their comfort zones… for only then would they discover the questions that might unveil the truth.

The popular philosopher was careful not to sway or influence opinion. This was his nature. Like the Buddha, he encouraged people to discover the truth for themselves, for he knew that self-discovery created stronger convictions.

He was also well aware that those who held power were spiritually unconscious and insecure and would lash out at any attempt to weaken their authority or discredit their laws. He knew that speaking publicly would bring him under scrutiny, regardless of his intentions. But he pressed forward, convinced that it was his obligation to challenge and educate in regards to mandated beliefs, despite the risks.

Suddenly there was a commotion at the south entrance of the square. A parade of men in white cotton robes entered to a chorus of cheers. Their cherished savant had arrived, riding unchained on a simple donkey drawn cart. There was no need to tether him down, for he had no intentions of fleeing. His was a life of honour… of speaking the truth. He would not run.

Growing up, the young Elpidios had not accepted things at face value. He asked questions and he encouraged others to do the same, for he believed that there was more to human existence than what could be seen, heard, smelled, tasted or touched. What is more, like the great thinkers before him, he believed that there was more to life than living by the edicts put forth by those fearful small-minded men in power.

His need to question, to wonder, was not the product of education; rather it was born of the naturally inquisitive mind that exists within all of us. His curiosity could not be quashed by malicious, uninformed bureaucrats whose goal was to protect their own positions of wealth and power.

The cart stopped in the middle of the square and the crowd hushed. The humble philosopher rose gracefully and held up his hands as if to summon the wisdom of the heavens above. He stood silently for several moments, dignified, smiling at the assembly gathered before him. "You can snatch away one's wealth. You can take away their freedom. You can even take away their life. You cannot however, take away their love or their compassion or their will. You cannot break the spirit of those who have unshakable faith and hope.

"Nor can you control thought, just as you cannot control the wind or the rising of the sun. To attempt such a thing is as insane as to condemn a man to death for doing so. There will always be people who will contemplate, particularly those disposed to introspection. They will ask questions. This cannot be denied."

It seemed rather odd to many of those in attendance that the authorities had not accompanied Elpidios, allowing him ample opportunity to address the gathering. Given his popularity, one would have considered it absurd that he be allowed this freedom to speak and incite. It gave them cause to worry, but despite their concerns they had no intentions of leaving the square.

"The mysteries of the universe are many and man's desire to unravel them is undeniable," he continued confidently. "This too cannot be stilled."

"We love you," a voice shouted, prompting loud cheers from the assembly.

Though this was a solemn occasion, there was much affection and Elpidios could feel it. He was about to continue when the crowd suddenly hushed. In the distance, the methodical pounding of a drum could be heard and with each successive beat, it drew nearer and nearer. Slowly, a nervous tension began to take hold in the square and people became increasingly restless.

"Hold your places. Stay calm. You are safe," the philosopher assured them. "It is me to whom the council wishes to dispense its justice."

As the drummer entered the square followed by members of the council, the crowd turned. The council members were followed by many lines of hoplites, fierce helmeted warriors armed with shields and spears.

The sight of the hoplites shocked the crowd and many shrieked in terror as they withdrew into a mass in the center of the square.

Then lines of archers suddenly appeared on the surrounding rooftops and balconies throwing the crowd into a panic. To their credit they held their ground and after several minutes, peace was restored.

Elpidios knew that his followers had been betrayed and although he feared for their safety, he dare not speak it, for he did not want to create pandemonium, which surely would have led to their slaughter. And so, he held his tongue.

"In defiance of the authority of the supreme council," began the council chief, getting right to the point, "you have endeavoured to influence the people of our noble city with your malicious notions. For your contemptuous behaviour you have been sentenced to death. Do you have anything to say before this sentence is carried out?"

Elpidios stood bravely and drew his arm over the crowd from left to right in a gentle sweeping motion. "You see before you, evidence of the support for the views of which I speak. It cannot be denied, just like that of which I speak cannot be denied. For you cannot refute the truth. It will always live on. You may silence my voice but others will follow. Is it your intention to silence all of these voices? For if it is, your efforts will be futile, for you will never quash them all, just like you will never quash the nightly hoot of the owl. That is all," he concluded, slowly taking a seat in the cart.

The head of the council lifted an arm and snapped his fingers. An orderly stepped forward and marched silently towards the man in the cart. He stopped in front and removed the gold silk cloth covering a woven basket. Without speaking, he reached into the basket and retrieved a clay goblet. Placing it on the cart, he then withdrew a copper container and poured its contents into the chalice. Finally, he retrieved a small vial and emptied its contents into the goblet before handing it to Elpidios.

"Farewell my friends," the philosopher declared raising the mug in a gesture of assurance.

These were to be his final words. He lay down quietly, held the goblet to his lips and slowly swallowed its lethal contents. For the next few moments, he lay still. Then he began to spasm, writhing in pain as the crowd gasped. Finally his body tensed and was stilled.

One of his aids approached the body, held two fingers to his throat, before turning to face the crowd. "He is dead," he said softly, bowing his head.

Many people began wailing as the gathering pressed forward to pay their respects and catch a glimpse of the body.

Then, suddenly without warning, the archers unleashed their deadly arrows on the crowd. Many were killed instantly. Those who weren't made a frantic dash towards the entrance to the square where they were met by the fierce hoplites. Surrounded and unarmed, they had no chance.

The hoplites stabbed and slashed as arrows continued to rain down upon them from the rooftops. In a few short minutes, it was over and the square fell silent.

John slowly opened his eyes. The first rays of light were beginning to illuminate the day. He looked around and realized he was in his bed. He had been dreaming. "I'm still alive," he said out loud, startling himself. Many times he had awakened from a dream needing a few moments for his senses to bring him back to reality.

His dreams were full of realism and this one seemed particularly so. It spoke to him of the need to speak; of the need to overcome fear in order to voice our views regardless of how different our opinion may be in relation to more popularly held beliefs. For people will never be silenced by fearful men in authority wanting to maintain the status quo and preserve their positions of power and wealth.

The dream was also related to the hidden cameras and the attempt to coerce Matt into setting him up. Somebody wanted to silence him. Who, and why, was a mystery at this point. But whatever the reason, he would not be deterred. His message was too important.

John Stevens sat upright and swung his legs over the side of the bed. The floor felt warm to the touch of his feet; clearly a sign that the days were getting warmer. Scratching his chin, he felt confident, ready for the day ahead.

Teach sat on the stage quietly reflecting on the year just past. He was also thinking about the dream. It had been an enormously gratifying year and although he was feeling nervous, the dream had given him great inspiration.

He sat quietly listening to the speeches preceding him, applauding politely at their conclusion. Principal Clark then called upon him to speak, but before he could stand up, his entire class arose and walked up onto the stage. They stood side by side smiling at the audience who were suddenly abuzz with anticipation.

After everyone had quieted down, Jordan approached the microphone. "We have something we would like to share with you," he began. "I saw an old movie recently. It was about four murders that took place during the American civil rights movement in the nineteen-sixties. The senselessness of these killings inspired me to watch Martin Luther King's *I Have a Dream* speech. I had never heard the speech before and I was very moved by it. Mr. King's dream was born of faith. He had faith that things could change. He had faith in the basic goodness of people. He had faith in the indomitable human spirit. Listening to him, I couldn't help but think that I... I mean, we.... have our own dream. We too have faith and we would like to share it with you now."

Jordan stepped back quietly, as Tom walked up to the microphone. "We have faith that some day we will be able to walk down any street in any city in any country anywhere in the world, any time of day or night and not have to worry about being beaten up, robbed, raped or murdered."

Ryan was next to speak. "And we have faith that someday, all of mankind will live in spiritual consciousness and Oneness with all that is, celebrating our uniqueness and honouring our *choice* to live as we wish. Where there is no separation by gender, race, religion or country of origin. Only unity in all contexts."

Next, was Tracy's turn. "And we have faith that some day we will live in a world, free of borders and conflict. A world where there is no military because there will be no wars. Where there is no police and no police brutality because there will be no crime. Where there are no courts and no jails because there will be no criminals."

Adam then shyly stepped up to the microphone. He stood quietly for a few moments looking down at the floor of the stage, gathering up his courage. "Basically we have faith that some day we will live without medications, without hospitals and without health plans, because we will all understand that part of our reason for being here in physical form is to heal our emotional wounds and release our emotional pain, and by doing so, we will free our bodies of illness and disease."

As Adam stepped back to join the group he was met by Caitlyn, who gave him a big hug. Then she too took her turn in front of the microphone. "And we have faith that one day we will live in a world where there is no poverty, no starvation and no homelessness, because there will be employment for all. Everyone's work will be valued and we will all take an active interest in supporting those less fortunate."

Then Josh spoke. "And we have faith that one day we will live in a world where we live by simple guidelines, with clearly defined boundaries. Where there are no laws and no rules, because we will all be living in peace and harmony." Then he triumphantly raised his fists to the sky and shouted, "Hallelujah!"

The students chuckled knowing that Josh couldn't pass up an opportunity to do something funny. It was not in his nature and they would have been disappointed had he not.

Then Jessica took her turn. "And we have faith that one day we will live in a world where all children will be encouraged to express themselves, their feelings, their opinions and their beliefs because that would be so awesome!"

Blair then stepped up to the microphone. "And we have faith that one day we will live in a world where we no longer hold onto anger and where men in particular will know how to express themselves in a constructive way, free of self-judgment and guilt."

Matt high-fived Blair as he took his turn in front of the mic. "And we have faith that one day we will live in a world that no longer judges us according to our income or the level of wealth we have accumulated or the level of fame we have achieved or the amount of power we wield. But instead honours and celebrates each of us for the amount of compassion, acceptance and love we offer others and that honours us for our wisdom and our willingness to share this wisdom."

Matt was followed by Mike. "And we have faith that one day we will live in a world where men truly understand who they are. Who understand their sensitive nature. Who no longer abuse, bully or attempt to dominate and control. Who are able to openly love and nurture. Who honour the feminine aspect of our existence."

Terry spoke next. "And we have faith that one day we will live in a world where there is no betrayal, no abandonment, no persecution and no exploitation… a world where we understand the illusion of loss and where we grieve openly."

Then it was Travis's turn. "And we have faith that one day all governments will behave in a way that best serves the people they represent… where corruption and autocracy no longer exist."

Eric was next. "And we have faith that one day corporate greed will no longer exist and we will live in a world where corporations put the welfare of society ahead of company profits… where corporate CEOs no longer are rewarded for improving the bottom line by putting employees out of work."

Then it was Stuart's turn. "And we have faith that one day we will understand the importance of a healthy diet and the implications of using pesticides, chemical fertilizers and developing genetically modified organisms. We have faith that we will return to more traditional and humane farming practices."

Scott followed next. "And we have faith that one day we will live in a world where everyone will feel good about themselves. Where we will raise our children to feel good about themselves. Where we all feel lovable, worthy, good enough and empowered. Where we are all kind to one another."

Finally, Jordan returned to address the audience. "And we have faith that one day we will in fact create heaven on earth. A true oasis for all. Where peace of mind, joyful living and unconditional love reign supreme. Where we celebrate all aspects of life on Earth. Where we no longer have to experience the dark contrasts of life, but instead live in the wonderful lightness of bliss. Thank you."

As Jordan stepped back from the microphone, the entire gathering rose from their seats and burst into applause. In that moment, Teach couldn't have been prouder. He stood with the rest of the audience, clapping and cheering. One by one, the students walked over to him, shook his hand and hugged him. He smiled and cried the entire time.

After the audience had quieted and returned to their seats, John composed himself and took his turn at the microphone. "Socrates once said, 'What is justice?'

"Well, what is justice and what is a *just* world? I suppose if you live in a multi-million dollar mansion, work hard for everything you've earned, do well in the stock market, have a happy marriage, have raised well adjusted children and take vacations in the tropics every year, you might think we live in a just world. Or perhaps not.

"If you were an orphan living in a third world country, where there was rampant oppression, drought, homelessness and hunger, perhaps you wouldn't consider this a very just world. Or maybe you would.

"We live in a time of tremendous inequality, not just in terms of what is, but also, what is possible. Or so it seems.

"Since the beginning of time, our human world has had its oppressors and its oppressed. And it's had its share of revolutionaries; extremely courageous people who have stood up for the oppressed against the oppressor. From Socrates and Jesus, to Martin Luther King and Nelson Mandela," he continued, looking at Jordan, "people have given their freedom and even their lives for justice and equality.

"If I could add my voice to their cause, it would be to say that there is no need for this suffering to continue. We can end it now. Throughout our history, man has shown a propensity for turning valuable insights into tyranny. The teachings of Jesus and Muhammad, just like the philosophies of Marx and Nietzsche, have been taken out of context, misinterpreted or simply manipulated in order to fulfill personal agendas.

"But what is at the root of this behaviour? Why have we turned immense wisdom into terrible suffering? Perhaps it is due to what Mandela referred to as a collective psychological inferiority... spiritually unconscious men who quite simply do not feel good about themselves... and this oppression continues to be enacted as we speak.

"When we understand what I refer to as the five essentials of life, we understand the ingredients of blissful living... where justness is no longer a question... where suffering no longer exists. Here are the five essentials. First, when we know there is nothing more important than a positive self-image and that feeling good about ourselves is the most essential thing for our health and happiness. Helping people feel good about themselves... particularly our children... by being kind and honest in everything we do and by making them feel loved, wanted, accepted and appreciated, must become a priority in our homes, schools, communities and nations.

"Second, when we understand the purpose of our existence. When we know who we really are ... divine spiritual beings living in Oneness with all that is ... and why we're really here on the planet. Because this knowledge allows us to develop faith and trust. It tells us that there is a purpose for our being here and this awareness frees us from fear and gives us hope.

"Third, when we know that healing our emotional pain is a fundamental component of human existence. It's one of the reasons we are here in human form and it too is essential for our health and happiness.

"Fourth, when we know that healthy food, water and air is paramount to joyful longevity. We cannot continue to consume sugar, artificial sweeteners and processed foods and expect to live long healthy lives or eradicate cancer and disease. The human body was designed to function much longer than our current average lifespan, but until we purify our diets and environment, we won't get to enjoy a prolonged existence.

"And the fifth and final essential, is to focus on doing our best in the present moment because this is the one thing that we truly have control over. It is to get out of the habitual negative and destructive thinking that goes on in our heads in order to stay present. It is to focus on doing our best rather than winning and being the best.

"If you could have a conversation with God, what questions would you ask? What do you think God would say? I think God would tell us that we do live in a just world because we have a choice. We can choose tyranny or peace. We can choose lack or abundance. We can choose cruelty or kindness. We can choose fear or love.

"Perhaps God would say that to understand the justness of our world we need to go beyond form. We need to look deep inside ourselves and we need to look deeply into the natural world because in so doing, the truth of our spiritual nature and our divine existence is revealed. And it is this truth that will really set us free from the fear that so constrains us."

As John continued confidently, all eyes in audience were riveted upon him and they understood the significance of his words. "Perhaps God would say we simply need to teach each other to feel good about ourselves because if we did so, we wouldn't mistreat another being. Maybe God would tell us the power to change is within us and in fact, change is inevitable. For the truth is that those who live in fear can no more stop the forces of change than winter can stop the arrival of spring. Change is imminent. It is a certainty. It is the flow of life.

"Perhaps the real question isn't whether or not we live in a just world, perhaps it is simply what kind of a world do we want to live in?

"A few minutes ago, you heard the students tell you that they have faith that some day we will live in a really awesome world. Let's all work together to create it... a kind, loving, compassionate, accepting world where people live joyfully, with peace of mind and endless love. Thank you!"

Driving home later that day, John Stevens couldn't take his mind off the students' impromptu speech. He had become convinced that humankind is heading recklessly towards extinction, but their understanding of the causes of our suffering and their determination to create change was inspiring. It gave him hope that perhaps we could alter our destiny. Our ignorance and arrogance seem unstoppable, but maybe we have the will to end our suffering. As daunting as the challenge is, it was a comforting thought.

As he drove casually through downtown, heading towards his apartment above Sammy Wong's, his mind was drawn to his children. He hadn't seen them in a long time and although they were scattered all over the world, he felt it was time to take a trip. He wanted to see them. It was the start of summer vacation. Two months of freedom lay ahead. What better time for an adventure!

John knocked on the door, then turned to look up into the night sky. It made him think of Matt's poem... *the wisdom of the night sky*. Its incredibly profound words were penned by a young man who had been written off by society... misunderstood like Machiavelli and cast aside carelessly like an unwanted toy. How ironic! It seemed as though much of our wisdom was born of great suffering. From the birth of Buddhism, the result of Siddhartha Gautama's determined effort to experience transformation through intentional hardship, to the present day. Heck, even his favorite song, *Layla*, might not have been written were it not for Eric Clapton's anguish.

Standing alone on the front step, Matt's words echoed in his head... *finding light in the darkness.* Teach had experienced many dark moments... the end of his marriage, the closing of the art store and the end of his relationship with Sandra. And yet each dark moment had led to something bright. Now he was teaching and loving it, and he had found a new relationship with new potential and new hopes and dreams. He had developed a sense of trust that no matter what happened, he would be okay.

The door swung open and Marnie stood before him, her beautiful eyes glowing in the darkness.

He stepped inside and held her in a long embrace. "I want to make love to you," he whispered.

"You're ready?" she asked.

He could feel her body trembling as he held her tightly. "Yes, I am."

She took his hand and led him silently upstairs.

The End

Dedicated to my mom and dad

Fred's Blog

Follow Fred's blog at:
fredphillips.wordpress.com

Printed in Canada